Mick,

Congratulations on your graduation from Tulane University. We are so proud of you.

Love - Mom & Dad

May 16th, 2020

GOD

an autobiography

GOD

_an_ autobiography

as told to a philosopher

Jerry L. Martin

CALADIUM

www.godanautobiography.com

**For media inquiries and requests, please contact
Sarah Miniaci, Senior Account Executive
SMITH Publicity, Inc.
856.872.2508 / sarah.miniaci@smithpublicity.com**

Page design: Trio Bookworks

Library of Congress Control Number: 2015960889

Hardcover ISBN: 978-0-9967253-1-6
Ebook ISBN: 978-0-9967253-2-3

Printed in the United States of America

20   19   18   17   16   1   2   3   4   5   6   7   8   9 10

For Abigail

Contents

The Beginning

The first time God spoke to me I didn't believe He existed.

Billy Graham once reported, "I know God exists—I talked to him this morning." Theatrical posturing, I thought. Graham may have been talking to God, but was God talking back? I remembered psychologist Thomas Szasz's comment: "If somebody talks to God, that's praying. If God talks to them, that's schizophrenia."

I had been raised in a Christian home, but those beliefs did not survive Philosophy 101, where arguments for the existence of God were shot down like clay pigeons. Since that time, I had been what one of my professors, Philip Wheelwright, called himself: a "pious agnostic"—respectful of belief in a higher reality but, when it came right down to it, staying eye-level with the natural world, the world of experience as I then knew it.

It is said you do not have to believe in God in order to pray. That is what happened to me.

I had been divorced for many years. I always thought I would be happier married, but as the decades rolled on without Miss Right showing up, I began to think she never would.

Then one day, the phone rang.

It was Abigail Rosenthal. She was a professor at Brooklyn College, a school with an outstanding liberal arts curriculum. The new college president had decided to replace core courses that opened students to the whole world of learning with—telescope from wide vista to a keyhole view—a focus on the borough of Brooklyn, the one thing the students knew already, in fact knew better than their professors.

Rosenthal and a colleague in the history department were fighting the change. They had succeeded in rallying most of the faculty, but the administration was driving a steamroller. She called the higher education organization I ran in Washington, D.C. Could we help? "Yes, that is what we do," I said.

Our only hope was to take the issue to the public, and we did. The battle raged in the press through the spring and into the summer. Abigail and I talked almost daily, strategizing and getting the story out. None of the talk was personal, and we never met, yet I found myself thinking, "This is a very remarkable woman."

In fact, I fell in love with her on the phone.

And we won the fight. In September, *The Chronicle of Higher Education* published a front-page story on the Brooklyn Connections fight with a full-page photo of Abigail and her colleague, along with a small, smiling photo of me on the inside.

A week later, I went to New York to give a talk about the struggle and, for the first time, we met in person. I brought her up to the front to field questions. She was funny and articulate and smart— and really cute! So cute, in fact, that I was overcome with shyness and, instead of lingering, made a quick getaway.

I feared I had missed my chance. I had to get back to New York. In December, I made a point of going to the city "on business" and made sure we had dinner. We mainly talked about issues at the college, but I thought I might have struck a spark. Her diary entry the next day, she later told me, was "Dinner last night was disturbingly interesting."

The pace of our phone calls quickened and grew more personal. But, other than hanging on her every word, I was not fessing up to my feelings. And she, of course, was playing her cards close—as much as her impetuosity permitted. Thinking to maintain her feminine elusiveness, she nevertheless warned, in a stream of modals, "If there may be or might or possibly could be something personal, at some point perhaps, between us, we should make sure it doesn't interfere with our efforts for Brooklyn College." My lips said, "Of course, the college comes first," but my heart said, "She loves me!"

I was not just in love; I was completely overwhelmed. I suppose it's a well-known phenomenon. Poets have sung about it ever since poets learned to sing; yet I had never really believed in love, not romantic love. Being in love was a delusion, based on projection—even the poets call it a form of madness—the kind of thing you expect to outgrow as you get older. I was only looking for compatibility, even had a Myers-Briggs personality profile in mind.

Instead, I found myself so totally, deeply in love that it did seem like a form of madness. "If you knew how much I love you, you would think I was crazy," I told her. I was a pretty buttoned-down, levelheaded guy, but on one occasion I said, "I feel as if I have always loved you." I am not sure what that meant, but I know it is how I felt. I would have been in sad shape had Abigail not had similar feelings, but she too responded to what she called "the summons of love."

Being in love was so strange to me that—what does an academic do?—I read books, mainly relationship books, but also an interesting collection of love letters by famous writers over the ages. The contrast was striking. The relationship books reflected something like my earlier attitude. They warned about projection, talked about the ups and downs of relationships, cautioned you against your own feelings. The love letters were the opposite—sometimes sweetly so, sometimes tragically so, as when Edith Wharton writes desperately loving letters to a man not worthy of her. The love letters testified to the reality of love but also justified the warnings issued by psychologists.

Women are supposed to be the experts in love. What do *they* think it is? Ah, I thought, they read novels, love stories. One had been left in a place I was staying. It was the first book that really told me about love. Love is not a set of psychological triggers firing off wildly. In a sense, it's not subjective at all, not a mere feeling. It is an ontological fact, a bond between two people that is deep within the structure of reality itself. That is what women, or at least some of them, know.

Being in love was not only a profound new experience; it shook my worldview. My whole life took on a new meaning. No, that is not quite right. My life went from a collection of purposes to *having* a meaning. It went from black-and-white to Technicolor. No, more radical than that, it went from a two-dimensional universe to a three-dimensional—or, as it turned out, n-dimensional—universe. I felt surprise and joy and gratitude. I did not know whom to thank, but an extraordinary gift had come into my life.

One summer morning I felt an urge to express my thanks, to pray—to Whomever. I did not see any reason not to express what I genuinely felt. So I fell to my knees, as I had been taught as a child, and thanked "the Lord."

I now believed in love, but not much else. I did not know if I was praying to the God of Israel, to Jesus of Nazareth, or, for all I knew, to the Lord Krishna worshipped by Hindus. Or simply to a benign universe. I didn't worry about that. I just poured out my heart in prayer.

A few weeks later, I felt this same urge and said another prayer of thanks, still addressed to a Lord I did not actually believe in. This time, to my surprise, I offered to be of service. To a God I didn't believe existed. Inconsistent of course, but not insincere.

Toward the end of a long summer day, Abigail and I were sitting on a park bench along the Potomac, across from the Lincoln Memorial. She was writing in her journal and I was pondering the challenge of making a future together. Without thinking about it, much less expecting an answer, I prayed again, this time asking for guidance.

Immediately a visual image appeared, like a hologram, a few feet in front of me—a rising, sparkling, multicolored fountain. It radiated vitality and promise, an answer to my prayer. But there was more.

A voice spoke . . .

Listen

I am the God of All

The voice did not sound particularly different from my own inner voice, but *it wasn't me talking*. I looked at Abigail to see if she heard it, but she continued writing, undisturbed. I asked, not out loud, "What is this voice? Who are you?"

The answer came back:

I am God.

"The God of Israel?"

I am the God of All.

The questions that led me to pray evaporated. Then the encounter was over. For the moment.

The historian Paul Johnson writes in his spiritual memoir about having once called the prime minister's office when, instead of getting the secretary's secretary, the prime minister herself answered. "It happened to me once with a prime minister," Johnson writes. "But with God it happens all the time."

I don't know if Johnson's experience is like mine, but from that day on, when I prayed, I almost always received a verbal response, often with quite specific guidance. At first, it just seemed an oddity that went too much against my agnostic worldview to be taken seriously. Once my son had classical music playing in his ear all the time. It turned out to be an ear infection, causing buzzing signals that his brain skillfully translated into Mozart. Maybe my prayers were like that.

I would tell Abigail about these odd experiences. While I always disdained paranormal reports, near-death experiences, and the like, she did not. I assumed she put the voice in that category. I didn't really know, because usually she just took in what I told her and didn't say much. She explained to me later that she thought I was engaged in a sensitive communication and did not want to create static.

Then, one day, she did speak up. "Are you going to take the voice seriously, or is this just entertainment?"

She had put her finger on the contradiction I was living. The voice was too real and benign and authoritative to ignore. Yet I could not imagine acting on it. Well, actually I could and did act on it, but without taking it seriously. I would be told to do this or that. Sometimes the guidance was about some matter facing me that day, and following the guidance usually worked out pretty well. Other times I received arbitrary directives which, since harmless, I followed. For example, one morning Abigail and I had just sat down to breakfast when I was told,

Don't eat.

So I just sat there for maybe fifteen or twenty minutes.

You can eat now.

I always did as I was told, but it was still more like a game of Captain-may-I than a life imperative. I was not ready to answer Abigail's question.

On a visit to Boulder, where I used to teach, I told a former colleague about my experiences. I was afraid he would think, "Poor Jerry, he has gone daft." But he listened with interest, and recommended that I read American philosopher William James's classic essay "The Will to Believe." An influential British scientist had declared, as a principle of the ethics of belief, "It is *wrong*, always, everywhere, and for every one, to believe *anything* upon insufficient evidence." The scientist had religion in his crosshairs.

James responded that there are some beliefs that, if you accept them, will shape your whole life. And shape it in a different way if you do not. You cannot remain neutral; yet evidence is inconclusive either way. You just have to decide which belief you would rather live with.

My situation seemed to be exactly what James was describing. Facing a similar choice between belief and unbelief, the seventeenth-century philosopher Blaise Pascal had seen it as a wager. If I believe in God and am wrong, well, I'm dead anyway, so I haven't lost much. But if I don't believe in God, and there is one . . . well, you might say, there's hell to pay.

I faced my own wager. Either I follow the voice or I don't. If I follow the voice and it is *not* divine, what is the worst that can happen? Well, I would be a fool, maybe a laughingstock, and would say good-bye to an excellent career. But if I decide not to follow the voice and it *is* divine, then I would have missed my purpose in this life. What if Moses had done that? Or George Fox, the founder of the Quakers? The Old Testament is full of people called by God, who at first demur and only reluctantly heed the call. Even Moses worries ("Suppose they do not believe me") and feels inadequate to the task ("I have never been eloquent. . . . I am slow of speech and slow of tongue").

I am not comparing myself to these great religious leaders, but all of us in our lives face moments when we have to decide whether to respond to a certain call—be it the call of duty or service or simply, as Joseph Campbell puts it, to "follow your bliss"—rather than continue a more conventional or comfortable course. If I had to live with one worst-case scenario or the other, I could live with being a fool, if that's what it came to, but I could not live with having refused God's call.

Making a decision to believe is not quite the same as accepting that belief in your bones. It is more like the first step toward believing. My philosophy still had no place for God—especially for a God who talks to *me*. Outside the Bible, who talks to God?

Another notable book by William James, *The Varieties of Religious Experience*, helped answer this question. The founder of pragmatism, the only distinctively American school of philosophy, James also taught physiology and psychology. He was a man of science but, for him, empiricism did not mean restricting our understanding to what science registers. He looked without prejudice at all kinds of human experience. He talked about famous people such as George Fox as well as ordinary people who has received answers to prayer or psychic intuitions or visitations from recently departed family members.

Many people have had moments of divine or nonnatural awareness, probably more than feel comfortable talking about them publicly. Duke English professor Reynolds Price writes about his own battle with cancer. During the course of his treatment, he had an encounter with Jesus in a vision or, as it seemed to him, in another dimension. After he published his story, he received letters from many people with similar experiences—experiences that they had never told anyone. My experience was not as out of line as I had thought.

I decided to follow the voice and see where it would lead me.

Listen to Me—
even when I whisper

It seemed to be a training in obedience. One day, after breakfast at a little café in Alexandria, I was told,

Don't go to work.

"Lord, do You know we have to get that grant proposal in today?"

Of course.

My organization lived on grant money. But the voice said not to go in. What to do? Well, the sky was not going to fall if the proposal went in the following day. I would go back to my apartment.

As I turned on the ignition, the voice spoke again.

You can go to work now.

I remember that incident because something was at stake, but usually I was told do something trivial, such as to listen to a different radio station or sit in a different chair. As these arbitrary commands continued—mounted as it seemed—Abigail expressed concern. This sounded more like boot camp than spiritual guidance. Maybe I shouldn't do *everything* I was told. Maybe I should, as she put it, "use your intelligence." I was puzzled. Was I supposed to second-guess God?

The next day I stopped at Borders bookstore near Pentagon City. On the way out, I felt guided to move in a particular direction, like a dowser following his stick: first straight ahead, next to the right, then straight ahead, now stop. I was at the religion section. I felt guided down to the third shelf on the right, and finally to a particular book. It was a book I never would have chosen on my own: John Calvin's commentary on the Gospel of John. I know that Calvin is one of the great theologians of the modern era, but I had an impression of him as stern and rigid. I picked up the book and it opened to John 8:28, where Jesus says, "I do nothing on my own." Calvin explains that "Christ wants to prove that he does nothing without the Father's command. . . . He depends entirely on his will and serves him sincerely. . . . He does not just partially obey God, but is entirely and without exception devoted to his obedience." It was a lesson in obedience.

Near the register, there was a display with another book I never would have bought on my own: *The Ten Commandments*, by Dr. Laura Schlesinger and Rabbi Stewart Vogel. Many people like Doctor Laura, but the few times I had heard her on the radio, she seemed harsh rather than loving. I believe in tough love, but she just sounded tough. However, I opened it and my eyes fell on a line boldfaced in the text. It was where the people of Israel accept the covenant: "Everything that God has spoken we will do!" Another example of total obedience.

I had been led to one other passage in Calvin's commentary. John 9:4 says, "We must work the works of him who sent me while it is day; night is coming when no one can work." Calvin comments, "As soon as God enlightens us by calling us, we must not delay, in case the opportunity is lost."

The note of urgency reminded me of the story a village chief in eastern Brazilia told of his own encounter with a divine being. He had encountered the being while out hunting, but was too scared to speak and the being left. "At night while I was asleep he [the divine being] reappeared to me. . . . He led me some distance behind the house and there showed me a spot on the ground where, he said, something was lying in storage for me. Then he vanished. The next morning I immediately went there and touched the ground with the tip of my foot, perceiving something hard buried there. But others came to call me to go hunting. I was ashamed to stay behind and joined them. When we returned, I at once went back to the site he had shown me, but did not find anything anymore." He had missed his moment. I did not want to miss mine.

So I began to take the prayers more seriously and started writing some of them down. Sometimes the voice would speak to me even when I was not praying. One day I was driving to New York, running behind schedule. Along the Baltimore-Washington Parkway, I kept hearing a faint sound, not much more than a gnat in the ear, and I kept trying to "brush it away." But it was persistent, and so I finally paid attention. It was the voice telling me to pull over and pray. I don't remember the rest of what I was told, but the first words I have always remembered,

Listen to Me—even when I whisper.

I have tried to do that ever since, but it is not always easy.

In spite of the voice, I wondered why, most of the time, God is irritatingly elusive. But I was told,

You see Me all the time.

I looked around and tried to see God, but nothing registered. Martin Buber talks about saying Thou to nature, and that was about as close as I could get. If God wants to be so coy, why does He bother to get our attention at all? How, I asked, could our response possibly matter to Him?

It is very important. It is at the heart of My being.

Human recognition is at the heart of God's being? I found that intriguing, but it only heightened the paradox of an invisible God who wants to be seen.

Abigail was still teaching full-time in New York, and I was working in Washington, D.C. We saw each other only on all-too-brief weekends. Come summer, we were spending more time together. She needed a car. I looked at the ads and found a nice little white used car. The guy selling it was the youth minister at his church. I started to explain I was buying it for my girlfriend. No, that would not sound right, and it was not true. I was buying it for my future wife. "I'm buying it for my fiancée."

There had never been any doubt that I would marry Abigail. I never considered anything short of that. But, in my methodical way, I had held off for six long months. It was time to pop the question. I took her to a dark, romantic Spanish restaurant in Alexandria. I don't know how we behaved in those days, but the waiters called us the lovebirds, and they put us in the "lovers' cove" upstairs. I had written her a little poem, a bad poem. I can't write poetry, but I thought the effort might soften her up. But it was not our night. A thunderstorm came up, and just as I was warming up to ask her, drip-drip-drip right in front of us. Ink in the poem ran. We scooted the table to the side. And then I told her I loved her and wanted to "spend at least one lifetime together" and would she be my wife? I knew well the scene in Hollywood movies. The woman looks longingly into her paladin's eyes and gushes, "Oh yes, yes!" Well, not the philosophical Abigail. I asked, and waited. And waited. Then waited some more. She seemed lost in deep thought. Like an underwater swimmer, I was holding my breath. Finally, "You haven't answered my question." In the gravest of tones, she answered. "Yes." Why the long pause? "It was a serious question and I thought I should give it a serious answer."

By the time we went through the legal hoops, there were only three days before Abigail returned to teaching. The only solution was to "elope." No announcements, no visiting family, a weekend "honeymoon" in Annapolis. We would have a simple interreligious wedding with a rabbi and a priest (my upbringing was Protestant, but he was an old friend from grad school) and the mandatory two witnesses. We barely managed to reserve the chapel in time, and when we arrived, almost late, the severe young man guarding the entrance refused to let us in. "We're here to be married," I explained, thinking our wedding finery would speak for itself. "Yeah, likely story," his eyes said. "It's the old dressed-up-like-a-bride scam." Finally, we convinced him we were not disguised Visigoths.

To us, the ceremony was not just the last step of a legal process. It was important to be married "before God." *His* presence was required. Yet it all seemed so slapdash—the priest couldn't get permission to officiate and the rabbi forgot to bring the service we had agreed upon—that I actually worried that God might not be present.

"Lord, will You be with us?"

You couldn't keep Me away! My presence will be fully with you. I bless this marriage. I will be present in every pore of your being.

It was a simple and beautiful ceremony, and we did feel blessed. But, as time went on, I found I was praying but not really listening. I was avoiding something.

3

I am an evolving God

I had entered college a Christian and left an agnostic. I had no desire to be "washed in the blood" again. The question I had been avoiding was, "Do You want me to become a Christian?"

No, I don't want you to join any denomination.

"Is it okay for me to read about Jesus?" I asked about Jesus rather than Christ. Jesus is a historical person, who certainly existed, but whether he was the Christ, the Messiah, is a religious question. I did not want my question to prejudge the answer.

Yes, but reading through the Old Testament first is a good approach.

"The God of the Old Testament seems terrifying. You do not seem terrifying, Lord."

I was young then. I had not had much experience with people. I am an evolving God.

God was *young* then? He is *evolving*? I thought God was supposed to be perfect, eternal, and unchanging. I had been an agnostic, but I thought I had a clear idea of what I was agnostic *about*. I was usually disturbed to be told something that did not fit my preconceptions. Yet this bit of news, while puzzling, did not upset me. The God who spoke to me was very much a personal God. It was surprising but not out of character if, like other persons, He changes over time. Later I would learn this is why God wanted to talk to me.

I was relieved I did not have to become a Christian, but I still wondered whether Christian beliefs about Jesus were true. "Lord, is Jesus Your Son?"

Yes.

I wondered about the doctrine of the Trinity, that God comprises the Father, the Son, and the Holy Spirit. "Lord, is Jesus God?"

Yes.

I had trouble tracking these answers. "But You told me I should not become a Christian."

Yes, you should not.

"But You just said . . ."

To believe that Jesus is My Son is not the same as being a Christian. Christianity is a sect, with some truths but many limitations. Study Jesus, learn from him, but do not become a Christian.

So Jesus is God. Or is he *a* god. Perhaps all highly spiritual people are godlike. "Lord, does Jesus have a unique role, or is he one of many manifestations of God?"

Unique.

"Is he the key to saving or healing the world?"

Yes, he is an important part of it.

"Is the language of 'believing in him' apt?"

Yes.

"Should I pray to Jesus or to God?"

It is the same.

The same! That certainly sounded Christian to me.

Protestants don't "worship Mary," as they suspect Catholics of doing, but for some reason I asked, "What about Mary?"

The feminine side of God—the healing side—is important in healing the world. Mary is a good embodiment, representation, reflection of that side of God.

My wife is Jewish and I was afraid all this talk about Jesus would upset her. But, like someone who talks too much about the very thing he wants to avoid, I asked, "Lord, did the Jews make a mistake in not being open to the new covenant announced by Jesus?"

Yes.

Oh, no, here it goes!

They became wedded to the covenant, the covenant with the people of Israel in their Messianic destiny. That was, and remains, a valid covenant.

But it is not the only covenant. I make many covenants with human beings. They are all valid and have their own destiny, and work together toward a common destiny for mankind.

The new covenant of Jesus is not as incompatible with the covenant with Israel as Jews tend to suppose. It is compatible, but does not supersede, does not erase or nullify, the old covenant.

I wanted to nail this down. "Does Jesus replace the covenant?"

No, he fulfills it.

That answer was consistent with the New Testament. In Matthew 5:17 Jesus says, "Do not think that I have come to abolish the law or the prophets. I have come not to abolish but to fulfill."

Like an attorney driving a point home, I asked again, "Does Jesus fulfill the covenant in a way that *replaces* it?"

No, it remains fully valid.

But, back to my first question: "Should Jews, in Jesus' day, have accepted him as Messiah?"

Yes.

Okay, Abigail would just have to live with that answer. "Lord, why didn't they accept Jesus?"

Many different reasons. He was too radical, flouted their traditions, spoke a language they found uncomfortable, alien. It's not easy to believe. It is easier to pray for a distant Messiah than to accept a present one.

I didn't seem to be able to stop myself. "Lord, was it a *sin* for Jews to reject Jesus?"

No, no more or less than all those years you did not believe. It is a sin in a sense, but it is also much of the human condition not to believe. People are skeptical for good reasons, having to do with their intelligence, as well as bad.

Finally, I went over the top. "Did Jews kill Christ?"

That's a silly question. Did Americans—or Southerners—kill Lincoln? Some Jews, some Gentiles were equally implicated. That is a nonissue.

Good. At least that issue was taken off the table.

I had also heard that St. Paul redefined the people of Israel to include all people who believe in Jesus. "Lord, are Christians part of the people of Israel?"

People who believe in Jesus are members of My people.

I would often tell Abigail what I had been told, and usually she reserved comment. But, when she heard that Jews should have accepted Jesus, she burst into tears. Two thousand years of pogroms and persecution, ghettos and exile—all for a mistake? I don't know if that is really an implication of what I had been told, but it was certainly a natural reaction. She later told me that, "mistake" or not, the people of the covenant, as the "suffering servant" identified by Isaiah, will always be susceptible to persecution.

After that, I wondered whether I should share everything with Abigail. Perhaps I was supposed to keep it to myself. She is a sensitive person—feelings shoot right through her body. I was told to use discretion.

Do not break the vessel.

Judaism, Christianity, Jews, Jesus—all this upset me, so, for a time, I concentrated on day-to-day matters. One morning I started to ask some trivial question and was interrupted.

You stopped asking about Me because some of the answers disturbed you. They shook your faith.

That was true. When answers upset me, I would start thinking that, surely, this was not the voice of God. "Lord, why is faith like that? Why is Your interaction with us so tenuous and subject to doubt?"

First, it is not. During most times, people have not had trouble believing. Believing in Me or in some gods was—is—the most natural thing in the world.

Second, My "invisibility" has to do with the kind of Being I am. It's like asking why we can't see neutrinos. Nobody can see your "mind." You believe in "other minds" with no greater "evidence."

God was alluding to the topic of my doctoral dissertation. One of the great philosophical puzzles concerns skepticism with regard to knowledge of other minds. The problem arises from the fact that we do not have direct access to other people's thoughts and feelings. We only observe their outer behavior. In fact, we do not have any proof that others really have inner thoughts and feelings at all. Yet it is reasonable to believe they do. Is God any more elusive than minds? Well, He certainly seems so.

Suffering is the law of growth in the universe

4

I was trying to be flexible, but my mind was being stretched out of shape. Some days I would doubt the voice. It was, after all, in my head and talked a lot like me. But I was told,

My words are coming to you for a reason. Do not worry that it (My voice) sounds like you. It is bound to sound like you (and to use) your vocabulary, your concepts. That is how revelation works . . .

As I listen, I have a sense of what God means and spell that out in parentheses.

But notice that what you are now writing is completely different from what you believed prior to prayer—so different, much of it is profoundly uncomfortable and disturbing to you.

Just relax, and put yourself in My hands.

Being reassured by the very voice I was doubting seemed circular. How can you tell whether a message is really from God? I sought advice from a philosopher at a religious college. Did he know of any writings about how to tell if an answer received in prayer is really from God? I learned that my question had an official name, the Problem of Spiritual Discernment, and that indeed it had been addressed. Now I would get to the bottom of it.

The classic text on the question is *The Spiritual Exercises* of St. Ignatius, founder of the Society of Jesus (Jesuits). I read it eagerly, but the section on Rules for the Discernment of Spirits sent a chill down my spine:

"It is characteristic of the evil one to transform himself into an angel of light, to work with the soul in the beginning, but in the end to work for himself. At first he will suggest good and holy thoughts that are in conformity with the disposition of a just soul, then, little by little he strives to gain his own ends by drawing the soul into his hidden deceits and perverse designs."

Evidently, the evil one is a very good con man. Could my voice be a clever deception leading me down the garden path? How could I tell? St. Ignatius explains:

"We must pay close attention to the course of our thoughts, and if the beginning, middle, and end are all good and directed to what is entirely right, it is a sign that they are inspired by the good angel. If the course of the thoughts suggested to us ends in something evil, or distracting, or less good than the soul had previously proposed to do; or if these thoughts weaken, disquiet, or disturb the soul by destroying the peace, tranquility, and quiet which it had before, this is a clear sign that they proceed from the evil spirit."

My prayers did suggest "good and holy thoughts." God had certainly not told me to do anything wrong. On the other hand, the prayers did disquiet my agnostic soul. Well, it is actually more complicated than that. The moments when I most "dwelt in God" were calm and reassuring. But I was not always comfortable with what I was told. And I was most disturbed when I was not actually praying, but wondering what people would think if I told them I talk with God—and He talks back!

So I continued to investigate the problem of discernment. I looked for something more recent and found it in *The Art of Praying: The Principles and Methods of Christian Prayer*, by Romano Guardini. According to Monsignor Guardini, "It may happen in contemplation that we have a strange experience. We may have been reflecting on God in faith alone. Suddenly, God is present . . . a wall which was there before is there no more." Okay, this spoke directly to my situation.

According to Guardini, there follows a period of divided reactions: "Our intuition tells us that this is God or at any rate connected with Him. The intimation may frighten us. ['Yes,' I thought.] We do not know whether we dare presume that this intuition is true and we are uncertain what to do. ['Yes, exactly.'] However, the intuition becomes a certainty, even an absolute certainty which leaves no room for doubt. ['That is true also.']"

However, Guardini says, doubts may return "when we discover that other people have no knowledge of these things." Yes, the problem of what will other people think. This, he says, can lead to total unbelief. "It may also happen that one doubts whether the whole experience had not merely been a delusion or temptation." Well, I never went that far. But all is not lost, he says, if one follows this advice. "In the face of these difficulties and doubts one should remain calm and trust in God. One should submit to His will and pray for enlightenment." "Thus," he concludes, "faith is fortified and love becomes pure."

In short, there is a problem in believing every voice you hear. But there is also a problem if, having sensed the divine presence, you give in to doubt.

Unfortunately, since Descartes, doubt has been the preoccupation—perhaps the occupational disease—of us epistemologists. "Lord, I am skeptical by nature and that worries me."

Don't worry about doubting unless it interferes with faith. Doubting is a natural response of a thinking mind to conflicting evidence. You may doubt—you might always doubt—but faith must transcend doubt as it transcends knowledge.

I determined to follow that path, maintaining a critical distance from my experience of God while at the same time yielding to divine guidance. It is not an easy balance to strike, but it seems to be a challenge at the heart of the life of faith.

Is God a Person? When I asked, I was given a complex answer.

Yes and No. I come to you—but not to raindrops—as a Person, and therefore I *am* a Person. One cannot be a Person in some modes without *being* a Person.

But I am also much more than a Person. Just because I seem so

familiar to you—we talk just as persons do—should not mislead you into thinking I am "just a guy." It is true that I have many of the attributes of a person—desires and a history, for example. But again do not assume that desire and history mean just the same for Me as they do for human beings. Keep in mind that I am definitely *not* a human being.

"But Jesus is."

Yes.

"Then how can it be right to say that Jesus is *identical* with God, that he *is* God? Two beings cannot be identical if one is human and one is not, one is mortal and the other is not."

This notion of identity is not helpful here. Jesus' whole heart and soul and mind were one hundred percent infused with Me. What he said, I said—just as what you are writing now is what I am telling you. And some of your thoughts are put there by Me, which means they are Mine, because they are put there by an indwelling of Me in you, a partial merge, if you will. This is not just inspiration. When I enter something, I really enter it—become infused—"intermingled" is too weak a word because the elements are no longer separately identifiable.

Well, that was a lot to take in. I would have to "let it percolate" as Miss Finley, my high school Latin teacher, used to say.

Reading the New Testament, I came to the story of an angry Jesus driving the money lenders from the Temple (Mark 11:15-17): "And he entered the temple and began to drive out those who were selling and those who were buying in the temple, and he overturned the tables of the money changers and the seats of those who sold doves. . . ."

"Lord, what am I to make of Jesus' temper?"

People often irritated him.

"Irritated him? If he is God, wouldn't he be above that sort of feeling?"

Yes and No. You don't understand. Jesus is a human being, though he is also part of Me. He is subject to limitations as well as benefits that result from that. He has feelings and emotions. That is why he can save the world so effectively. He is a model of how a finite creature, with all the pushes and pulls of emotions, can nevertheless give boundless love.

"Okay, that makes sense to me."

Like others before me, I wondered how a Supreme Being could possibly care about us human beings. Job asks (7:17-18): "What is man, that you make much of him, that you fix your attention upon him—inspect him every morning, examine him every minute?"

"Lord, what are we to You?"

You are My face onto the world. And onto each other—you, whom I love. I want you to love each other. Christ's two commandments are right.

Matthew 22:37-39: "You shall love the Lord your God with all your heart, and with all your soul, and with all your mind" and "You shall love your neighbor as yourself."

They are rooted in the Old Testament. It is hard for Me to love people directly—hard on them, that is. I need people to do it for Me.

It seems that we open the world to God. He experiences the world through us. I remembered French phenomenologist Maurice Merleau-Ponty's argument that, since perception is essentially perspectival—from a vantage point—there is literally no God's-eye point of view. We are His eyes and ears.

"I have read that our grace or salvation had to be 'purchased at a price'—namely, God's giving up His only Son. I really don't understand this, Lord. Did You really suffer from giving up Your only Son?"

It is more complex than that. God as Son takes on the suffering of mankind, takes it on quite literally and co-suffers with mankind. *I* **co-suffer with mankind. Otherwise, I would have put creatures into a fallen (limited) world and watched them suffer from a distance.**

Moreover, My growth requires that I suffer. Suffering is the law of growth in the universe. There is even a form of suffering for subatomic particles—the constant disequilibrium and disruption of particles. Like muscles, things grow by being torn apart and healing.

Okay, so we suffer, Jesus suffers, and God suffers, but the question remains: How does the fact that suffering is divinely shared make anything better?

You got a glimpse of life after death

5

I don't care whether there is life after death. That may seem odd, but I tend to be a contrarian with regard to my own feelings, a habit since childhood. I do not live a roller coaster of hopes and fears. My emotions are like the plains of Kansas, so flat water doesn't know which way to run. That includes the afterlife.

Still, as long as I had God on the line, it seemed like something I should ask about. When I asked, I was reprimanded. I was told that I didn't really want to know, I was asking merely because I thought I should, and I should figure out why I didn't want to know.

At first, I had no idea, but then it came to me. As I pictured the afterlife, it was boring and lonely, like driving all night on one of those long western highways.

Then I was given a series of images—more accurate ways to picture the afterlife. The first image was of being immersed in wonders of nature of incomparable beauty. The second was of being an Einstein whose mind now grasped fully all the vast mysteries of the universe, having the ultimate "aha!" experience over and over again. Another was of listening with full intensity to music more lovely than any the world has ever known. And finally, it was like being in love, but with a vaster compass, sustained over endless time, and receiving boundless love in return.

That night I had a dream.

I was a young man in the Navy. We were told we would ship out the next day, but were given a few hours' leave the evening before. My buddy had to go do something first—fix a ship or something. So I went to check out with the "sergeant." You needed to turn in two forms. I had misplaced one and assumed they would give me another, but, no, they were teaching me a lesson in Navy discipline. I saw my friend's forms lying there, so I "borrowed" one of his, thinking that, savvy in the ways of the Navy, he would know how to get around the problem. Later I felt I had done the wrong thing.

The scene changed. I was driving through Kentucky, heading home to my family (though, in real life, I have no family in Kentucky). Somehow I found myself in an institutional compound of stark concrete buildings enclosed by thick walls. The inhabitants—inmates?—seemed friendly. But some began to suffer mental decline and animal-like deformities. First there were just a few victims—we all had the condescendingly charitable attitude, "poor Joe"—but the condition kept spreading, and finally afflicted me. I looked grotesque, my head oversized and apelike, and I began losing memory and focus.

It became evident that the people in charge meant us no good. That night, I escaped over the wall, and was hunted. I came to a Hindu monastery run by women, perhaps nuns. I felt God guide my words, and to my surprise I said, "I need help, but more importantly, I can help you." They were in financial trouble. I said I could get $10,000 for "each one."

About this time I woke up. It was the middle of the night, but I sat up for a few minutes. Abigail was asleep by my side. The dream continued even as I was awake. As people visited the monastery, I told them my story—I was still deformed—and they were moved by it. I began giving advice and helping people, and then praying for their healing, successfully I guess. My personal story was published, and more people came. Although I was still ugly, my face took on a look that was pleasant for people to look upon. The main nun and I became lovers or soul mates. Then I died.

I expected the dream to end there, but it continued. At some point, I had lain down and gone back to sleep.

I found myself in heaven. There were glorious lights and an airy openness. From that vantage point, one could survey the whole universe, seeing everything through God's eyes, as it were, and with His understanding. I could see all the people on earth, past and present, but I saw them, not as a crowd, but one by one and felt a God-like deep personal concern for each person.

The nun, along with a lover from a different life (a version of Abigail from the times of ancient Israel), were with me, very loving, but without a sexual dimension and without jealousy. And I thought the dream had come to a conclusion.

But, no, I found myself in the world again, in some faraway land, perhaps China, first as a baby in a basket in a field. A moment later the baby turned into a peasant working in the field. As the peasant, I forgot the previous experiences, but I had an attitude of kindness and benign understanding that seemed to carry over.

And then the dream ended.

It could probably be read as an allegory—my having done something wrong, suffered for it, offered service which was redemptive, and enjoyed an afterlife characterized by love. I did not think about it that way at the time, but two aspects did stay with me: first, looking at all of humanity from a God's-eye view and seeing and loving each person in his or her particularity; and second, the surprising rebirth in which I start all over again but with some kind of retention of life's lessons.

A few days later, I started praying about daily matters and was interrupted.

If this were our last conversation and you could know only one thing, what would it be?

I thought, what is it that affects me personally? "Lord, is there life after death, and if so, what is it like?"

You flunk. You have asked Me a question I have already told you the answer to.

"But not what life after death is like."

The dream I sent you told you that. You got a glimpse of life after death.

There is a second reason you flunk. Your motive is honest but

wrong. You ask only what concerns you. You ask out of desire, and fear of not getting what you desire. You should ask in terms of the good of life, of all life, and of what I want for you, not in terms of what you want for yourself. You should seek understanding.

I tried to step back to see what question my "soul" would ask. "How can I merge with You? I'm not sure if that's the best way to put it, Lord: be at one with You, at rest with You, at one with Your will?"

The question is adequately formulated. The goal—one way to describe the goal—is to be at one with God, the God of All. At bottom, the Soul's will *is* the will of God. The Soul is at one with God.

It is not that you and I are literally the same substance, the same particular. It is that we are "at one," in perfect harmony, and not accidentally so. It is in the nature of what the Soul is, that it is at one with God. Remember that these metaphysical (philosophical) categories are crude and inadequate in the first place.

Back to your question: How can you become at one with God? Of course, the answer is that you already are—your Soul, that is. The task is to come to realize that this is so, to realize it not merely in theory, but in intuitive, felt understanding, in your emotions and feelings, and in practice.

"That's the goal, Lord? It sounds simple. The oneness is already inside. All we have to do is to bring our conscious selves along."

That is right. It is the simplest thing in the world. And everyone, at some level and at some moments, knows it, at least glimpses it. But it is very difficult to actualize in practice. The empirical world—the world of desires and the senses—seems so real and is so powerful that it is extremely difficult to redirect one's energy.

And the empirical world *is* real, in its own way. The world is not an illusion, a mirage. If it is a mirage, it is one from which you can drink water. No, you must respect the empirical world while at the same time emancipating yourself from it, not letting yourself be identical with your interests in this world.

So the world of our experience (and desire) is quite real—it is the arena in which we live our lives and loves, joys and sorrows. In spite of that, we should not let ourselves be ensnared by it. How are we supposed to pull that off?

I was in
the drop of water

6

I wondered if the traditional "divine attributes" were accurate. "Lord, are You infinite?"

I am boundless.

"Are You omniscient?"

I know everything that is important.

"Are You omnipotent?"

I can do everything I want (care) to do.

God had just contradicted every key attribute in the conventional definition of God. He is not exactly infinite, not exactly omniscient, and not exactly omnipotent. All this was so new, I just didn't know what to think, but I was beginning to sense that one reason God spoke to me was to clear up some misunderstandings.

I decided to try a different approach. Philosophers have also conceived of God as Being, the very ground of reality. So I asked about that way of understanding God.

Being, pure Being, Being itself, and the like, are not quite right. You need to keep reading and thinking about this.

The great Catholic philosopher St. Thomas Aquinas defined God as that being whose very essence is to be, to exist. "Lord, is to-be—the *esse* of Thomas Aquinas—right?"

Close but not quite right.

"Why the guessing game?" I wondered. "Why don't You just put the answers in my head?"

That isn't the way the human mind works.

That made sense to me. As a teacher, I understood that minds are not just storage bins you drop things into. Learning is an active process. So I continued the questioning. "Lord, do any of the gods of the world's religions fit You correctly?"

Some—many—come pretty close.

"Lord, is the God of the Old Testament one of the accurate depictions?"

Yes, that is certainly Me. And that is what I was like at that time. I led you to the Miles book because that is something he got right.

I had read and liked Jack Miles' award-winning book, *God: A Biography*. Though a trained theologian, Miles reads the Bible like a novel in which God is the main character. That may sound as if it would fail to do justice to scripture, but it avoids the worries that theologians and historians usually bring to it. He just lets the text—and the character of God—speak for itself.

One day, a New Age friend gave me a mantra that was supposed to "center" one's self. I thought I would give it a try. I don't remember the mantra now, but it was addressed to "the Lord." I asked, "Is the Lord in the mantra You?"

There is only one God but many "lords," many spiritual beings for whom that is not an inappropriate title. Your early prayers—which were addressed to "Lord" and you thought perhaps Lord Krishna or who-knows-Who—were about right. When you address "the Lord," you do not have to specify or have in mind a particular spiritual entity. The Lord who is right for you at that time will respond. The Lord that was right for your early prayers was Me, and so I answered.

I had a very basic question. The God who speaks to me is personal, and in human experience, persons are either male or female. The voice I heard was definitely a masculine voice but sometimes, in some indefinable way, also had a feminine aspect. To my surprise, the answer came in a female voice.

There are many sides to God, some of which *you* might call feminine.

Then one day I had an experience that felt like the feminine presence of God—like a powdery shower, perfumed talc being sprinkled over my whole being.

"Lord, is there a special meaning to the feminine presence?"

You need both (masculine and feminine). What you call the masculine presence gives you strength and energy. It is a bonding in My service. The so-called feminine gives you grace and peace. It is a healing between you and Me.

Abigail asked if I had ever had any spiritual experiences in the past. At first I said "no." I had forgotten two events early in life. Well, not actually forgotten, but set them aside. That's what people do in our secular age. A woman I know recently took a boat trip up the Amazon. One night, she awakened when everyone else was fast asleep, and went up to the deck. The entire galaxy was splayed across the sky. She was enveloped by the dark sights and murmuring sounds of the jungle, teeming with life in the midst of tranquility. It was an immersion in the universe itself. She did not call the experience mystical or even religious, but it was certainly an epiphany, a moment of intimate connection with the Whole, full of awe, wonder, and reverence.

My friend's experience was in a more impressive setting than my two moments. The first occurred when I was just a kid. One of my chores was watering the lawn. I had run water in the shrubs and bent down to turn off the faucet. I don't know why I lingered for a moment, crouching down, looking at the tap, but as I did, a last drop of water slowly formed on the bottom edge and hung there. I looked at that drop of water in a way I had never looked at anything before. I saw it—how to describe it?—in its full presence, its suchness, its integrity as an independent existent in the community of being. When I later read in Buber about encountering Nature as Thou, this experience came to mind. It was not as if the drop of water had a mind or soul or was looking back at me or anything like that. Yet I no longer saw it as merely an *it*, merely an item in the inventory of the universe. I saw the drop of water as, in a sense, a member of what Immanuel Kant called the Kingdom of Ends—the community of all beings who should be respected as ends-in-themselves, not just as means for the use of others. This is, of course, language I now use. I don't know how I would have described it at the time. I was just a kid, after all, and it didn't seem worth telling.

The other experience was more arresting and consequential. It was a balmy evening during my senior year at Riverside Poly high school. We used to go downtown to one of those old-style, elegant movie theaters. My friends and I were outside, standing around and joking, waiting for others to arrive. Suddenly, I was in a world of my own, enveloped by concentric circles swirling around a center, like a small spiral galaxy. Just as suddenly, the experience was over. It would have been hard to describe even then, but its meaning was crystal clear. Time had disclosed its essence to me. I did not mention it to my friends, who had not noticed my "absence." I did not tell any-one—whatever understanding I retained I could not have articulated even to myself—but the moment left an imprint. Though not much for poetry, I found myself responding to T. S. Eliot's *Four Quartets*, a deep meditation on the nature of time, and particularly to the lines:

> At the still point of the turning world. Neither flesh nor
>   fleshless;
> Neither from nor towards; at the still point, there the dance is,
> But neither arrest nor movement. And do not call it fixity,
> Where past and future are gathered. Neither movement from
>   nor towards,
> Neither ascent nor decline. Except for the point, the still point,
> There would be no dance, and there is only the dance.

I developed an interest in philosophical questions regarding time and years later published a phenomenological analysis of the experienced "now" that provided a way of understanding Plato's insight that "time is the moving image of eternity."

These two moments—and that of my friend in the Amazon—were divine shafts of light breaking through the clouds, as are many experiences people gloss over and relegate to their mental attics.

Later, I was told,

Think about epiphanic experiences. When did you feel close to Me or most spiritually open?

"I can only remember the two experiences. The first was the I-Thou with a drop of water."

Yes, that is *very* significant. What did you understand from that experience?

"I understood the subjectivity of all things . . . but I'm not sure that is quite right. I did not imagine the drop of water looking out at me or having feelings or the like. I just encountered the 'suchness' of it, its full independent integrity, my respect for it, that we were in some kind of relationship . . ."

That was an encounter with Me. *I* was in the drop of water. Why not? Where else would I be? I am in everything. You suddenly became open to My presence in that drop of water. You did not think of it that way, and you were right. It is not that I as a great mystical being somehow inhabited this tiny object, but you rightly experienced the drop for what it was, and that is precisely how I am "in" things. As you can tell, I am in each thing "fully."

"Lord, if You were in the drop of water, then are You in each of us also? Are we all part of You?"

You are both other and same (as Me). I need you to be other so that I may encounter another self. I am a Person and, like other persons, define Myself by responding to other persons, and being responded to (by them).

But I also need union, not distance—just as other persons do. You and Abigail are both other and same. You need to be different people—love is a bridge between differences. You also merge spirits at certain moments, though not totally. That is also a kind of completion or fulfillment. Life, including My life, is the dialectic, as you might call it, of same and other, confrontation and union.

We are both other than God and yet the same as God? But same and other are opposites. This did not go down easy for a former logic professor, but I went on. "Lord, are those moments of union with God the goal, or are they just nice accompaniments?"

Neither. You shouldn't strive for moments of union *per se*, for peak experiences. That is self-indulgence, and a mistake of some who seek mystical experience. It is like orgasms—you should not seek them for their own sake. That is an abuse, a kind of idolatry. They happen naturally as the outcome and expression of love. But the experience of union is not just the accidental accompaniment of loving God. It is the essential expression.

Then, late at night, I felt the boundary between me and the world becoming thinner and less distinct. Slowly, subject and object were blending, becoming intimately bound, not standing apart from one another. I was noting this intellectually, but it was not an intellectual experience. It was an ontological experience, an experience of my whole being. Finally, for a few moments, it approached total oneness, the complete loss of awareness of self. At that point, I pulled back.

"Lord, what is the meaning of this kind of experience?"

There are many levels and kinds of experience with Me—including music. Do not make too much of it. It is good; just let it happen. It does not mean that you are about to become a mystic or anything unworldly. It is not unlike—it is on a continuum with— a wide range of spiritual experiences, in and out of religious practice and sensibility, that people have all the time. But it is definitely good. It will give you energy and peace and insight, so let it in.

Many times one "loses oneself" in an experience, but those moments are less threatening than merging with God. I pulled back, but felt a nagging sense I was not supposed to. "Lord, I feel You want me to do more of the mystical stuff, 'entering' You and so forth."

Yes, and you can remove the scare quotes. There is nothing strange about it. That is how the universe is. The parts can communicate with the whole. It is no more mystical or mysterious than your ability to move your arm.

Actually, since Descartes introduced a sharp mind-body distinction, how the mind moves the body has been a philosophical mystery. But, in actual life, it is not. The parts can communicate with the whole and vice versa. I had never thought of the universe that way.

My Story

I want you to tell My story

7

Memorial Bridge was lit by the morning sun, white and bright. The Lincoln Memorial rose up in front of me, also white, but grave and rich in national meaning. For me, crossing the bridge was a daily call to purpose. But the voice broke today's silent entry by announcing, out of the blue:

Your work here is done.

My work here is *done*? I thought I was right in the middle of it.

After teaching philosophy for fifteen years at Boulder, I had come to Washington on a Congressional Fellowship and stayed, working first on a Congressional staff, later at the National Endowment for the Humanities, finally at the nonprofit organization where Abigail had first reached me. When these prayers began, friends and associates were moving into the highest levels of government and I was being asked to consider positions, just below Cabinet level, that would have crowned a career like mine. But now, suddenly, I was being told, "Your work here is done." *Done.*

About that time, I felt guided to look at Matthew 16:13-14, where Jesus asks the disciples, "Who do people say that the Son of Man is?" "And they answered, 'Some say John the Baptist, but others Elijah, and still others Jeremiah or one of the prophets.'"

Then I was directed to the very last verse of the very last book of the Old Testament. Malachi 4:5 promises that Elijah, the prophet who was taken up to heaven in a fiery chariot, will return with God's message, "Lo, I will send you the prophet Elijah. . . ."

Abigail's train was late. I had been waiting at Union Station for over an hour and stood to stretch my legs. Some now-forgotten images passed before my eyes, and then,

I want you to be My new Elijah.

"Your new *Elijah*?" I didn't know whether to feel flattered, or overwhelmed, or just crazy. I protested, "Lord, I am not worthy."

I will decide who is worthy.

I didn't know what a new Elijah was supposed to be, but I knew I did not want the job. "Lord, I don't have faith enough."

You have more faith than you know.

"Who is Elijah?"

He is the prophet.

"What is he to me?"

He is you.

I didn't think that meant that I was literally a reappearance of Elijah, but still I objected, "No, Lord, this is just crazy."

He is you.

I remembered Abraham Lincoln's story about the man who was tarred and feathered and run out of town on a rail. "If it weren't for the honor of the thing," the man said, "I would rather have walked." And I had seen the war movies: "You will have the honor of leading the assault." Some honors aren't worth it.

I did feel the honor. God was about to put His seal on this role for me, a role more suitable for a real Elijah. I felt a swell of pride, as I was being told this, and immediately the line went dead. Ego had broken the connection.

Abigail's train still had not arrived. I paced back and forth, no longer seeing the other people in the station. What to think? What to feel? Finally, I forced a deep breath and, with irritation mitigated by resignation, asked, "Lord, what exactly do You want of me?"

I want you to describe the inner life of God, what it is like to be God.

The *inner* life of God? What it is *like* to be God? I didn't know what this could possibly mean, but I forged on. "Lord, why is that important for us to know?"

Mankind sees God only from the outside, and that leads to distortions in its view of God, as it would of anyone—too distant, awesome, oppressive, Other. Even mystics are very one-sided. They experience oneness, but that is not the same as empathizing with My subjective experiences.

Okay, I could see that if God is too distant, it would be hard to relate to Him, but there was a problem. "Lord, we think of God as being so infinite and ethereal that 'subjective experience' doesn't even make sense."

Exactly—that's one of the distortions. Although I am much more than a Person, I am a Person, a soul, like you. You—people—cannot relate properly, constructively, to Me unless you understand that. (Take) love, for example. My love comes across as impersonal, generic, oceanic wallowing, but (in fact) it is quite specific, concrete, with feeling, with response to the particulars of your being, of your life.

I want you to tell My story.

Thinking of the Bible, I said, "Lord, hasn't Your story already been told?"

Yes, but it is time for it to be told anew, and not in the same way. We are entering an unusual time in the history of the world. The old religions are coming apart. Yet there is a renewal of religious spirit. Many of the great religions rested on a relatively clear reception of messages from Me. The new spirituality does not. It is aimless, made-up, impressionistic, psychologized, sometimes flaky and even dangerous and demonic. Not all "spiritual" forces are from God. Some are evil or distorted. A purity of message must be regained.

But there is gain here as well. The old revelations were limited. They fit the understanding of people at the time. The messages were sometimes garbled or misunderstood or distorted over time.

Also, I have evolved since then. There is new information to impart.

There it is again: God evolves.

There is a long history, that has not been chronicled, of My development. I would like to tell you that story and perhaps have you publish it.

My message is evolving over time. You will carry it forward. Do not credit this to your ego—it will be My voice. (Just) focus on the task. The world's religions have spent themselves. They need renewal.

Believe the inspirations I send you. Do not worry about any other standards than communicating correctly what I reveal to you. It may seem crazy to others. It (revelation) always does. This is the courage of the messenger.

I felt like Dorothy swept up in the whirlwind. And poor Abigail, would she be swept up too?

Her train had finally arrived. Over dinner, I broke it to her. She just listened, unfazed.

"I felt submissive; it sounded like orders from Above," she explained later. "I thought: Jerry is clearly not making it up. What it means in my life is, of necessity, open-ended. To receive such a directive is to move to a realm or level not foreseeable. In other words, it is a blessing."

There is a spiritual reawakening

8

The next day, the words "an instrument of revelation" came to me. "Lord, is this what You want me to be?"

Yes, that's right.

"What kind of revelation?"

And what kind of instrument. First, I want you to model the spiritual life. Live it deeply. Theology is not just an intellectual exercise. It must be grounded in an intimate relationship with Me, an intimate openness to My Word.

"Aren't I already open, Lord?"

Yes, but you turn away. You know the problem. You hold Me at arm's length and listen to Me only part of the time, and only partially, not as a whole person. You need to draw Me into yourself totally—live through Me—and let Me guide you totally.

"But that sounds miserable. I couldn't have fun and enjoy life anymore."

No, it doesn't mean that. You will find life perfectly pleasant. This is not a renunciation. It is an affirmation, a growing in a certain direction, in a certain domain.

This reminded me of saying a sad farewell, before getting married, to all I would be giving up—having my apartment as messy as I wanted, living on pizza, watching the *Late Late Show*. It's amazing what a bachelor can cherish as the good life.

"Lord, what do You want me to do?"

Nothing dramatic. Just pause in the course of the day to take Me in. It doesn't mean you have to interrupt other things you're doing. But I will be copresent and a coparticipant. Try that now, as you eat your lunch.

"Okay, Lord." I drew Him in and unwrapped my sandwich. "Let me share this with You, Lord."

Good.

That day I ate lunch "with God." But most days I do not.

"Lord, it sounds as if You want to announce a new revelation. In this day and age?"

There is nothing surprising or shocking in further revelations. I reveal things to people all the time in many different ways—in prayer, inspiration, intuition, ethical insight, even aesthetic response. My revelations evolve. I reveal different things now than millions of years ago.

"Millions of years ago?"

Yes, I revealed things to prehistoric people, though they had a limited ability to understand. My revelations to Abraham and Moses were unusual, because they marked the first of the clear messages that got through and were really understood.

But the current situation is different. I have been revealing things always to individuals who asked, but this was piecemeal, fragmentary, and usually added by the recipients as interpretations of previous texts and old revelations.

Now we need new systematic revelation, from bottom to top, almost to start over again—with (a new) Genesis, one might say, with a new Gospel of John. And a new philosophical understanding of God. The old one was only partly inspired and contains too much of the arrogance of human reason.

Mankind does not live in a period for a Great Prophet. There can be no new Moses or other Deliverer. There can at best be Elijahs—prophets and seers—people who explain My story in a form that can be understood by this age.

A time of mending is needed, but the nature of the world today prevents the presentation of a single, unitary vision. The best I can do is to share visions with particular individuals and let them articulate these visions in their own voices.

It is difficult being God. One is not well understood. One is even ignored, neglected, and denied. Yet I need to be known, to be recognized. The world needs for Me to be known.

My nature, the true nature of the universe, of Being, and My relation to human beings, to their role and destiny, is complex. Einstein's theory of relativity is child's play by comparison. An adequate understanding cuts across some of the categories human beings find most natural, though they are really profoundly "unnatural"—and I mean that in the eerie sense. They are warped; they often represent disorders of the soul, distortions of Being.

It is your task, as one of My messengers, My Elijahs, to straighten out some of the errors and distortions, and also to broadcast these particular revelations to others.

"Lord, how will I get myself heard?"

You will be heard precisely because there is a spiritual reawakening. Many are listening, waiting, open to a new word. It will be most hard for two groups—the atheists, secularists, who have set their hearts against Me, against hearing, and (followers of) the old religions, who are set in their ways, very attached to specific forms and formulas. The latter pains Me because, in many ways, these have been My most faithful servants. Like a servant whose master has died and faithfully carries out his last wish—but misheard the wish. The old religions are mostly based on insights, revelations I gave them. But they became rigidified. Partial insights were mistaken for the whole. Ritualism and creeds have been overemphasized, and I am Myself partly to blame, since at one point those were the most important thing in the world to Me. I am hoping I can open their hearts to something new, without unduly disturbing their good and faithful practices.

One other thing, besides the new spiritual openness, will help. The testimony of the speaker, by which I mean the witness of his character, makes the message credible. You have a good (sound) character. People can see that. You are not a nut or a fanatic or a self-important impostor. People see that. That is why it is important that you write in your own honest, authentic voice—not as some oracular imitation of Me.

Following that instruction, I have not tried to "improve" what God told me.

When I was told to "tell God's story," I was cautioned against claiming divine authority.

I give you information, insight, but I am not bequeathing any authority. Pass it on in that spirit.

"But, in fact, having this line of communication with You does make me feel superior, Lord."

You are not superior. You have drenched yourself in sin for fifty years. Do not feel superior to anyone. Your only superiority is your willingness to obey, and that I have given to you. I opened your heart to love and to Me. You did things to prepare, but I have opened the hearts of some who did not. It is neither deserved nor a gift—it is a fact about Me. I am expressing Myself through you—neither more deserving nor more blessed than the paint used in the *Mona Lisa*.

Well, okay, no matter who the artist is, paint is just paint. But I couldn't help thinking that, if you're paint, what could be better than to make it into the *Mona Lisa*?

Still, I did not feel like a prophet or seer. As I started reading about different religions, I found an endless cast of characters— priests, saints, mystics, apostles, evangelists, gurus, shamans. None seemed to fit me. "Lord, what is my role supposed to be?"

Just to be a serious reporter of what you are told when you pray.

Okay, *that* I could do.

Still, it all seemed intolerably bizarre. I thought I should talk it over with the wisest people I knew. One, a distinguished medical ethicist, responded, "First of all, this is not weird." Nothing he could have said would have been a greater relief to me! Another, a well-known author, said, first, "That's great—now you *know* there is a God," and then added, "You have had a Kierkegaard moment," recalling that philosopher's question, "If you encountered Jesus on the streets of Copenhagen, would you follow him?" A prominent lay theologian said he was "touched" by my story and suggested some reading while I waited for my "big" assignment.

While there were also cautionary responses, no one seemed to think I was crazy or a fool to take the voice seriously.

Still, I was not prepared for the next experience.

I want you to enter My heart.

"*Enter* God's heart? This is weird, Lord, and scary, like out-of-body travel."

I will protect you.

For moral support I asked, "Lord, first give me Your love."

Let Abigail love you. You will feel My love through her.

"Then strengthen me, be with me, for this."

I will.

He took my hand, as it were, and led me into the "heart of God." I had expected it to be an overpowering, perhaps terrifying experience. But it was more like the eye of a hurricane. I was at the center of something vast and powerful, but here it was quiet, calm, and peaceful. I surveyed the things I feared—the end of my career, loss of reputation, financial insecurity, and a book that went nowhere. In that calm that is God, each concern disappeared.

9

I want nothing other than your fulfillment

The brash display at the front of the bookstore announced *Conversations with God*—the first of three volumes in which God tells all . . . to *somebody else*. I thought I was the one anointed to carry God's message. "What's going on here?" I thought.

Before my own experience, I would not have thought for a minute that the author, Neale Donald Walsch, actually heard from God. But, if God spoke to me, He could surely speak to anyone He pleased. In fact, I had been told that He communicates with people all the time. Walsch too reports God as saying, "I talk to everyone. All the time. The question is not to whom do I talk, but who listens." Just what I had been told.

Had God appointed two messengers? With different messages? Or was this guy not on the up-and-up? I have to admit I was skeptical. My own prayers were herky-jerky and the voice I heard spoke in my own casual vernacular. Walsch's conversations are reported in polished prose. That looked rigged.

Nor was I impressed with what Walsch reports having been told. It sounded like pop Buddhism—feel-good stuff that sells books but is unlikely to be God's authentic word. Wasn't Walsch just a charlatan?

When I asked, I didn't like the answer. I was told,

He got most of it right.

"Got most of it right? But, Lord, some of what Walsch reports contradicts what You have told me."

They probably are not contradictions, but merely appear to be. Of course, you are both fallible receptors.

"Walsch reports You as saying that 'you can do whatever you believe you can.' Lord, that is just silly."

Give Me an example.

I started to describe the case of a woman I know who has clear goals, strong convictions, and great force of will, and yet often fails.

No, (give Me an instance) from your own life.

"Just winning a tennis game, for example."

Give Me a break. (A) You always have mixed thoughts in those situations and (B) I said you can't alter physical laws. If you completely wanted to win at tennis and believed you could, you would practice, exercise, and so forth. When I say you can do anything, I don't mean that you don't have to take the necessary steps. Napoleon was charismatic, but he still had to train troops, plan logistics, and so on. Stop being simpleminded. You are fixating on a single meaning of "you can do anything" and trying to rebut it. Instead, think about what meaning could be true. It certainly does not mean wish-fulfillment. Think about it.

"Walsch reports You as saying, 'God will grant whatever is asked, without fail.' Whatever is asked!"

The trick is in "ask." Not everything you "want" has been "asked" in the right way, with fulsomeness of soul.

"But then the statement is completely misleading. It depends on a verbal sleight of hand."

Not so. Some might be confused by it, but it is a way of focusing attention on the right way to ask, to believe and feel fully, and to motivate this change in people. But it is not a lie, not even a Noble Lie. It is the direct truth. When you come into the fullness of Being, of partnership with God, everything you truly seek will be granted. That may seem like a bait and switch, but that is not the way you will see it when you get there. You will see that this is indeed what you really wanted all along.

"But it still seems misleading since it suggests that you can win the lottery by wishing for it."

But don't you see? That's not what your soul wants. If it did, *per impossibile*, it would win it. But it doesn't, because your soul has no true desire for such things.

"But, Lord, don't You see how misleading the statement is? It certainly will be read as wish-fulfillment."

Then it's a mistake. That is not what I meant. People want God's will to conform to theirs. Others try to conform their will to God's. But, at root, the two are the same. The goal is to get to the point that you surface your true will, which will coincide with God's. Remember that I want what is good for you. I do not have some arbitrary plan and then demand obedience to it. I want nothing other than your fulfillment. That is what you want too.

You will develop more and have a greater impact for good if you trust in Me and believe in yourself—not in your ego, your will, but in your spirit and your destiny.

"Destiny?"

Yes, there is a goal for you (for each person)—an individual path of evolution—that I want to help you along. Believing that you can progress and trust in Me to help you is very helpful in achieving that goal.

"Walsch reports that everyone will achieve union eventually, through many lives."

That is true, but that does not mean that it is automatic. Everyone will succeed because eventually everyone will do the right thing. In a sense, it doesn't matter who gets there first—there is no prize for speed—all lives are equally valuable. But it matters to the individual, and to the amount of earthly suffering he or she will experience.

"Lord, Walsch says that God has 'no preference' with regard to 'how you live your life.'"

Wrong. I want you to become your best self. What is true is that I accept your need to do whatever you do and (to) take many lives to achieve fulfillment.

Many lives? That sounded like reincarnation, in which I had zero interest, so I didn't ask about it. I don't think I took it seriously.

I didn't pray about Walsch after that. Whatever God was or wasn't doing with him was between him and God.

10

Ego is destructive, separatist, defiant

"Lord, what exactly is my assignment?"

The world needs to understand My story, or at least to understand it better. I have given parts of the story to different people at different times. The whole now needs to be told. Your effort will be part of telling that whole story.

"Do You want people to piece the whole together out of the parts?"

What I most want is for people to listen to Me.

"And to listen to what You have told various people over the ages?"

Yes, that is part of listening to Me.

"What exactly do You want me to write?"

God: An Autobiography. My story is the history of Me—how I came to be.

"The story of Your interactions with various peoples?"

That but not only that. Tell it from My point of view, not the history of people's experience of God.

"Lord, the total story of Your interaction with people would be too vast."

No, all history is selective. Use a different word—like episodes—if you like. But it is history in the sense of being chronological, developmental, and dramatic in some sense. There is a subjective point of view (Myself), intentions and concerns for the future, regrets about the past, and so forth.

"What are the materials for this history? The great religious texts?"

Yes, of course. That is one side of the human-divine (interaction), like hearing one end of a telephone conversation. So that is one starting point. But there are others as well, and I have been leading you to them—the physical record, the geological record, the biological development, the stars and galaxies, time and creation, and so on.

And I will tell you many things Myself—that is the "new revelation" aspect. Nothing overly dramatic there—I reveal Myself all the time.

"So I should read the scriptures of the major religions?"

Yes, I want you to read the early spiritual history of mankind. I will lead you to which readings. I would like you to pray as you read them and take notes as directed.

I grew up at a time when "man" and "mankind" referred to both men and women, and God spoke to me in my own vernacular.

"Lord, You said I was to tell Your story 'from the inside out.' But reading the scriptures is 'from the outside in.'"

Yes, tell My story as I tell it to you. The only purpose for reading is to give you reference points for understanding My story.

"Lord, if I am going to 'get into Your head,' it would be helpful to know what You are up to, what Your ultimate goal is."

No, your job is not to "get into My head." Remember, I am *telling* you what is "in My head." You are not trying to empathize with a fictional or historical character. You have the living Person right here, and I will tell you.

"But, as I prepare for the work . . ."

You are making this falsely complicated because you are not trusting Me. You think you will have to do this on your own by deciphering the cultural forms and so forth. But it is exquisitely simple. You ask Me what you are to read or to study. And then You ask Me what I was up to in relation to what you are reading or studying. And you don't need to worry about the total compass or overall story, because I will lead you item by item.

"Lord, how should I approach the ancient scriptures?"

Get into the frame of mind for reading the (particular) work. That frame of mind is reverential, quiet, respectful, openhearted. It does not consist of analyzing metaphors and stories of gods. Just take in what comes to you.

An ego rush always broke my connection with God. So I tried to keep a cold watch on this ego of mine.

When I was still in Washington, D.C., a matter came up about which I needed the assistance of an eminent intellectual with whom I had a limited acquaintance. He was completely forthcoming, and I felt flattered by his response.

"Lord, how should I take this? Is it wrong for me to feel flattered?"

No, it is not. This is joy, the joy of being yourself, which is proper to (appropriate for) human beings. I want you to be happy, to feel the fullness of your own being, its bounty. I blessed you with certain gifts. Of course, you recognize them as gifts, as benefits, as talents. That is okay. It is not the same as ego.

Ego is destructive, separatist, defiant of My will, self-satisfied and self-lustful. A proper appreciation of yourself opens your heart, binds you to Me, to those you love. Remember that I love you—I love all human beings—without reservation. Ideally, you would love yourself as I love you, as I loved Jesus. But that is not normally possible for human beings, because there are many obstacles.

"But it is possible for a few?"

For some, yes. I have blessed them with the ability to transcend those limitations. They can love themselves fully, and this permits them to love others.

One week I testified before a U.S. Senate committee. It did not go well and my ego limped out of the hearing room.

Get your ego out of it. Stand back and look (at it) at a distance.

"A 'God's-eye' view?"

No, just objectively, as if it were someone else.

That helped. If it were someone else, I would know that, even on a good day, a Senate hearing is unpredictable. But there was still an ego wound.

"Lord, what can I do about that?"

Look, you are encased in a body and a personality, and it requires ego strength and self-respect. When I say, "Get the ego out," I mean the second-order attachment to ego. The ego, like desires, is a fact, a necessary fact. Like the body, it gets bruised. You just nurture it and let it heal. Don't deny it but don't dwell on it either. Accept it and don't attach it to blame. That your ego has been embarrassed is not the same as "doing something wrong." Don't blame yourself. That is an example of the wrong kind of attachment.

"Then I should just say, 'I wish it had gone better,' and leave it at that?"

Correct.

Think about your own
times of suffering

11

I had now accepted the assignment, but God wanted more.

You need purification. Transformation is a good word. It is obedience, which at its fullest is transformation.

"What does that involve, Lord?"

Putting Me first rather than last. Living every moment, making every decision, in response to My call.

"How do I go about doing that?"

You know this—start every day with prayer and let prayer guide you through the day.

There is another way to listen to God. One day, when I was fatigued from travel, I was told to take a day to rest.

"But I have so much work to do, Lord."

Always listen to your body—it is also My voice.

I have not found it easy to live my life fully in tandem with God. Every day there are items on my personal radar, and I usually attend to them first and fit God in when I have a chance.

One morning Abigail called me to breakfast and I held off, due to one of God's seemingly arbitrary commands. "Is my husband becoming a holy man?" she asked with more exasperation than reverence. "I already am," I said, in the sense of having a divine call, "just a very bad one."

"Lord, I know I should try to live each day in response to Your purposes."

That is right. Not just to do it mechanically, like a soldier following orders, but to do it as an organic flow, wishing to be in touch with Me and to live in accord with My will, My love.

"Yes, I always think of You 'pushing' me, rather than my being 'drawn' to You. I respond to orders rather than seeking union."

That is good. The shallow seeking of union with Me is a delusion. The goal is to be "in tune" with Me. The work will flow from that. This is not just a matter of doing your duty. It is coming into alignment with Me—like two singers doing a harmony.

Any person who believes in God has to confront the problem of human suffering. Why does God permit it?

"Lord, does suffering have any purpose or meaning?"

Of course, suffering is what makes life serious. Imagine a world in which actions never resulted in suffering. Imagine a world without the pain of regret, without feeling bad about doing something wrong (or) shameful.

"But disease serves no moral purpose."

Now you are fencing with Me on "the problem of pain." Just listen. You will never learn from fencing.

Disease, disaster, aging, death are essential aspects of suffering. "We" live in a physically vulnerable world. That is the essential condition that makes life serious.

"All that's rather abstract, Lord. What exactly does disease do for us?" I thought of Job's boils.

Suffering is the test of your humanity. There is no greater test than pain—how one copes with it. It is easy to be nice, faithful, and such, when things are great, but very hard under adversity.

"But, Lord, that just seems perverse—or cruel."

No, that's not so. Think about your own times of physical suffering—in the hospital, for example—the shots, the clumsy aide, the itch, the nurse about urinating, those were full of growth.

Those examples brought back memories. A couple of years before these prayers began, I suffered a mild heart attack and was rushed to the intensive care unit. They took blood tests, day and night. There are a limited number of places from which blood can be drawn, and the same spot cannot be used again right away. The wrists are ideal, but mine are sensitive and a needle there smarts. One does not have much power as a patient, but safeguarding my wrists became my prime imperative. One after another blood drawer would come, and I would plead, argue, wheedle, and insist they find some other place to puncture me. Each resisted, then managed to find a spot.

I was transferred to another hospital for the surgical procedure. I was met by a technician who said his name and stuck out his hand— while looking the other way and standing on my oxygen tube. When it was time to go into the operating room, he snatched away my blanket with so violent a jerk it would have ripped out the intravenous insertion if I had not by now been on high alert.

Once in the operating room, I was placed on a slab with my arms flat at my sides. Medical equipment loomed above, posing an impressive threat. "Don't move!" I was told. My nose chose that moment to itch. The itch grew intense, then more intense, dreadfully intense, until nothing existed but me and that itch. Then I understood. I couldn't fight it. I just had to live with it, until the procedure was over. I don't know if the itch went away or what—I forgot all about it.

The procedure went smoothly. I watched the monitor as the surgeon snaked a catheter through an incision in my groin up to a major coronary artery where a stent had to be placed.

Opening an artery is a very serious matter. Bleeding can be life-threatening. The patient has to lie flat and immobile for twenty-four hours. Nurses at my first hospital had been angels in white, but here I was attended by Nurse Ratched's less charming twin. She seemed to resent patients needing her help. Finding it difficult to manage the bedpan flat on my back, I asked for assistance. She acted as if it were a dirty-minded request and responded by threatening me, "If you can't manage the bedpan, we will catheterize you!" Finally, I did manage, and it was time to close up the artery. Another patient had told me the closing could be dangerous as well as painful.

"Who is to perform this delicate operation?"

Nurse Ratched gave me the grim news: young Mr. Scissorhands, the technician whose previous efforts to hurt me had been foiled, would now have another shot. I asked for someone else. "He is the only technician available."

"I am not going to let that guy lay another hand on me."

She made it a battle of wills. We went back and forth. Finally I said, "Let me speak to the doctor."

She said she would see what she could do, and after a time she returned with a young Asian-American attendant. He had magical hands. I didn't feel a thing.

My body was recovering nicely, but the whole experience—starting with "indigestion" in the night (I didn't know that was a heart symptom), calling the office the next morning to find out what nearby doctor was covered by my health plan, driving myself (fool that I was) to the doctor's office, filling out forms and waiting for some time before going up and telling the receptionist, "I may be having a heart attack," the quick examination and discovery that I was at that very moment in the throes of an incipient attack, an emergency medical team rushing to my side trying to head it off, being shoveled into an ambulance, the sirens, intensive care, the surgery, the whole ordeal— left me feeling fragile, as if I were made of spun glass. A sharp tap and I would shatter.

They (these moments) were not empty suffering; they even had to do with leading you to Me.

"How so, Lord?"

They focused your attention on your mortality, which (led) you to open your heart fully to Abigail because you realized how precious this love was. And it led to your prayer to serve God.

I am the medium through which people understand the world  12

"The external world and consciousness are one and the same thing," writes Erwin Schrödinger, the great twentieth-century physicist. In *My View of the World*, he sees the deep meaning of quantum mechanics expressed in the Hindu philosophy of Vedanta. This sounds important, I thought. "Lord, I am reading Schrödinger . . ."

No, that is not the way truth lies.

"But, Lord, I felt You wanted me to read something scientific and . . ."

You didn't pray for guidance about what to read.

"What do You want me to read, Lord? . . . I get the sense that You want me to read something that cuts against scientific orthodoxy."

Yes.

"But what does that?"

History of science. History of views that didn't work out.

"Like astrology?"

Something like that.

Paul Feyerabend was a philosopher-scientist. On the cover of one of his books, where others list their degrees and honors, he gives his astrological chart. I had known and liked him. He had a remarkable appreciation for the unpredictable vitality of the life of the mind, and hence great respect for "views that didn't work out." On one occasion, he heatedly denounced a certain philosopher for trying to resolve philosophical issues by translating them into logical notation. "What a pitiful, rigid, anemic approach!" Abruptly, the denunciation ceased. "Hector should keep at it," he said in a mellow voice. "Who knows? He might come up with something."

In his iconoclastic *Against Method*, Feyerabend, a physicist himself, assembles a fascinating array of examples from the history of science to show that science does not depend on canons of rational method. Rather, the practice of science "can stand on its own feet and does not need any help from rationalists," he wrote. And "non-scientific cultures, procedures and assumptions can also stand on their own feet and should be allowed to do so."

Elsewhere I read about the three traditions in Renaissance science—Aristotelian, Neo-Platonic, and mechanistic. At the time, the mechanistic mindset provided an obstacle to progress in medicine and biology, but it was extraordinarily fruitful for physics and chemistry and established itself as scientific orthodoxy. However, the mechanistic approach to biology has never fully succeeded, and certain trends in recent physics have Neoplatonic overtones. Science remains unpredictable.

I read about the great scientific debate of the eighteenth century: Is space absolute or relative? Today, the standard view is that science and religion are opposites. But it was his theology that led Newton to regard space, "the sensorium of God," as absolute, and a different theology that led Leibniz to uphold relativity, two centuries before Einstein made a fateful decision to study physics rather than music.

"Lord, what does this reading have to do with my assignment?"

The history of science is My story. The history of man's efforts to understand the world is the history of man's relation to Me.

I am the point of interaction between man and the world.

"Lord, what do You mean by point of interaction?"

I am the medium through which man understands the world.

"Is mind the medium?"

Yes.

"Lord, are You saying that, in addition to the human mind and the natural world, there is divine mind somehow essential to the act of understanding?"

The answer I received addresses one of the deep mysteries of philosophy. How is it that consciousness relates to or "intends" an object such as the Liberty Bell? For example, what is it about a thought that makes it the thought *of the Liberty Bell*? The thought is "in your head" and the Liberty Bell is in Philadelphia. What "connects" them?

There is a parallel question about language. How is it that a word relates to or refers to a particular object? The word is itself an object, a vocalized sound or a mark on a page. What connects the word *bell* to the bell? Sometimes it is said that one "points" to the other, but that is a figure of speech. As Ludwig Wittgenstein observes, the same question arises with pointing. When you stretch out your finger, why does it direct attention to an object across the room, rather than to itself?

Follow along, and open your mind. Mind is like a fluid in which human beings and the natural world exist. By participating in the fluid, minds can understand. Think of the problem of intentionality. How is reference possible? How can essences be grasped? How can objects be seen? There must be an interaction, and it is not only causal-physical. How *could* it be? Mind, understanding, is not just physical. It is a conscious, fluid medium.

"Is it somewhat physical?"

Those categories are not helpful here, but it exerts physical force, has physical consequences.

Later I learned that there are some interpretations of quantum mechanics that use a similar concept to explain how an electron in one part of the universe can be in perfect sync with an electron in another part of the universe without any physical interaction between them. I was not aware of that at the time, but I had just read about dark matter and dark energy, "dark" because they cannot be seen but only inferred from gravitational and other effects. The mass of these previously unsuspected components are now thought to far exceed the total visible mass in the universe.

Yes, you should look into those. Think of it—most of what is in the universe is unnoticed. It is inferred from gross phenomena, but it is inferred as force. Think of the human body. It is moved by the mind. How? Where is the mind? The mind is throughout the body.

Its actions are registered, but it is not noticed. I am not noticed. But in fact I am seen everywhere, and I am in the innermost being of man and in the innermost being of matter. Do not have contempt for matter. It is not the inert stuff of certain old theories. It is vital and alive and a part of Me. The interaction of mind and matter is part of Me, and I am the vehicle through which it takes place.

"Lord, I have the feeling that You want me to read and think less, and to listen more and just write down Your story."

Don't stop thinking, but think in a different way. Don't work so hard to figure everything out, to make it rational, to make it fit your categories. Just listen and think through the implications of what I tell you.

"But, Lord, some of what I learn from You comes from worrying over what You say."

Sometimes yes, but often no. Sometimes your questioning just gets in the way. The main point is to open your mind, to try to understand what I am saying on its own terms, and to see ways it might be true or understandable to you.

If something doesn't make sense to me, how am I supposed to "see ways" to make it understandable? Where is that vantage point to be found?

Pure Being is not an abstraction but a living force

13

My experiences with God were personal and intimate. Philosophers drain the life out of Him. God the Person becomes God the Abstraction—the Unmoved Mover, the One, the Absolute, infinite substance, the Ground of Being, the being whose essence is to exist. William Butler Yeats describes the result: "High on some mountain shelf / Huddle the pitiless abstractions bald about the neck."

The great Jewish scholar Gershom Scholem explains the phenomenon.

> The philosophers and theologians were concerned first and foremost with the *purity* of the concept of God and determined to divest it of all mythical and anthropomorphic elements. But this determination to . . . reinterpret the recklessly anthropomorphic statements of the biblical text and the popular forms of religious expression in terms of a purified theology tended to empty out the concept of God. . . . The price of God's purity is the loss of His living reality. What makes Him a living God . . . is precisely what makes it possible for man to see Him face to face.

Feelings, along with other affects, are taken to be weaknesses. So God is regarded as passionless, so passionless that it is difficult to see how He can love. St. Anselm puzzles over how a passionless God can be compassionate. His solution is that "we experience the effect of compassion, but Thou dost not experience the feeling." You can see the logical puzzle: we experience God's love even though God feels no love for us. For the philosophers, even to speak of a personal God is at best a metaphor or analogy. But in my experience, God is not a metaphor. He is a Person to whom we can pray and who can give us guidance about our lives. However, I was told,

They have some aspects of Me right.

"What do they have right?"

They understand that I am pure Being, Being unto itself. They understand My metaphysical essence. They do not understand My dynamic existence, a force . . .

"A Person?"

. . . yes, and a Person. They use these categories in a way that makes them mutually exclusive, but they are not. Pure Being is not an abstraction but a living force, focused personally. Do not avoid metaphysics, but always listen to Me or you will go on the wrong track.

I had read Martin Buber's *I and Thou* when I was a college freshman and had not looked at it since then. But when I fell in love and realized that she loved me back, the opening words of Part 3 came back to me: "The extended lines of relations meet in the Eternal Thou." Love between human beings has a trajectory toward the Divine.

That recollection rekindled my interest in Buber. Returning from New York, where Abigail still taught, I started reading Maurice Friedman's highly praised biography. Buber's philosophical awakening occurred during adolescence, prompted by "the fourteen-year-old's terror before the infinity of the universe." Buber wrote, "A necessity I could not understand swept over me: I had to try again and again to imagine the edge of space, or its edgelessness, time with a beginning and an end or a time without beginning or end, and both were equally impossible, equally hopeless. . . . Under an irresistible compulsion I reeled from one to the other, at times so closely threatened with the danger of madness that I seriously thought of avoiding it by suicide."

I stopped reading for a moment, and as the train rumbled on, I pondered the "edge of infinity." I was taken over by a powerful image, visual and visceral. I felt and saw space at its edges, rushing, expanding outward, unfurling itself with vast force and at almost instantaneous speed, without stop, neither a completed infinity nor merely finite. The vision had a tremendous feeling of life-force, of Being unfurled, bursting forth at reckless speed.

Buber was saved from the brink of suicide by reading Immanuel Kant. Unsolvable questions arise, Kant argues, from trying to reason about space and time as if they were characteristics of reality in itself. They are really just forms of our experience, he says, or, as a Kantian might put it today, features of our scientific paradigms or theoretical frames. This reassuring view gave Buber "philosophical peace."

There now came to Buber "an intuition of eternity," not as endless time, but as "Being as such." I moved deeply into myself to get some sense of what this might mean. I felt a great rushing, gushing, like a geyser, welling up inside me and rising up through all tiers of reality, an energy or life-force, creative and growing, but more basic and undifferentiated than these terms suggest, as if it were the very Being of these forces, running through the whole of reality. It rushed, expanded, created, grew not just outwardly but in a vertical dimension as well, from the primordial base up to the creative spiritual edge. It was, in some sense, erotic energy from bottom to top, with no level, not even the most elemental, ever eclipsed. The vision ended. I slumped back, breathing hard.

I wondered what it could mean for Being as such to be a Person, a Thou, as surely, from my own experience, God is. Then it struck me that this rushing Stuff, this force of Being, is also the being of me. And I am a person. So why shouldn't the rushing Stuff, the Being of—of what?—the World, of Being itself, be a Person writ large? I don't mean the World merely in a physical sense, since my own being is not merely that of my body. Similarly, the Being that animates everything could be a Person.

As I looked out the window at the passing trees, it struck me that their very leaves are full of Being as such, the Being that is also a Person, and that it made sense for them to be a Thou for me. And, more remarkably, for me to be a Thou for them. I felt that Being facing Being, not necessarily speaking but simply facing, is what personhood is.

I slumped back again and put the book aside. Later, I read on for several pages. I was struck by how many thoughts that I had received had also occurred to Buber. He entered a Nietzschean phase with an emphasis on "dynamism" and "a creative flow of life-force." Later Buber thought eternity "sends forth time out of itself" and "sets us in that relationship to it that we call existence." To achieve wholeness as a person, he said, it is necessary to direct the creative force of the Evil Urge, the erotic energy that I had felt to be at the center of Being itself.

I reached Washington and returned to my apartment in Alexandria, then resumed reading. I had left off with Buber speaking of the quality of "fervor with direction, all the awesome power of the 'evil urge' taken up into the service of God, [seventeenth-century visionary theologian Jakob] Boehme's 'ternary of fire' [symbolizing desire] spiraling upward into the 'ternary of light' [symbolizing love] without losing any of its power thereby." This was "one of the truly decisive moments in Buber's life": "Overpowered in an instant, I experienced the Hasidic soul," he writes. "At the same time I became aware of the summons to proclaim it to the world." I knew how he felt.

I had received visions of the explosive expansions of time and space, and of divine energy rushing up through all levels of reality. Were these intimations of Creation? I was told,

The work I want you to begin involves reading and writing about My nature. Start with the Creation. I have given you some clues already. Follow up on them.

One day, in quiet reflection, I was taken deep into the Self, taken back, it seemed, to the Beginning. Here is how I described it right afterward:

There was a sense of things shattering, like crockery breaking, or like the shell of an egg breaking. (I think of Kabbalah and its image of Creation as divine vessels breaking.) Then there is a river, or milk, flowing out from amidst the shards. The river is clouded in mist and flows a long way down canyons of shards or rocks. Until it settles in a pool below. Tranquil waters. This is when Life begins. Cool, calm but rippling waters.

All this was taking place on a flight to California to visit my ninety-year-old father. Sitting beside me was a nine-year-old girl, traveling alone. She kept looking at me, wondering what I was up to. Ignoring her was unkind, so I stopped praying and chatted with her.

After that, I returned to my own meditations and received a stream of visual images, a vision: the sun cracking up, solar flares that zoomed out into the reaches of space. I then saw, through the mist, an ethereal caravan of camels and their riders, coming up a valley, their long line stretching behind, down a winding road into the distance. I followed the road back to the source. I came upon vast winds, like a monsoon, then a world exploding—and then the vision abruptly stopped. The caravan seemed to represent the long course of human history, traced backward, all the way to the beginning, and then nothing.

I had received hints about the moment of Creation. Then, one day, He told me more. This is where God's story really begins.

Creation

I am in the midst of Nothingness

14

We should go back to the Beginning. Enter into Me, and experience the Beginning as I experienced it. Record what I say as I reexperience that moment.

I tried to still myself and yield to whatever experience I was about to be given.

I am in the midst of Nothingness . . .

"In the midst of Nothingness?" My logical alarms went off. "Lord, how can I make sense of this?"

Don't worry now about making sense of it. Just listen.

I tried again to still myself and yield.

I am in the midst of Nothing. I don't know who or what I am—I am like a baby in a womb. I hear nothing, see nothing—because there is nothing. I feel alone, very alone, except that I don't yet know what alone means. I feel growing strength, and Myself being drawn toward the light, just a glimmer at the "edge." I am in a kind of "pain," like stretching aching muscles.

Suddenly, it is as if I punch My arms and legs through the sides of a bag I'm in. It is like an explosion. In a split second, fragments are zooming out in all directions. I am at a throbbing, pulsing center. I am not sure what's happening. It is like a tightly coiled spring being suddenly released and springing out into a vast space instantaneously.

I scramble to take control, to provide order.

I tried to picture all this in terms of the Big Bang theory. In the first trillionth of a trillionth of a second, the universe expanded faster, much faster than the speed of light. "Within a fraction of a second," writes physicist Michio Kaku, "the universe expanded by an unimaginable factor of (10 to the 50th power)." It became 100,000,000,000,000,000,000,000,000,000,000,000,000,000,000, 000,000,000 times bigger than it had been less than a second before.

"Lord, were there already laws of nature, or did You have to establish those regularities?"

At this point, I know nothing about laws of nature. All is chaos.

Slowly I reach out to extend Myself over the whole, to infuse it. It becomes calmer, but still full of flux and dynamism and outward expansion.

I relapse, as if tired. I have done all I can do at that stage.

"Lord, You have taken me through a story that is completely unorthodox and embarrassingly anthropomorphic. What am I to make of that?"

I am not interested in what you make of it (or) in conforming My account to your prior, fixed beliefs. Be more specific in your future questions.

I am using literal language because that is the only way to explain the experience of being God.

"But 'experience' is also anthropomorphic."

Not really. I am a Person, but I am not only a Person. I am also much more. There is something you might call "what it is like" to be God. That is what "experience" refers to.

"But, Lord, You are admitting serious limitations as You scramble to create order out of chaos. This is not our idea of God."

Limitations only from My perspective. Don't be misled. By your standards I already had unimaginable power and knowledge.

"But You say You knew nothing."

There is another side to the story. In one sense I knew nothing. But, in another sense, I was viewing everything from another level—as when your senses are confused but your mind is clear and is noting with precision and even analysis the nature and contours of the confusion. Think of waking from a dream while analyzing the fact that you just had a dream.

"Perhaps like a researcher taking a hallucinogen and carefully noting its effects."

Before I was a Person, I was around "for a long time." First there was Nothingness, not just empty space—there was no space and time either. Out of Nothingness I erupted, "created" Myself. At that point, I was just pure energy, pure creative force, pure Being, Being itself. Space and time were created as a result of My Being. They were the frames of My existence. The physical universe spun out of Me by My overflowing. I am the to-be of all things. I was not yet a Person. I was not yet self-aware. I was amorphous energy flowing out radically in all directions. (Before Creation) I am pure spirit, sufficient unto Myself, and have no "body." And I did not exist in a world with physical bodies. I felt I was lacking something—grounding, facticity, the blunt materiality, the standing-against, the hard edge to push oneself against, the resistance and friction that physical objects have. So, out of My Being, a world was spun.

"Lord, I don't understand what existed at the Beginning. It sounds as if You are describing Your own birth as well as the birth of the universe. What were You before the explosion of Creation? A pregnant Nothingness?"

A passable description. There was a Self, timeless, without reflection, still and at peace, like calm waters, lucid, not nothing, but not something either. The universe contains many things, not just some-things and nothings.

What kind of Nothingness can explode into Being? Ah, I thought, maybe a Nothingness that is not just nothing, but is the Plenum of Potentiality for All Things. Perhaps the possibility of all things cannot fail to spill over into some actuality.

I could not settle any of these questions in my own mind. All I could do was to continue to ask questions. "Lord, what was there before? What motivates the act of creation?"

I received the following words and images, which I recorded in my notes.

"A feeling of loneliness, of searching, reaching—not yet a Person. Expanding into the great emptiness of Nothing, which is 'infinitely empty' far beyond (far more empty than) empty spaces. 'Who am I? What am I? Am I an I? What is an I?' A chaotic feeling of the infinite rushing at the edges."

"Lord, why did eternity 'shatter' in this way? Did the still, self-sufficient stuff explode?"

I received the sense: "Brittle, crystalline, too perfect, static, isolated, removed, alone, bored, incomplete. The eternal already had the potential to be a Person but could not do so without creating time."

"Lord, do I understand this correctly: You are emerging, self-creating perhaps, out of Nothing?"

This is correct. It is not quite right to say that I "always" existed. I did come into being, and before Me, there was only Nothing, and there is a sense in which I was present in the Nothing. There was no time, in the usual sense, then. There was no matter, no energy, no events.

As I emerged, I had to figure out Who I Was, and What Was to Happen. You (human beings) talk about God's plan, but I am enacting the Plan, a Plan binding on Me and not just made up by Me. The Plan is the scheme, as I have figured it out, of how things should be. My role is less (that) of (an) organizer than of (the) goal or telos.

Telos is the Greek word for aim, purpose, or function, as in "teleological."

I *draw* things in the right direction, like flowers to the sun.

15

I am pulling life forward

Go back to My loneliness. Feel it along with Me. The universe has exploded into being, and I scramble to order it. Then there are long eons, though remember that "long" doesn't mean exactly the same to Me.

The following came to me as God's experience: "I am dwelling in the vast loneliness. It is the loneliness of a huge figure who does not know He is alone, since the idea of others has not yet appeared, so it is just this huge unexplained emptiness."

I was beside myself. I had reluctantly given up my happy agnosticism—and for this? I had higher expectations. "Lord, that doesn't sound like much of a god."

You are diverting yourself from the task of describing My life because of fears that you will say something wrong and embarrassing. Don't let your fears guide you. Just listen to Me and dwell within My heart and tell My story from that vantage point.

However disappointing, the voice was still authoritative. I relaxed and, once again, was taken back to the Creation, in (for me) uncomfortably anthropomorphic language.

I am awake. I rise and shrug off the cramps of night. I stretch My arms, move My feet. It is good to be alive. I look at the world, matter, around Me. Dead. Nothing there. I am ready for action, for interaction, but there is nothing. Just whirls and splashes and explosions.

Matter has a subjective side, a "within," that subliminally experiences its surroundings, but that is too limited to interact with, too limited to be satisfying. It is like the story of the tar baby—you can poke it but you do not get much of a response. The Mayan myth of making men out of clay and wood is not far off.

In *Popol Vuh*, God aims to make men who can "walk and talk and pray articulately." He first tries making them of wood and then of clay, and finds those don't work very well.

So I infuse My spirit into matter, as if trying to blow life into it. (Like blowing bubbles) I blow and blow molecules, complex molecules, the building blocks of life.

This was a meaningful image even if anthropomorphic. Even for scientists, the origins of life—even the answer to "What is life?"—is a profound mystery. If there is a God, then surely He would be part of that story, and "blowing life into it" might be about as precise as anything.

Life is at first of a very low level—something like bacteria and viruses—tiny bits of life—moss and slime.

I asked, with some edge, "Did You interact in a personal way with moss and slime?"

It is better if you don't interrupt with questions. Just listen. Questions can come later.

Remember that I am learning all the way. I do not know what the final product may be. Man, as he now exists, is not the final product—only the future will tell us, including Me, that. I feel My way, pulled forward by a felt telos or goal emergent in each step, the way an intellectual project often develops from one insight to another. I am pulling life forward, eliciting the development of its potential, drawing it to more complex forms.

In this process, consciousness is quite a miracle, even from My point of view. I had consciousness before, but I didn't think of it that way. I just *was*, and matter *was*. It was quite startling to see *other* consciousness develop. Previously (all) consciousness had been coextensive with and hence identical with Me. It did not make sense to think of there being others as well.

Consciousness developed very slowly. The first glimmer is found in the lowest molecules, in their ability to interact with, to respond to, their environment. Whitehead and Teilhard are on the right track in this regard. Leibniz is not.

I had to look again at these thinkers to see what God was getting at. Rejecting the mind-nature dualism, Alfred North Whitehead held that, even at the micro level, every event is a pulse of existence, feeling and responding to its environment. These "prehensions" are not so much states as vectors, arrows pointing to connections with the surrounding world. The Jesuit paleontologist Pierre Teilhard de Chardin spoke of the "within" of things, their interiority, which "appears at the heart of beings." Thus "the exterior world must inevitably be lined at every point with an interior one." Both Whitehead and Teilhard thought that nature itself was imbued with something like consciousness. By contrast, the seventeenth-century thinker G. W. Leibniz believed that only minds, centers of consciousness, exist. What we think of as the natural world is actually just the totality of the streams of consciousness of many minds. Each mind's states of consciousness are divinely synchronized (by a "pre-established harmony") to give the appearance of an independently existing material world so that, you might say, the movies played on your mental screen fit coherently with the movies on mine. His theories of space and time were set within that metaphysical framework. Put simply, for Whitehead and Teilhard, nature is quite physical but has a mental aspect within it; for Leibniz, there are only minds.

As God went on, He sounded a lot like Teilhard.

What happens is that reactions have an internal dimension— responding to the environment, the molecule begins rearranging its internal parts and configurations and processes. This is the beginning of interiority. Ultimately, interiority involves the second-order process of monitoring and directing inner processes. But, even at the beginning, prior to the emergence of second-order processes, there is an emerging consciousness. To be conscious is not the same as and does not require self-consciousness. It can be very dim and limited and still be consciousness, because something new and remarkable has arisen—the presentient and then sentient awareness of the environment. Don't worry at this point about what is meant by

"presentient" awareness. Your understanding is necessarily anthro-pocentric, using human consciousness as the standard by which to understand all forms of consciousness.

I breathe life into matter, and matter starts responding. As one translation of Genesis puts it, I "flutter over the waters" and nurture, incubate life. And I am filled with joy. It is like a child picking up a harp and being surprised to find that strumming it makes beautiful sounds—and delightedly playing with it.

At the beginning, the cosmos was My playpen, My garden of delights. It was beautiful, dazzling. I could play it like a vast organ, but one attached to laser shows and fireworks.

"But You felt all alone?"

Yes, I wanted more. In retrospect, the inanimate years feel very lonely. The emergence of life is a delight. With life, spirit comes into play. Wonderful to see amoeba, moss, and so forth. The frogs (and other creatures), each with a soul and personality, each in a sense in tune with God. I can play with the animals, "walk among them." I love their myriad forms. I am not alone anymore.

The creatures that began to stir on the earth are amazing, more amazing than anything that had yet occurred in creation. They move on their own; they have "internal principles of motion" as Aristotle said, have dramatic lives—even the worms and fishes.

There is birth, growth, death, mating, offspring, colonies and flocks, emergent social orders—ideality as well. There is telos and pur-pose, success and failure, standards of perfection and imperfection.

And over time, further developments in the species, a most amazing, creative ramifying of the evolutionary ladder. New species emerge that could not have been imagined before. Your paleontol-ogy tells the story: the first horses could easily fit into the palm of a hand, and so forth. Can you imagine the spectacle?

"Yes, I think I can."

Personality develops—think of your own pets—and intelli-gence, problem-solving, lives with continuous purpose and plans, individual recognition of one animal by another, lifelong mates. Now I have not just a playpen, but a menagerie, a zoo, of My own, a private jungle where I can be Tarzan.

There is nothing wrong in this world.

"But can the animals respond to You?"

It is not true that the lower forms have no spiritual response. They are sensitive to and in tune with nature and hence with Me. They even have teleological aspirations, including spiritual growth.

They are in harmony, in attunement with nature and with Me. Their capacity may be limited, but they (have the advantage that they) do not have any filters. Their world is much less dualistic, more holistic, with less individuality and separateness and hence less separateness from Me. It is mainly an instinctual un-self-conscious rapport that we have. But (I feel) a great excitement at the process of life and evolution itself.

"Why isn't that enough?"

In a sense it is. Animals do have uniqueness. Each animal is distinct, has its own soul. But they lack self-awareness, and that is true even of cats and dogs and apes. You can interact with them but there is no second-order reflection, hence a very truncated sense of time—just a sense of temporal motion, of passage from an immediate moment-just-passed to a next moment anticipated. And even that cannot be thought about, represented symbolically, or made available to self-consciousness.

So I cannot develop solely through interacting with them. It is static, inert. We just *are* together. I could not become a Person without there being other persons. The personal is essentially interpersonal. Like a child who first lives in an undifferentiated world, in which other people are merely contents of his or her own oceanic flow of consciousness, I needed to separate Myself from other persons. And so I created mankind.

16

They were aware of My presence

What I had been told about Creation still bothered me. I was relieved when God started talking about the process of evolution.

"Lord, do You have to will creatures to evolve into homo sapiens, or does it just happen by natural processes?"

That's not a well-conceived question. It rests on a false dichotomy. Remember that nature is itself teleological, except it is much more complicated than that apparently simple statement. I provide—I am—the telos or purpose, and I follow the telos as well. However, I draw man forward to greater development in the very process of interacting with men (people). At the time of early man, I am not yet sure what is missing. I am not fully developed Myself yet, since I have not encountered beings who can call forth My full latent nature. For the moment, call it a dialectical evolution responding to My need for development.

Here and elsewhere, "man" has the older sense inclusive of both women and men.

"And so, Lord, You call forth the first human beings?"

Yes, the first inklings, forerunners, of man. The great apes are wonderful creatures, full of intelligence, energy, and drive. But it is frustrating to interact with them. They are so close and yet so far from having full interactive personalities. They have teleological urges but they are only effective, for the most part, at the biological level. Their social life is rudimentary and their spiritual awareness is diffuse and inarticulate. They lack a symbolic order. They can't project ideals beyond the sensual. They can't respond to Me either.

"But they evolved?"

The transition to early man is both slow and sudden. At first, you couldn't tell them from animals, but I could see their potential. They didn't have language, but their sounds and marks had representative purposes. They could connect one thing to another, one thought to another. They could remember their past and replay it in their minds. They slowly developed a sense of the future.

What happens with the first form of man is that they have symbolic capacity, developed only crudely at first, but still it is an enormous leap over previous consciousness.

"And this made a difference?"

Take the symbolic system of counting—keeping records of the number of cattle or bushels of wheat. The first step in this is letting a single mark or object stand for something else. A stone might stand for a head of cattle, for example. But this is not much beyond just lining up marbles and saying this one is Daddy and this is Mommy. It is phenomenal to be able to make a representation at all, but some prehumans do something that is very close. They make marks that have a significance.

Symbolic capacity makes everything different. Events, bodily motions, things no longer just *are*; they have *meaning*. Before, a stone just was a stone; scratches on a clay tablet were just scratches. Now they may stand for cattle, or for the king, or for past and future events, or for the deity.

"And this helped them to think about those things?"

For the first time, thought can be detached from objects. Plans can become abstract, long-term, not just emergent possibilities inherent in situations, as they are for animals. The response to other creatures can be evaluative, normative. It becomes possible to notice that a particular action falls short of the best or right action, that a particular human being falls short of the ideal human being. Beauty also becomes possible, as you see in prehistoric cave paintings. Creatures from a very low level enjoy and appreciate sensory stimulation. In that sense they find a scene (though not quite a "scene" for them yet) "beautiful." But true appreciation of beauty is seeing an ideal form in something material. What they are drawing on cave walls are ideal bulls.

I found a very fine collection of cave paintings and other prehistoric art in *Images of the Ice Age*, by Paul G. Bahn and Jean Vertut. There is a breathtaking simplicity and grace to many of the paintings. A bison or horse may be depicted by just a few well-chosen strokes of neck and back lines—"a kind of Palaeolithic 'shorthand' in which a part stands for the whole." Others have naturalistic details reflecting precise observation and artistic execution. "The technical, naturalistic, and aesthetic qualities of European Palaeolithic images remain almost unique," the authors report. "The fluid, effortlessly drawn and well-proportioned animal figures . . . suggest that the artists carried everything in their mind's eye. . . . They never took a measurement—they projected onto the rock an inner vision of the animal." The figures, portrayed as motionless, with no visible weight on the legs, are "nevertheless imbued with an impression of life and power."

Study the cave paintings and other artifacts. They respond to, reflect, *how* I was presenting Myself to them. You will be able to see or infer what My experience was like, what I was trying to do.

"Lord, these cave paintings also have an aura of holiness."

That is right. My first approach is to give humans the sense that nature is special, sacred, that there is something more than trees and clumps of grass, that there is also a spiritual presence.

"What does this mean for You, for Your life?"

For Me, it means the first spark of real interpersonal interaction, not just vague spiritual rapport. From very early, humans—protohumans—have a sense of something more, something higher. (Their sense of) the Divine is not just fear and wish-fulfillment, though there is plenty of that. There is a real sense of relating to Me as a Person, not just as the vague spirituality of nature.

It is hard to convey in retrospect, but at this point I do not quite know I have a personality, an individual personhood. Events pass through My consciousness. I have a sense of My intelligence pervading the world, of fulfilling a universal telos. I feel a spiritual rapport with life. But none of that constitutes a sense of personhood, of an I

standing opposite a You. The protohumans gave Me that, or I developed it or became aware of it in relation to them.

For the first time, human beings mirror Me, look at Me eyeball to eyeball. And I try to draw them forward, to be more evolved, more fully human and fully spiritual.

17

A self requires another self

Early man was a whole new phenomenon, not entirely expected.

"How can that be, Lord? Weren't human beings part of Your plan from the beginning?"

Remember that I am following a plan, not inventing it. I don't know the whole plan Myself.

"So the emergence of human beings was a surprise?"

Yes. Even though I saw the unfolding of life and understood its trajectory, there is a discontinuity between animal life and human life that's surprising. People are not just smarter animals. It is not just that they have souls—animals have a kind of soul too—it is that they are creative, free, self-reflective, open-ended, have a yearning to go beyond themselves. They are in fact like little gods, though I do not like the usual use of this notion. But people are much more of the same substance and kind as God. That is why I can communicate with them so effectively. The mind is a little reflection or mirror of God.

Early man I can communicate with. So it seemed to Me at first that I could communicate with them directly, that I would not be so alone. Hegel was right: A self requires another self in order to define itself.

Rene Descartes had based his philosophy on the *cogito*, the thinking I, an isolated pinpoint self. Two hundred years later, G. W. F.

Hegel argued, in *The Phenomenology of Mind*, that a sense of self is possible only through an encounter with another self.

With man, I can send dreams, give intuitions, stir love, frighten if necessary. I began to develop My arsenal of ways to deal with man. But I too am primitive and undeveloped. I know little about how to be effective in bringing man forward. And I am meeting My needs as much as theirs, My need for companionship, for being worshipped.

Early man seems primitive to you, but there were Einsteins among them. They represented a tremendous leap forward. And they certainly had some capacity for the Divine, some spirituality and openness. But My messages came through either with great vagueness because they lacked concepts or in very simple physical images that lacked transcendence. They were not subtle enough, and they lacked the means, such as cultural memory, to become subtle.

Scholars believe that there was a cultural, creative explosion in the late Paleolithic period over thirty thousand years ago. *The Oxford Illustrated History of Prehistoric Europe* calls it the Upper Paleolithic Revolution, "a major watershed in cultural development."

Part of the "revolution" comes from Me. I am always whispering things, ideas, to people. Much of mankind's creative development comes from Me, from these inklings I send.

"Even in areas other than religion?"

Yes, decidedly. I am not just interested in the so-called spiritual side of man that allows people to communicate, but with (their) overall development.

"But these whisperings sound like efficient (push) causes rather than final (pull) causes. You are prompting people to act, not just relying on some ideal to draw them forward."

Yes and no. Yes, in the sense that they (the whisperings) are "inputs." No, in the sense that I do not *make* them happen. I do not put the theory of relativity into Einstein's head. I give hints, direct attention, open minds in certain directions, like a good teacher coaching a class.

According to the *Oxford History*, DNA studies "point to the conclusion that all of the present-day populations throughout the world were most probably derived from a single common ancestor, within the span of the past 200,000 years."

"Is this the same as Adam and Eve, Lord?"

Don't be too mythological. That is, they were not in a Garden of Eden and so on. But the Garden story captures with great precision the prototypical experience of human innocence, and of Divine innocence and awkwardness. In that sense, the common ancestor is Eve, a creature of a higher development than ever before, with a new level of interaction, able to hear and respond to a higher level of whispering, and hence, over time, of much greater development.

The story of Adam and Eve portrays the first kind of experience I had with human beings. I created them in My image. As essentially creative force (Myself), I gave them creative force, the power of sexuality and the ability to create other human beings. I gave them objects of beauty, in nature and in each other, and pleasure in eating, moving about, and enjoyment of each other. I had been all alone and I enjoyed the company.

At first I imagined I could walk among humans and enjoy their company. This required that they obey Me, while not being in awe of Me, and that they retain a certain innocence. This was My first experience in discovering that humans cannot interact with God in the simple, direct way they interact with one another. Like children not separated from their mother, at first they had little individuality or purpose. They enjoyed the good things I had given them and did not understand the power of good and evil or the power and complexity of their own sexuality.

I had also underestimated the power of love. First, I created Adam and I could see that he was alone, as I had once been, and this was not good. He did not see it because he did not know anything different. But, as he tried to befriend various animals, he would quickly reach the limit of those relationships and be frustrated and unfulfilled. So I created woman and made her lovely in his eyes. They were naked and knew no shame. And their sexuality was intense and profound.

And, frankly, I felt left out. I had no such consort. And, while obedient, man loved woman more than Me. Though understandable in light of the human nature I had given them, it was not right. And they knew it was not right and began to disobey Me. They hid their nakedness, which is to say, they hid their creativity and sexuality from Me, detached it from My purpose and used it solely for their own pleasure and intimacy—innocently enough, as children might do, but still wrong. And so, with regret, I expelled them to a life of hardship. Detached sexuality, hiding from God, has its own intrinsic price, the loss of the full bounty and blessing of God.

"Do You need the world for completion or does the world need You?"

Both. Neither of us is complete or perfect in ourselves. I can only develop a self-consciousness and hence become a Person by interacting with the world and hence with people.

For the first time, the dim outline of an overall story was emerging. If we and God develop together, in interaction with one another, then the drama of history and of individual lives begins to make sense. We are not standing still; we are moving forward together.

"Lord, is there an aim, like perfecting the world or uniting us all into the Godhead?"

No, not exactly. There is a purpose but not an end-point. The notion of an end-point derives from the model of the human will and its desires, getting what it wants. The purpose of singing a song is not to get to the end.

There is no end-time. The purpose of eschatology is to portray something about the meaning of the world.

Eschatology denotes religious ideas about the final purpose or culmination of history.

There are endings to particular worlds, but they are not apocalyptic, any more than an individual death is.

So history comes to nothing? I found this answer distressing, and Abigail was even more upset. One of the Jews' gifts to the world is the very idea of history, not as a series of endless episodes or cycles, but as a progress, with a Beginning (the Creation) and a Grand Finale (the Coming of the Messiah). Abigail doesn't even like movies without happy endings. And we weren't talking about movies. We were talking about whether life had any meaning or purpose at all. This was a concern neither of us would let go.

Any religion that does not allow for this aspect of My presence is missing something

18

I had been told that God manifests Himself in many ways, and He often mentioned art. I did start sensing the divine manifestation in things, not only in beautiful things like sunsets but also ordinary things in their bare particularity. I am notoriously insensitive to art, particularly to painting. I could appreciate three-dimensional art—sculpture and architecture—but not what I call "flat stuff." Until I encountered Andrew Wyeth.

Between the melting of winter and the flood of tourists, Abigail and I took a long weekend in the Brandywine Valley, not far from home. This is Wyeth country. His farmhouse still stands, and we had breakfast at Andy's favorite diner. His granddaughter gives lively tours of his paintings at a nearby gallery. I don't know if it was a change in me or something unique in Wyeth, but for the first time, I saw paintings that meant something to me. By capturing the textured surface of things, Wyeth allowed their grainy suchness to come out, which is another way of saying he let the Divine show through.

As early peoples caught glimpses of the Divine in art or in nature, it must have been natural to think there were gods in things. In fact, I had been told,

Some elements of polytheism are merely superstitious, but other aspects are genuinely responsive to the many ways in which I present Myself. It may seem odd to your modern mind to think of fire as a god, but why do you think I made fire mysterious and fascinating?

It is a physical metaphor in itself—it is created out of nothing and disappears into nothing, grows and dies, gives life and warmth as well as pain and destruction, and it looks both hypnotically attractive and frightening.

As you know, I am very powerful. I do manifest Myself in storms and thunder, in the ocean and great waves—in the power that drives the universe and that manifests itself in each particular event. The large cosmic forces are divine and so are their concrete manifestations. That does not mean that every rainstorm is a specific communication or is there to advance or retard some particular action, but it does mean that every rainstorm expresses an aspect of Me.

Early peoples saw My presence everywhere, saw the spiritual indwelling of things, their powers and potencies and the divine element in all that. But there was always an awareness, however dim, that there was a single spiritual reality behind them all.

I have told you that there are many gods but only one God, and I am He.

"What do You mean by many gods?"

In a sense, the wind and seas are gods. The elemental forces of nature are gods.

"Why gods rather than impersonal forces?"

They are not impersonal. They are agents of Me. They help direct the world toward its goal.

"What is Your relation to the God of Israel?"

The God of Israel is one face of Me. It is really Me, and I really did undergo the development recorded pretty accurately in the Hebrew Bible.

"You have other 'faces'?"

Of course. I came to all peoples, but arrived in different guises. I came to the American Indians as the Great Spirit, to the Moslems as Allah, and so on. I came to the Hindus in many different forms, and hence their many stories.

"Some of their stories are about gods as forces of nature, aren't they?"

Yes, some of those gods are (indirect) manifestations of Me, and some are more direct appearances by Me.

"Lord, this sounds like the Hindu view, that everything is God or is a manifestation of God. Is that so?"

Yes, that is correct.

"Then I am God and a manifestation of God?"

That is true.

"But I also interact with You, and according to the biblical story, You interact with peoples and act in history."

That is all true. But the fact that I am you and you are I does not prevent us from interacting.

"Is that why I sometimes have trouble telling whether I am hearing Your voice or my own?"

Yes, but there is still a difference between your voice and Mine, since you are a specific manifestation of Me and I am in fact a specific manifestation of Myself. So we still have to talk, and can misunderstand each other.

Did this mean there is something true in polytheism? But I had been taught, "Thou shalt have no other gods before Me." And that Me was not Baal or some idol or clump of trees. The Old Testament campaigns against polytheism, against "whoring after strange gods." This required further investigation.

Abigail's father had been a professor, and I married into his library. It included Martin P. Nilsson's *Greek Popular Religion*, a classic on ancient Greek polytheism. According to Nilsson, anything that had potency or an aura was regarded as holy. Spirits lurked inside striking features of the landscape such as trees, forests, lakes, and mountains. River crossings and cave entrances would be marked with stones or statues.

"Were these valid responses to You, Lord?"

You lump them all together. We would have to take them one by one. You see them as generic types of actions. I see them as specific communications or acknowledgments. One person looked at a stream and saw the current of My energy running through it and marked the spot in homage. Another was superstitious and marked the spot for good luck. Some were fearful and thought they might drown crossing if they did not place a token on the bank. Some actually stopped and prayed or meditated or sang a song of praise. These are very different kinds of communications, with different degrees of reality.

If your question is whether streams and mountains and so forth do in fact embody My presence, the answer again is not so simple. Of course, everything embodies My presence and it is always a good thing when someone pauses to acknowledge that. But some things do embody it more. There is truth to the sense that I am more distinctively present in aspects of energy and force than in matter that is relatively more inert. We would have to go into physics, into the physics of the future, to discuss that in detail. At particular times, I am especially present in a certain place or to a certain person. It is not mere superstition that causes (people to) pause before the fact of death, for example. That is a moment and place of particular interaction between Me and the deceased and their survivors. However, there are some dramatic elements of nature, such as lightning, that might be appropriate symbols for divine power but are not in fact times and places of special presence or interaction.

But, in general, did polytheism respond to a divine reality? Yes, it did. And any religion that does not allow for this aspect of My presence—My presence in nature, in objects, in places, and in forces—is missing something.

The Greeks also thought of "the great forces of nature (such as sky and seasons) and of human life (such as love and death) as gods," says Nilsson.

It is quite apt, and not incompatible with understanding a single divine reality behind them all. In fact, seeing them as gods—as personal beings with desires, plans, loves, and so forth—is a step in the right direction, of acknowledging that God is a Person and one with whom one can interact.

There can be no love without difference

19

"Lord, did the polytheistic response affect You in any way?"

Oh yes, in many ways. When someone sensed My presence in a place and responded respectfully, it increased My awareness of My presence there, and of what it was about Me that evoked and deserved respect.

Then I was given an analogy.

Sometimes someone might be the pillar of a particular institution and not realize their distinctive role until a crisis. And they notice that everyone rallies around them or sees them as their savior or seeks their advice or expects them to get them through it. In a sense, they were the pillar all along, but it was almost latent and not fully actualized until the occasion arose and they saw it reflected in the eyes of others.

I gather that God's experience was something like that.

I am ever-present—let's say for now and not get too picturesque about what this means. Put it negatively: there is no realm from which I am absent, no realm I do not have a direct relationship to.

Did the so-called polytheistic religions realize this better than the so-called monotheistic? Not necessarily. They certainly gave it full-bodied expression and awareness to the point of insanity— there were fears about every wind and so forth. But Judaism and Christianity have not failed to understand My presence everywhere, and they have understood this not just as an abstract concept but in many ways as a concrete reality.

You can explore later how these different approaches or communications—polytheism, monotheism, the Way, and so forth—relate to one another and to some meaningful whole, but don't get caught up in trying to make a metaphysical scheme out of it. Think more of both-and and less of either-or. Logic is helpful for some things, but not for everything.

"Zeus had changed into Eros when about to create," writes the early Greek thinker Pherecydes, and, "having composed the world from the opposites, he led it into agreement and peace and sowed sameness in all things, and unity that interpenetrates the universe."

"It is an arresting image, Lord, Zeus changing into Eros in order to bring opposites into a unity."

It reflects the dynamic in the universe, in being, the dialectic of otherness and sameness. There is sameness in all things and I put it there. It is equivalent to order. Otherwise things would fall apart. A similar image is centripetal and centrifugal—there need to be forces of attraction and forces of repulsion.

I understand that, if gravitational pull were slightly stronger, all the galaxies would collapse into a single lump. If it were the slightest bit weaker, nothing would hold together. "Lord, could gravity, if this makes sense, be a kind of love or an expression of love?"

Yes, love exists at all levels, just as spirit or soul exists at all levels. At the physical level, it is things like gravity. At the level of human personality, it is integrity; it is the "transcendental unity of apperception" for consciousness (personality). It is institutions and mores for society, balance and harmony for art, and so forth.

"Transcendental unity of apperception" is Immanuel Kant's term for the principle that makes the jumble of sensory impressions into a unified field of consciousness.

"Lord, Pherecydes also says the world is composed of opposites."

There can be no love without difference, no harmony or balance without opposing items or forces, no magnetism without the magnet and its object, and so on.

Mystic merging is not quite right. You (people) need to live out your lives in relation to, in concert with Me, but it would serve no purpose, karmic or otherwise, for you to get lost in Me, like a drop of water in the sea.

I knew that I wanted to love Abigail, not to merge into her, or to have her merge into me. There is not just unity, but creative tension as well.

The ancients posed the question: Do the gods rule the world, or does the world, in some respects, rule the gods? Perhaps even the gods are subject to Fate and to the whims of Time.

"Is that view right, Lord?"

Yes, something like that. There is a rhythm, a framework, a pattern to the universe that I must yield to, work within, accommodate to, (and) respect. I work within fixed patterns, patterns larger than the laws of nature in this world, to achieve My goals.

"That makes You sound small, Lord."

No, that is not accurate at all. I am very large, very large indeed, about the largest "thing" you can imagine. But I am bounded. Remember that I can do anything I care to do. In that sense, My will is not limited. But what I care to do is shaped by, exists in light of, boundary conditions.

"And some of these conditions involve time?"

Yes, that's right.

"Do the actions of human beings affect what is 'timely' for You?"

Yes! That is correct. I cannot move at a pace greater than the human reactions. That is why it is important for you to tell My story, My history of interactions with humans, from My side. You will see that a development in God is really a response to, (and) conditioned by, the development of men (human beings) and their response to Me.

I started to study other ancient cultures and religions. I began attending meetings of the American Academy of Religion. To make time for these activities, I phased back at work. I put a colleague in charge of day-to-day operations.

Abigail was still teaching at Brooklyn College. She got a Tuesday-Thursday teaching schedule, and I cut back to three days a week in the office. We needed a place from which we could both commute. We found a lovely town with historic grace in Bucks County, north of Philadelphia, within easy reach of Amtrak. We would drive to the station together and then split, one going north, the other south, and come together again at the end of the week. The days apart made the heart grow fonder—and more frustrated. We couldn't make a life together that way.

I am not the kind of person who, if God tells me to jump off a cliff, will jump. And now I had Abigail to take into account. Thanks to what I call her gift of belief, she was supportive of my new calling, but she thought it best we not go broke. "Money is a person's lifeblood," she said. I gradually cut hours and reduced salary until it became clear how much we needed. After a couple of years, Abigail was able to retire and draw an annuity. When our financial advisor said it was okay for me to quit as well, I resigned my position. A few months later the stock market collapsed.

20

I communicated something more personal

My first impressions of the ancient Egyptians were formed in Sunday School, put to music by gospels such as "Go Down, Moses," and brought to the silver screen by Cecil B. DeMille. It was not a pretty picture—false gods, harsh rulers, fake magicians, and slave-drivers wielding the lash. Egypt was on the wrong side of everything.

But now I was told that God was sending divine messages to every culture. So I had to look at the land of the pharaohs through different eyes, Egyptian eyes.

Written in hieroglyphs that were already old when Sumerian cuneiform was young, the Pyramid texts date back almost five thousand years. Chiseled into the walls of the dark corridors beneath these monumental tombs were how-to lessons to guide the deceased pharaoh to a successful afterlife. One strategy was to enter the cyclical course of the cosmos and accompany the sun god in the barque that transverses the sky each day. In one "success story," a deceased king kicked the sun god overboard to make room for himself.

The complex mythology of the Egyptians far surpassed the simple piety of preliterate polytheism. But, however complex, these greedy efforts to compel or trick the divine powers seem spiritually retrograde compared to the sensitive cave paintings and the humble peasant honoring a stream with a pile of stones. "Isn't that right, Lord?"

Yes, it is a fundamental mistake of man to try to control God rather than the other way around.

I found that, over time, Egyptian religious consciousness became more high-minded. The god Re, it is written, had "put Maat in the place of chaos." Maat represents social and cosmic order, truth and fidelity. Human beings sustain the divine order by living in harmony with it. All change is a threat to order but can be tamed by ritual, repetition, and regularity.

"Lord, don't the Egyptians have a deep sense of harmony with the Divine?"

Yes, that is right. Now flip it and look at it from My side.

I prayed, but instead of hearing an answer, I was given a feeling—a sense of divine distance and a kind of monotonous pulse. Something was missing. What was it?

I communicated also a sense of the numinous, a sense of My holy presence—which is a way of saying My accessibility to human beings—in certain places, at certain times. But I communicated something more personal, more epiphanic than this, a sense of My personal concern with individuals and a sense of the importance of being in direct harmony with Me. You need to read and pray about passages to flesh this out.

The early Egyptian gods are quite distant, but then I found a stela that declares:

> You are Amun, lord of the silent,
> Who comes at the call of the poor.
> I called to you when I was in sorrow,
> And you came to save me.
> You gave breath to the one who was imprisoned,
> And saved me when I was in bonds. . . .
> You are the one who is gracious to him who calls on him,
> You are the one who comes from afar!

This is a vibrant response to a personal God. It reflects what cultural historian Jan Assman calls a new "dimension of divine presence," a "new sphere of religious experience . . . whose horizon was the human heart and personal history."

The following hymn reflects this new dimension:

Every face says, "We belong to you!"
　　Strong and weak together,
Rich and poor with one mouth . . .
Everyone turns to you, beseeches you,
　　Your ears are open to hear them and fulfill their wish.

"When they weep, he hears," declares the *Instruction for Merik-are*. Now God is personal as well as cosmic, near as well as far.

He is distant as the beholding one,
　　Near as the hearing one.

"Lord, these sound like genuine responses to the divine call."
Yes.

Then there was Akhenaten. He may have been the first monotheist. We have his own words, carved in stone. The young pharaoh reports having been divinely guided to the exact place the Creator had manifested Himself at the beginning of the world. It was a plain near the Nile, bounded by hills except on the east, a great amphitheater facing the morning sun.

There he founded a city of magnificent vistas dedicated to the Aten, the solar disk. The city was called Akhenaten, "the Horizon of the Aten," a name he also took for himself. There he swore an oath—to "the great and living Aten . . . rising and setting each day ceaselessly."

The Aten was symbolized by an image of the sun with rays reaching out in all directions. At the end of each ray is an open hand, ready to give and to receive gifts. "Thou art remote yet thy rays are upon the earth," writes Akhenaten. "Thou art in the sight of men, yet thy ways are not known."

It was a breathtaking vision and it shook Egypt from its moorings. The other gods were denounced as lifeless idols, their images replaced by the austere hieroglyph for the Aten, increasingly understood not as the sun or even the sun-god, but as a distant and unrecognizable divinity understood only by his "son," Akhenaten.

This was gross impiety to most Egyptians, an insult to the gods. It "offended their reverence for the phenomena [through which the gods made themselves present] and the tolerant wisdom with which they had done justice to the many-sidedness of reality," explains Egyptologist Henri Frankfort.

The result was perhaps predictable. Upon the pharaoh's death, priests and people alike turned against this strange, remote monotheism. The old gods and their "idols" were brought back. It was no longer their names which were erased, but his.

"Lord, what is the meaning of Akhenaten?"

Akhenaten was an extraordinary recipient of My inspiration (and of My) presence. He was, as all are, bound by his culture and the symbols he had available. But he got the main message—that, in a sense, I am One, that I am not to be equated with the sun or any other natural phenomena, that other gods are lesser or "mere" manifestations of Me or, in a sense, nonexistent compared to Me. The problem he ran into is that he was alone in his receptivity. Others were not prepared, were not open. The most spiritual Egyptians of his era were attuned to the old religion and could not jump the traces. It would have seemed impious to them.

"What was the difference between them and the people of Israel?"

The people of Israel were a *people*. They—the mass of them— had an intuitive understanding of a Covenant. Remember that the mass of ancient Jews were not faithful, or (they were) faithful only periodically. But they all lived under the Covenant and understood that they so lived. Akhenaten tried to impose a spiritual vision from above, through imperial authority and example. But there was no way for his vision to communicate more broadly. He would have deprived the people of the gods they could devoutly worship—and, through them, worship Me—without giving them a version they could appropriate (make use of). His rejection of other gods became mainly a negative force.

I had prayed about polytheism and the Egyptians, but there were other, bigger questions on my mind.

Get more anthropomorphic

21

If there is one God, why are there so many religions? Philosophers call this the Problem of the Diversity of Revelations. But I was told,

(There is) no reason to think (the) diversity of revelations is a problem, any more than for a therapist to say different things to different clients (whose needs and situations differ).

That analogy didn't take me very far. The therapist, like a doctor, is giving advice depending on the needs of the client. But God is giving different people contradictory stories about Himself, and also about how they should live.

"Lord, why not just give everyone the whole truth?"

Your question has presuppositions—that I have given different, incompatible stories to different cultures. This is only apparently true. If you think them through, they are different pieces of the same puzzle. Names shift but that is superficial.

"Even though one says 'God' and another (thinking of Buddhism) says 'Nothingness'?"

No religion puts Nothingness in the place of God. If it appears to, think again. What is the role of each (name)? Is one a substitute or replacement for the other? And (think about) the meaning of each. Are they really incompatible once you examine their properties?

"Perhaps each religion is like a single eye-witness report of some strange event such as an alien landing. The reports might be wildly different from one another. The challenge would be to sort them out and put them into a single coherent account."

Not exactly. It's not to blend the religions into a single synthesis or theology. It's to put them into one story.

I didn't see how to put the pieces into any kind of story. "I'm not getting anywhere, Lord."

Get more "anthropomorphic." Look at what kind of Person I must be from My interaction with man.

Get more anthropomorphic? What a thing to be told! It is just the opposite of what the Big Thinkers tell us to do.

The story begins with creation, the evolution up to life, animals, early man. Then to the very ancient communications that require language and memory.

As I have explained, I grew as a Self in response to the interiority of others, and I wanted to communicate, interact, more fully and at a higher level. This (communication) is somewhat possible with early man, who recognized My presence in nature, in life, and also heard, if somewhat dimly and inchoately, My other promptings such as conscience, (the sense of) right and wrong, fine sensibility, appreciation of nature and beauty, love amongst creatures, and mystical union.

"The next phase is what I wonder about. It looks to me as if You communicated some sense of moral order and hierarchy, reverence for life and death, a sense of the meaning of life . . . I am feeling that this is Your voice, not mine, Lord."

Yes, it is. They were understanding Me well enough to understand that life has meaning—a beginning and an end and the sense of a meaningful movement from one to the other, summarized (judged, reckoned) at the end. Death and the hope of immortality, which isn't merely the fear of death but the understanding that there is a vertical dimension to life and (that) its meaning does not stop with death, that there is a larger story the individual is part of, and his (and her) spiritual development in fact is not limited to just one life.

"Please go on, Lord."

My presence in a person, when felt, results in awe, conscience, appreciation of beauty, humbling before the cosmic order, and so forth. Don't think of My relations to people as tapping out telegraph messages that already have a precise meaning.

I understand My nature better as I articulate it or, better (a better way to put it), as humans hear it, process it, and articulate it.

Is this the key, then? Not so much God's trying to communicate something specific, as people themselves responding to some aspect of the presence of God.

I started making a list of great spiritual leaders to pray about. I thought the question would be, for example, What was God communicating to Martin Luther? But when I asked, I got a different answer.

Suppose you brought a guy in—say, Luther—and cut him up (looked at the elements that make him who he is). What would you find?

"Not just a solitary individual, I suppose, but someone immersed in a tradition, institutions, and a culture."

I act over the centuries in reference to individuals, but also movements, cultures, and the like.

"But only individuals receive communications."

Just listen for the moment. I interact with mankind, with the universe, in many different ways. Do not assume that the only interaction is the same form of the interaction I have with you. With some it is conversational, but with others it is by inspiration, by My spirit moving through them, infusing institutions, cultures, art, music, dance, symbolism, ideational systems, thought forms . . .

"So, looking at each cultural form, I should be able to figure out how it reflects You?"

The starting point is not the cultural forms and asking, "What kind of God or transcendent order does that imply or suggest?" but start with Me and ask, "What am I doing with that culture, individual, art form, or whatever. What is it to Me?" Pray and I will tell you.

"Why is culture so important?"

That's like saying, why language? If I am going to communicate with people, they need a language. For the same reason, they need a culture.

"They need a culture, but why such a variety of cultures?"

There are many ways of realizing (actualizing) the human story. Culture enables lives of different (types of) significance (meaning).

"But why, in terms of Your story?"

I need to come to people in all their particularity, not to mankind-as-such. The Chinese is one way of being. The primitive is one way of being. I come to each in its own terms. Each enables Me to show a different side of Myself.

Do you think I could come to the ancient Jews in the same way I came to the seventh-century Chinese? to Americans today? to you?

"So any single conception of God will grasp only one of Your aspects?"

Yes, you see the problem. My nature is quite variegated. People see one aspect and not another.

I wondered how many aspects there were to God.

The Way

You could tell My story through the history of love

22

I had never read the Bible cover to cover before. When I got to the end of the Old Testament, I told Abigail, "This is not a success story." Over and over, the people of Israel lapse into faithlessness. When I prayed, I was told,

Indeed, in a sense, no story of man's interaction with God is a success story. However, that is only half the picture. There is also enormous success, both individually and at a larger cultural level.

"Wouldn't it help if I had some sense of the overall direction of the story?"

It is too soon to really go into this. Let Me just say this. It is not progressive (simply); it is paradigmatic, iconic. Do not look for one thing (one religious phase, for example) to build on (or) advance on a previous stage. Look for iconic moments in which something unique is realized. These are breakthrough moments. Think of it like an author's oeuvre: a sonnet here, a tragedy there, a comedy, a play that achieves one set of insights, another achieving another. Not everything meaningful has a developmental pattern, not even a meaningful story or history. Imagine a tale in which first the hero acquires courage, then wisdom, then compassion.

I take it that the hero is not moving up a scale of virtues. The opposite order—compassion, then wisdom, then courage—would be just as good.

1108   Jerry L. Martin

To some extent, the desire for a direction is a product of human attachment to will. People want the satisfaction of getting somewhere. Step back from will (willfulness) and you will see it differently, and (that it is) like first learning music and then studying French.

Okay, it is good to learn, say, French after studying music, but that does not mean that French is superior to music.

"But, Lord, I thought Your story didn't move randomly from one moment to another but to higher levels of development. Is that wrong?"

No, not at all. I have evolved, developed, like a child born into a new life. The learning for man is also a learning for God. But much learning has the pattern I have described rather than a precisely developmental one-stage-leading-to-the-next quality. As you develop My story, this will become clearer.

One day I learned more about God's story when I asked simply, "Where should I begin today, Lord?"

Start at the beginning.

I felt drawn into God, once again at the Creation. "Lord, we seem to be at the point where the world has been unfurled and life begins."

Yes, and that goes on as we have discussed. Don't you feel My loneliness, My searching, questing for something alive, yearning for interaction?

"Yes, I do, Lord."

Ask yourself what I am looking for.

"Love?"

Well, yes, but what is that love?

"Interaction, communication, understanding?"

Yes! I long to be recognized, to be understood, and then to be taken in.

I wondered why a great being like God would need to be loved by mere mortals. "Why does that matter to You, Lord? You've got it all, just being God."

That is silly. This is what I am. I am like a function looking for a variable. I am only half the equation.

I looked for a humbler analogy. "Like cement looking for bricks to hold together?"

Okay.

"Is that connection only what You need, or is it also what the world needs?"

Both, obviously. In your analogy, the world is like the bricks that need to be held together.

"But, Lord, I sense that Your yearning is not just an incompleteness, like needing a pair of gloves. It feels like a craving."

Yes, it is a deep internal dynamic that drives Me forward to do the things I do. I unfurl the world and call forth life and send signals to people.

Sometimes words came so fast I could barely keep up, and some of my notes are little more than scrawls. Also, I sometimes rushed because of an underlying fear I was somehow just making all this up. I was trying to write it down faster than I could possibly have thought it up myself. God picked up on that.

Don't be so frantic. You are writing this down fearfully, rushing in hope that you are not just making this up and that something will come up that looks insightful or profound. Relax and let Me tell you what I have to say, My story.

"Yes, Lord. But, You see, it all sounds quite ungodlike, undivine to me."

Where do you get your idea of what's divine? What makes you think you know what it is like to be God? You wouldn't presume to tell a bat what that is like. Just listen, and feel.

"The feeling that comes to me is Your desire to call into being a corresponding being. It seems a lot like the dialectic of self and other in Hegel. Subjectivity desires to objectify itself, as it does in artifacts, and to subjectivize the surrounding world, as it does in interpretation, and, even higher, to encounter another subjectivity."

Yes, Hegel is very insightful on this score, not so much from his understanding of God, which is limited, but from his understanding of the human dynamic and of the dialectical nature of thinking. But I am not working out a dialectic. I am not a sublation of a sublation.

That is Hegel's jargon for stages of the dialectical process.

I am a Person, searching for . . .

"That's what I wonder, Lord. I can't quite imagine what You are searching for. Just interaction? That seems too limited and, in a sense, too easy."

You are right to be puzzled. It is not just looking for company. Perhaps speaking of loneliness is misleading. Why does a human being look for love? It is not just for company. That is companionship, not love. You want to pour yourself, your concern, your destiny into another person. And you want them to respond in kind, to understand and recognize and sympathize with and care about you, (and) to share your life story, so that I becomes we. And the result is not just good feelings or good times; it is ontological, it is virtually molecular. You know that, because you have experienced it. Imagine how puny your love is—not to belittle it, but just for comparison—compared to Mine. What is barely ontological or molecular in your case is fully so in Mine. The constitution of the universe is altered by My love and My being loved. You can't just say, "God so loved the world . . ." Love is a two-way street. Anything unilateral is merely an effort at love, not its fulfillment, not its achievement.

You could tell My story, one version of it at least, through the history of love. What has love meant and been over time? From Abraham's love for his wife and his son and his God, through the Ramayana and the compassionate Buddha and Jesus and Plato's philosophy as eros toward wisdom, to Christian chivalry and Buber's I-Thou—these are stages that reflect My development and My interaction with human beings and their developing response.

"Aren't these stages progressive then? Don't they move upward?"

That is not a helpful question. Let Me go on. The telos of the world is both immanent and transcendent. It is immanent in the sense that the seeds of love are planted in the world itself, in the human heart, in people's animal nature itself. That is the driving force of sexuality, which has an analogue even on the molecular level. It is transcendent in that there is an outward pull toward the ideal, toward love of the highest kind, so there is the telos in the thing's nature or person's nature pushing him (or her) forward and the telos as an ideal and an object of love pulling him (or her) forward.

Remember that love is what fully actualizes a thing. A person comes into full personhood only in a loving relationship, in loving and being loved. That is true of the whole world, and of Me as well.

If you go back over our prayers and your readings with this in mind, what do you see? You see My drawing the physical world toward life, and drawing life upward to greater possibilities of love; to creating man (and) drawing him (people) into loving relationships with his (their) fellow creatures, with nature, and with Me; to developing people into social relationships that are richer and on more stable grounds. Consider the invention of the hearth, of a home, of passing on such things as property, traditions, and values from one generation to the next, of coming to care about great-grandchildren one will never see.

"Lord, where do we go from here?"

Let's go to China.

23

There is a divine hum to the universe

To find the beginning, I looked for the Chinese Moses or Socrates. But books on China don't start with individual thinkers or religious leaders. They start with "the Chinese mind" or "the Chinese spirit."

"Lord, I am not finding a founder of Chinese religion."

Your approach is too individual, too "Protestant." I communicate not only with individuals but with peoples, and My instruments of communication include not just words and voices, but institutions, traditions, mores, historical currents and trends, and the like. The Chinese were collectively very responsive to a coherent set of messages I sent and they guarded them like the household treasure and passed them on from one generation to the next. Individual communication is one part of the story, but not the only part.

Remember, the focus is on My story. I speak to people through their cultures as a voice is through air. I am part of the warp and woof of men's (people's) mental lives. Culture is inspired.

"And to the Chinese in particular?"

I communicated a holistic, reverential attitude to Nature as a whole, which is the foundation for the idea of harmony with Nature as a guide to conduct and "salvation" (Taoist).

Nature is capitalized to indicate that what is meant is not nature in the sense of a picnic in the woods or nature as defined by contrasts such as nature versus nurture, nature versus convention, or nature versus human artifacts. Rather it is the overarching Nature that encompasses them all. For the Chinese, Heaven (*T'ien*) is a level, the highest level, of cosmic Nature. According to the ancient *Book of History*, "Heaven, working unseen, has decisively made men with certain hidden springs of character, aiding also the harmonious development of it in their various conditions." Virtuous rulers are said to rule with the Mandate of Heaven. Poor rulers forfeit it. The ancient *Book of Odes* advises, "Always strive to be in harmony with Heaven's Mandate."

"Lord, am I on the right track?"

Yes, but what you haven't picked up on is the Chinese aestheticizing of Nature, which is both broad and fine-tuned. Look at that poetry. The references to flowers and the like are not the kind of awe and fear that inspired early Greek polytheism, nor a vague holistic wonder at the universe as a whole. It reflects a sense of the expressive side of Nature, which is, of course, My expressiveness through Nature. They were subtle and picked up on that.

Looking at classic odes, I found that some of them are hymns, used in religious and state ceremonies. Others that arose among the common folk are simple songs, accompanied by a zither, that tell in a direct and honest way about life, love, and loss. The action is often set in nature, sometimes in the sense of Nature as an authoritative context, as in "South of the Great Sea."

> My love is living
> To the south of the Great Sea.
> What shall I send to greet him?
> Two pearls and a comb of tortoise-shell:
> I'll send them to him packed in a box of jade.
> They tell me he is not true [to me]:
> They tell me he dashed my box to the ground,
> Dashed it to the ground and burnt it
> And scattered its ashes to the wind.
> From this day to the ends of time
> I must never think of him,
> Never again think of him.
> The cocks are crowing,

And the dogs are barking—
My brother and his wife will soon know
[about the broken engagement].
The autumn wind is blowing;
The morning wind is sighing.
In a moment the sun will rise in the east
And then *it* too will know.

"Lord, what was special about Chinese culture?"

The Chinese are an unusual people. They resonate to Nature, feel its tones and rhythms, are attuned to it, "hear" it, listen attentively to it, and it "tells" them certain things. They catch its vibrations and try to match their vibrations to it. This is a deep affinity, with spiritual depth. This attunement provides rhythms and determinations (delimitations), divisions like quadrants, mapping orientations, spatial orientation like latitude and longitude, and orderings and a sense of what is fitting to their lives.

This in turn brings inner peace and harmony. This sense of order is something unique in human experience, a unique contribution. And it is a right response to the cosmos. There is a natural rhythm and ordering that is healing for the soul to conform to. It is not like Dike, some sort of divine law or righteousness or duty.

The Greek idea of Dike meant not transgressing the proper limits, hence justice or right order. This is not the Chinese understanding of order.

It is more like joining an instrumental group and fitting in with the harmonies, the patterns. For the Chinese, it is very intuitive, a sensibility, not like the Stoic logos.

The Stoic logos was a divine rationality that informs the universe and to which the rational soul conforms. For the Chinese, what is needed is not rationality, but a fine-tuned sensibility.

One of the things I put into the universe, one of the things I *am*, is the natural order and, like the standard measure (or meter), the prime "tone" or "metronome" or tuning fork. There is a "frequency" then, and I am it. This is one way I make Myself available to men

and animals. There is a divine hum to the universe, and that is one way I communicate.

So I "set aside" this whole people and communicate with them very profoundly in this way.

"And the Chinese were adept at picking up the signal?"

They have both a natural temperament and cultural, linguistic, (and) symbolic resources that lean them this way, much more than in the West. People cannot take everything in at once. They have to specialize and the Chinese have specialized in this.

"With little or no sense of a personal God, didn't they lose a lot?"

Everybody loses a lot. No one gets it all in. That is fine. They all help Me realize, express Myself. They are all part of the big story.

At this point, I was told just to sit with God for a moment. I was led into my inner self. Looking at nature from that vantage point, I saw it aesthetically. Samuel Taylor Coleridge said that fiction requires "the willing suspension of disbelief." The aesthetic attitude requires the willing suspension of *desire*. That allows the order and beauty of nature to reveal itself, uncoerced. That is the difference between art and decoration and, more radically, between the appreciation of nature and seeing it as something to be dismantled for other uses. It is the difference between inflicting ourselves on nature and letting the divine reality show through.

The Chinese had let the divine reality show through.

The great teacher of China was Confucius. The story has it that, as a young man, he went through a period of intense meditation on what he should do with his life. He began having recurring dreams about the Duke of Chou, one of the legendary patriarchs of China, the embodiment of wisdom and virtue. Confucius believed these dreams were sending him a message. He was to revive the ancient ways and the classics from which they could be learned. This was to be his most enduring legacy. It is a great story, but as I read it, I kept hearing,

No, (not from dreams).

"Lord, where did Confucius get his inspiration?"

He got it from his sense of fittingness. For him, duty was a kind of fittingness. It was fitting that a son pay appropriate honors to his father.

This is something the young Confucius, raised by his widowed mother, had managed to do in spite of great difficulties in even locating where his father had been buried.

It was fitting in an almost literal sense, like putting the square peg in the square hole, or putting each puzzle piece exactly where it goes without forcing it. It is the fittingness of an artisan, a craftsman, who knows, who virtually sees where each piece should go, where the edges need to be smoothed, where the joints need to be fitted together. He saw society in that way and was a craftsman of society. If fathers behaved fittingly toward their sons, and vice versa, and husbands to their wives, and kings to their subjects, and so forth, then all the pieces would fit, without being forced. You can understand his sayings in this light.

You often call the Chinese approach "aesthetic," and that is not wrong. But "aesthetic" means many things, and for Confucius, it means the aesthetics of the master craftsman, writ large. You will have to pray about what it means for Lao-Tzu.

Your approach is too individualistic, focused solely on My communications to individuals. I also shape cultural mentalities. The Chinese had their own mentality, an aesthetic sense of things, and I enhanced that through My communications with many, many Chinese. Their bias provided material that I used to shape a finely tuned aesthetic and spiritual instrument. You see the results, not only in thinkers such as Confucius and Lao-Tzu, but also in Chinese art, architecture, manners, family life, and so on.

Confucius describes the superior person: "In seeing he is careful to see clearly, in hearing he is careful to hear distinctly, in his looks he is careful to be kindly; in his manner to be respectful, in his words to be loyal, in his work to be diligent."

Proper behavior cannot be achieved by conforming to a general rule. One must pay careful attention to the situation and adjust behavior in the most fitting way, for, in the Confucian version of the Golden Mean, "To go too far is as bad as not to go far enough."

Words should fit deeds, with neither excessive pride nor false modesty. "A gentleman is ashamed to let his words outrun his deeds." And words must fit circumstances. "At home in his native village his manner is simple and unassuming, as though he did not trust himself to speak. But in the ancestral temple and at Court he speaks readily, though always choosing his words with care. . . . [W]hen conversing with the Under Ministers his attitude is friendly and affable; when conversing with the Upper Ministers, it is restrained and formal. When the ruler is present it is wary, but not cramped."

What to say, or whether to speak at all, depends on what words, or silences, are fitting to the person and the situation. "Not to talk [about the Way] to one who could be talked to, is to waste a man. To talk to those who cannot be talked to, is to waste one's words."

Confucius presented one version of the Way. There was another, presented by his older contemporary, Lao-Tzu.

24

These are all Me

The great work in the Taoist tradition is the *Tao Te Ching*, the Book of the Way and the Power. At first, I thought this would be the place to begin my Chinese studies but was warned,

Don't assume that every text enshrined in the history of religion is an authentic or pure communication from Me. The Taoism of Lao-Tzu reflects a great deal his own personality—shy, reticent, unassuming. I communicated a grain of truth to him. The rest is his own invention or elaboration. Find that grain of truth, or read him and the others (other Taoist texts) and pray to get My guidance in finding it. Read widely in Taoism. Do not assume that Lao-Tzu is the only worthwhile source, and do connect Taoism with the previous Chinese tradition.

I did read more broadly, and this is what I learned. Confucius had taught the rules of behavior appropriate to various social roles. Lao-Tzu was less interested in the ways of the world and more interested in the Way, the Tao, that lies beyond language and reason. The two men are said to have been contemporaries, living around the fifth or sixth century B.C.E., about the same time as Socrates. Writing a few centuries later, the great historian Ssu-ma Ch'ien, the Tacitus of ancient China, reports that the two sages met in the capital of Lo-yang, where Lao-Tzu, the older of the two, was curator of the royal library. Lao-Tzu told Confucius:

The men about whom you talk [the wise rulers venerated in the classics] are dead, and their bones are mouldered to dust; only their words are left. Moreover, when the superior man gets his opportunity, he mounts aloft; but when the time is against him, he is carried along by the force of circumstances. [The outcome depends, not on his will or talent or moral cultivation, but on whether he is attuned to the flow of the situation.] I have heard that a good merchant, though he have rich treasures safely stored, appears as if he were poor; and that the superior man, though his virtue be complete, is yet to outward seeming stupid. [Those in touch with the Way have no need or desire to flaunt their wealth or virtue.] Put away your proud air and many desires, your insinuating habit and wild will. They are no advantage to you—this is all I have to tell you.

After the meeting, Confucius is supposed to have said:

I know how birds can fly, fishes swim, and animals run. But the runner may be snared, the swimmer hooked, and the flyer shot by the arrow. But there is the dragon: I cannot tell how he mounts on the wind through the clouds, and rises to heaven. Today I have seen Lao-Tzu, and can only compare him to the dragon.

The historian adds his own epigraph.

Lao-Tzu cultivated the Tao and its attributes, the chief aim of his studies being how to keep himself concealed and remain unknown. He continued to reside at the capitol of Chou, but after a long time, seeing the decay of the dynasty, he left it and went away to the barrier-gate, leading out of the kingdom on the northwest. Yin His, the warden of the gate, said to him, "You are about to withdraw yourself out of sight. Let me insist on your (first) composing for me a book." On this, Lao-Tzu wrote a book in two parts, setting forth his views on the Tao and its attributes, in more than 5000 characters. He then went away, and it is not known

where he died. He was a superior man, who liked to keep himself
unknown.

Ching means not just a book, but the Book, an authoritative classic
or canon. The character *Tao* is composed of the characters for "moving on" and "head," hence, "going ahead." The original meaning
was "way" with the connotations of both path and method. In this
respect, it is similar to the Greek *hodos*, originally meaning "path,"
from which we derive the term *method* (*meta-hodos*, "according to
the path"). As method, the *Tao* also suggests such ideas as principle, rationality, or reason, hence the right way or truth, and finally
rational speech or word. In this respect, it resembles the Greek *logos*,
which means both "word," as in the opening of the Gospel of John
("In the beginning was the Word"), and "reason," which we retain in
such words as *logic* and *sociological*, reasoning about society.

But etymological analysis is not dispositive when one comes to
interpreting the *Tao Te Ching*. Take the famous opening line, usually
translated as, "The Way that can be spoken of is not the eternal Way."
I am told that, in Chinese, the line has only three characters, the last
with a negative indicator, each of which means Tao. Literally, it looks
like: Tao Tao not-Tao, which suggests that the Tao that is Tao-ed is
not *the* Tao. Another translation captures the repetition: "The Reason
that can be reasoned is not the eternal Reason." The "can be" is inter-
pretive, since there are no modals in Chinese, and no tenses. Alan
Watts suggests that the element that expresses "going" and forms part
of the character for Tao also has the connotation of rhythm. Hence
the Tao could be understood as intelligent rhythm, the rational pulse
of the universe. I remembered that God had described Himself as the
divine metronome.

Whatever the best translation, the Tao is elusive and clothed in
paradox. Whatever can be said must be said with a certain assertorial
lightness. What can we say about it?

First, the Way does not seem to be a Creator standing over or outside the world. For example (Alan Watts translation):

All things depend upon it to exist,
and it does not abandon them.
To its accomplishments it lays no claim.
It loves and nourishes all things,
but does not lord it over them.

But there is a kind of creation story, which has some resemblance to what I have received about God "before" Creation.

There is something obscure which is complete
before heaven and earth arose;
tranquil, quiet,
standing alone without change,
moving around without peril.
It could be the mother of everything.
I don't know its name,
and call it Tao.

The Tao provides everything without having to *do* anything: "The Tao does nothing, but nothing is left undone."

What about the other key term, *Te*? In Confucius, *Te* is virtue, character, or moral force, and requires moral cultivation. For the Taoists, it is virtue in a gentler sense. Lao-Tzu's great successor, Chaung-tse, writes:

When water is still, it is like a mirror, reflecting the beard and the eyebrows. It gives the accuracy of the water-level, and the philosopher makes it his model. And if water thus derives lucidity from stillness, how much more the faculties of the mind? The mind of the Sage being in repose becomes the mirror of the universe, the speculum of all existence.

The fluidity of water is not the result of any effort on the part of the water, but is its natural property. And the virtue of the perfect man is such that even without cultivation there is nothing which can withdraw from his sway. Heaven is naturally high, the earth is naturally solid, the sun and moon are naturally bright. Do they cultivate these attributes?

Before reading the *Tao Te Ching*, I had asked, "Lord, do You want me to pray first?"

Yes, for a minute.

I felt guided to look at the world through Lao-Tzu's eyes. "Lord, I get a feeling of great calm and peace, and of letting things be."

Exactly.

"It is quiet and beautiful, not like a spectacle or dramatic sunset, but more like the twilight glow on the desert or seashore—soft hues, at harmony with one another, not trying to command the eye. Lord, I think I have seen Chinese paintings like that."

Yes.

"Is the *Tao Te Ching* a metaphysical treatise, or is it a practical guide for living?"

Do you see how silly that question is?

"I see. It is a false dichotomy. I should just take it as it comes, not try to force categories on it."

Yes, now proceed (with) reading.

For some reason, I started with Book III, "The Imitation of Tao": "Looked at, but cannot be seen—that is called the Invisible (*yi*)."

This is reminiscent of what God told me when I asked why He didn't show Himself—*"You see Me all the time"*—not as a sensory item but as a presence. This "eludes all our inquiries," writes Lao-Tzu. "It cannot be defined."

"Yes, Lord, it does not so much mean 'ineffable and beyond all our categories,' as 'it just isn't the sort of thing to be defined; you just apprehend it.' This is said in several ways. Is that right, Lord?"

[silence]

"Shall I go on?"

[silence]

I went back to "looking through Lao-Tzu's eyes." I was having lunch at a little diner, colorless and a bit dumpy, but now I saw unity and a kind of beauty there, everything fitting together and benign, not in an active do-good sense but simply "it is what it is supposed to be."

"Is that right, Lord?"

[silence]

"Is there a message or implication in the silence?"

[silence]

"Am I trying too hard to put it into words?"

Yes.

"As I go back to looking, I find it hard to stay in a purely contemplative mode."

What changes?

"Well, desire, interest, the practical uses of things I'm seeing."

Now back off again.

"When I focus on objects as objects (as tables, as chairs, etc.) it is difficult. But when I just take in the scene and sense the life behind it all, including the 'inanimate' objects, then it is not so hard. There is a reality there that is more fundamental than things as objects. There is a unity and purpose, not in the sense of achieving an outcome, but in the sense of not being pointless."

Yes, that's right. . . . Now go back to reading.

I still did not grasp all the ways God comes to people, so I objected, "But, Lord, they do not report receiving any communication from You."

You forget that not all communication is verbal. There are dreams, intimations, a sense of the sacred, intuitions, promptings of the soul like conscience—these are all Me.

"Another question, Lord. One commentator says that the Tao precedes God. Perhaps this means something like what Paul Tillich calls the God beyond God."

Yes.

Well, I had asked the question and gotten an answer, but only later would learn what it meant. I had another task at the moment. I had been told to relate Taoism to what had come earlier. I now had to find out what that was.

25

You have to fight in life—not against the flow, but with it

Were these God's earliest verbal communications? For generations, Chinese farmers in Anyang would dig up "dragon bones" and sell them for medicinal uses. In 1899, an archaeologist discovered they were etched with markings—primeval Chinese characters a millennium older than previously known texts. On the bones were recorded a question and an answer, usually a yes or no. Will the king's child be a son? Will tomorrow be good for hunting? The king has a headache—has he offended a certain ancestor? In prehistoric times, priests would heat the bones with red-hot pokers and divine the meaning of the resulting cracks.

The oracle bones had come up in one of my first prayers. Rushing ahead without reading, I had asked simply, "Lord, what were You up to with the Chinese?"

You might say that the Chinese approached Me; I did not approach them. They explicitly consulted Me. That is the meaning of the oracle bones.

So the oracle bones were not a divine bolt out of the blue, like God speaking to Abraham. The Chinese sought divine guidance and God responded. What began as brief inscriptions on the oracle bones grew into a classic on how to behave in various situations.

The *I Ching* was a simple guide to action, trying to figure out what the situation was so they could know which virtue was appro-

priate to it. It is a very ancient work—one of the earliest—and represents an important moment in the conversation with Me.

Each section of the book opens with a beautifully drawn character, symbolic of its meaning.

"Lord, I seem to have two possible starting points on China—the discussion of the aesthetic appreciation of nature or the oracle bones as the precursors to the *I Ching*."

The two are really one. Correctly reading the oracle bones also required the "willing suspension of desire." That is one of the hazards of consulting oracles. Too often one wants only to hear good news or flattering reports or accept solutions with which you are comfortable. To correctly read the bones, or any oracle . . .

For a moment, I feared I had lapsed into just listening to my own thoughts. "I hope You're saying this, Lord."

. . . to correctly read any oracle requires not being attached to specific outcomes, not preferring, or not being influenced by preferring, one reading over another. That requires a restful, detached attitude—not very easy to achieve at court.

"With a ruler breathing down your neck."

Precisely. What the marks on the bone are doing is attuning the seer to the situation, letting it "speak" to him. This situation "wants" a certain action or attitude. The seer has to quietly "listen" to the situation.

"What did this do for Your development, Lord?"

It was a refinement. I had communicated with earlier man primarily by warnings and nudges to go one way rather than another.

"With the people of Israel, You gave commandments."

Yes, but this (the oracle bones) was much earlier. It invited Me to present Myself, not as an urging force, but just as a manifestation of the right order—and, like a patient being diagnosed, to "wince" if something was wrong. And, in a sense, it made Me beautiful. Obviously, the cave painters had seen My beauty too, but that response was primarily localized to seeing the divine presence in particular animals. The questions put to the oracle bones were about larger situations and pointed ultimately to the whole of Nature as a divine order.

"And a beautiful order?"

Precisely. And this was new to Me. There are two aspects here. First, that I am the right order of the universe, which is different from just being its organizer. We are moving from regularity, the laws of nature and human nature, to a moral and aesthetic order. Second, that My order is beautiful, that it can be sensed aesthetically, that there is encoded within it a fittingness, rules of fittingness, of what is right to do in different situations. The Taoists picked up on one aspect of this, the Confucians on another.

The oracle bones led to the *I Ching*, or Book of Changes, which in turn inspired both Taoist and Confucian commentaries. "Lord, which is closer to Your original communications?"

Both are equally old. The (Confucian) ethical terms predate *I Ching*, as does something like the Taoist sense of Nature.

Ching means an authoritative book or classic. *I* means "changes." Human situations are always changing, and the *I Ching* gives a taxonomy of the sixty-four kinds of situations a person can confront. It was studied for its wisdom, for divination, and for identification of one's situation and how best to respond to it. You toss coins or sticks to know which of the sixty-four sections will answer your question.

Years ago, a friend had talked me into trying it. At the time, I was drawn to a certain erotic adventure, to put it delicately. It could have been a disaster. I was looking for permission.

I tossed the coins and was guided to a section. It was the Chinese equivalent of Henry David Thoreau's "Simplify, simplify." Irritated, I did not do any more *I Ching*.

I wondered if I should try it again.

(No,) read it for the original (divine) encounter.

The book's ancient wisdom is contained in symbolic language that must be decoded. Like people for three thousand years, I found it fascinating. But I was told,

Do not overrate the *I Ching*. It is not the great Ur-source. It is valuable and important. As I indicated, it predates its use as an oracle. It is in part a visual representation. The signs themselves were important, and contemplation of them produced insights. They are really explorations of the situations in which one may find oneself. The oracle was added as a trick for identifying which situation applied to oneself at a given time. It is useful, but no more useful than seeking guidance from the Bible by opening to a random passage. It is not magic.

Nevertheless, I was told,

It might be My voice that they hear.

As I started reading the *I Ching*, my notes record, "This is what is coming to me: The sticks (represented as lines, symbols) may have originally begun as oracle devices, but the book is not an oracle. It is a way of listening to God (however conceived at that time), of seeking guidance, not predictions. The key is not in throwing sticks or tossing coins, but in letting God lead you to the relevant section." I began to understand how God's voice can be present even in a tradition that does not posit a personal god.

Congratulations. You have listened to what I have told you, which is to think, "What is God trying to communicate here?" Continue on that tack.

Each section of the *I Ching* begins with a brief poetic statement, called the Judgment, followed by the Image, an explanation couched in symbolic language.

In light of what you now know—your current sense—of Chinese and of Chinese symbolism, just contemplate each of the Judgments, just going through in order.

I was guided to start with Number 2, the Receptive, Earth, which emphasizes the "feminine." In the Chinese tradition, the feminine or receptive or passive is not considered less important; on the contrary, it is foundational. The section begins:

> The Receptive brings about sublime success,
> Furthering through the perseverance of a mare.
> If the superior man undertakes something and tries to lead,
> He goes astray;
> But if he follows, he finds guidance. . . .
> Quiet perseverance brings good fortune.

"The feminine, represented by the earth but also by the mare, is receptive, yielding. Lord, is this about life on earth?"

Yes.

"And that we need to live subserviently to God and allow His will . . ."

Yes.

". . . as reflected in the flow . . ."

Yes.

". . . to prevail?"

Yes, you just need to go along with My will. The universe has been structured to facilitate My will.

"But there are obstacles and negative forces as well?"

Yes, of course. But the feminine lays a substratum, just as the womb is crafted for life, to give proper life to a human being. The universe is the matrix of My will. It—the universe, the feminine, the receptive, the earthy—receives My will, takes it in, allows itself to be acted on by it, to express it (to be the expressive vehicle for it).

Quiet perseverance relates to the fight, as in the Mahabharata [the Hindu epic].

"So, Lord, sometimes, even in situations that involve conflict, the key is simply to continue quietly and persistently yielding to the will of God—and this relates to the plane of action?"

Sort of.

"To something more like the substrate of the plane of action? Not so much action—what one does or doesn't do—as the attitude, and the underlying spiritual reality in which the attitude is grounded, of an undeflected yielding to the divine will?"

Yes, better. Now go back to Number 1—the Creative.

Different responses are called for in different situations. Sometimes the "feminine" response in Number 2 is needed; other times the "masculine" response in Number 1 is called for.

Number 1. The Creative.

> The Creative works sublime success,
> Furthering through perseverance.

"Lord, this is the same as Number 2. Both say that 'sublime success' comes from 'perseverance.'"

Yes, but this is the active side of perseverance, struggle—not just letting be, letting oneself be the instrument of the Divine, but being the agent of the Divine.

I have asked you to be My instrument as in the Receptive (in telling My story). In the context of (your organizational work), you were an agent. They are two sides of the same coin.

"So the active is not 'working on' the passive—they are two quite different movements?"

Not exactly. Sometimes, in a sense always, the active is working on the passive, the matrix. The matrix or substrate is receiving form and direction. It is the instrument, but if I want something done, I need not only instruments but also doers, initiators.

Part of the complexity of the world is that I do not create what I want—My designs—directly, like a sculptor working in clay (that can be molded). I work through people.

"More like the director of a play?"

Exactly. The nature of the design is such that this is necessary.

"Lord, in the Creative, the Judgment is much shorter, perhaps symbolizing the directness of action."

Yes, the directness of the agent and of Me as well. If I say, "Do this," it gets done. If I say, "Let things happen," it is more complex.

"Because it involves a multiplicity of agents. Lord, should I move on to the next part?"

Linger over this. Think about "perseverance."

"Well, it means persistence, follow-through, not surrendering, not giving up."

Not surrendering. This is the combat aspect. You have to fight in life—not against the flow, but with it, against obstacles to it.

26

There are times
for just *being*

I moved on to other reading, but about six months later I was guided back to the *I Ching*, and told to pray in more detail about each section.

Number 1. The Creative.

> The Creative works sublime success,
> Furthering through perseverance.

It is always helpful to know the literal meaning, and fortunately the commentators provide it in the Wilhelm edition. "Furthering" means literally "creating that which accords with the nature of a given being." "Perseverance" is literally "correct and firm." So the Judgment could be restated as—here I am on my own—the Creative works sublime success, creating that which accords with the nature of the things (and people) involved, through correct and firm action.

"Lord, does 'correct and firm' action mean apt or appropriate action?"

Yes.

I sensed that the Creative refers to God's overflowing into human beings and into human action. "So the meaning of the Judgment is: The action is 'correct' in the sense of being attuned to God's will or general direction, flow, telos?"

Yes.

"Then the first line could be restated: God's overflowing moves toward sublime success, namely, success in what really matters. Is that okay, Lord?"

Okay.

So this is a situation where God's overflowing moves toward success in what is most important in this situation, creating an outcome that fits the nature and destiny of the people and forces concerned, through attuned, firm, purposeful action. This sounds like a situation in which firm action is called for, not action based on human choice or willfulness, but action that is an instrument for channeling God's overflowing presence into the situation so that there is a natural fulfillment of all parties concerned.

Now the Image.

> The movement of heaven is full of power.
> Thus the superior man makes himself strong and untiring.

The meaning is now transparent, isn't it?

"Yes, Lord. It is another way of saying the same thing. Sometimes the divine reality ('the movement of heaven') is flowing into a situation in a potentially powerful way. It behooves a properly attuned person to tap into that divine presence, to make himself or herself the instrument, and to engage in strong, purposeful action in accord with it. The result will be an outcome that fulfills or actualizes the individuals and forces involved."

Go on to Number 2.

Number 2. The Receptive. It begins:

> The Receptive brings about sublime success,
> Furthering through the perseverance of a mare,
> If the superior man undertakes something and tries to lead,
> He goes astray;
> But if he follows, he finds guidance. . . .

"'But if he follows, he finds guidance' seems to mean: If he follows like a dance partner, yields to the situation, and listens for God's voice, it will come to him, and he will know the right things to do."

Yes. Both situations occur. There are times you know what to do, what God wants of you, and there are times you do not, when the situation itself may be unclear, you don't know who are the good guys and who are the bad guys, or what action would be efficacious rather than risky or counterproductive or ineffective. In those situations, flow with the situation, staying attuned to Me, and sensitive to the forces present and the various actors, and the right action—or lack of action—will manifest itself.

Now go to Number 3.

The third of the sixty-four sections, each providing guidance for a particular type of situation, is called "Difficulty at the Beginning." Before I had a chance to read the Judgment, I was told,

Sometimes you don't know from the beginning what to do and, perhaps forced to act, you act wrongly—either morally or in terms of consequences. Then you need to rectify, to regain your footing, to seek advice and help from others.

I read Number 4 and then went to Number 5, "Waiting (Nourishment)."

Waiting. If you are sincere,
You have light and success.
Perseverance brings good fortune.
It furthers one to cross the great water.

Go to the Image.

Clouds rise up to heaven.
The image of waiting.
Thus the superior man eats and drinks,
Is joyous and of good cheer.

"Why the title 'Waiting'?"

This is all quite simple. The task is not always to fight or act, or to *try* to mobilize one's potential or effort to yield and follow God's will. There are times for just *being*, because you already are what you should be, and so is the universe, and you should enjoy, appreciate, understand that fact. The universe is a joy, not just an arena for action. It is a celebration.

Number 6 is about Conflict.

> Conflict. You are sincere
> And are being obstructed.
> A cautious halt halfway brings good fortune.
> Going through to the end brings misfortune.
> It furthers one to see the great man.
> It does not further one to cross the great water.

There are several elements here. It is not always time to "cross the great water," which primarily refers to spiritual growth. One has to accept one's situation and limitations. Often the goal should be modest, just putting one foot in front of the other.

"See the great man"—yes, that means to seek advice—but it is also a bit of a wrong instruction. It may not even be a time to run around and get advice. Just hold still, and mind your own business. Obstructions are meant to be there. Accept them and build up one's own resources, inner and outer.

The next is Number 7, the Army.

> The Army. The army needs perseverance
> And a strong man.
> Good fortune without blame.

This really refers, not to oneself lacking strength, but sometimes it is right to follow or rely on or seek the help of a strong man (person)—strong in forces or character or insight or whatever. That means your action is tied to his (or hers), which may sometimes err, but no blame attaches to you for that.

I had learned that there are two keys. You have to trust that your device for selecting the Number fitting your situation reflects divine guidance. Having found it, you have to meditate on the Judgment and Image in a prayerful, yielding way.

In *I Ching*, I had found another way God communicates.

"Lord, China is overwhelming."

You are looking at a massive culture that goes back thousands of years. You cannot expect to understand their relation to Me by building it up out of pieces. You need to step back and take a look at the whole.

"Lord, I don't see the whole."

Yes, you do. You just have to relax, and not feel you have to understand, in the sense of mastering, everything. Try it.

"When I step back, keeping in mind the ancient classics I have read . . ."

No, you don't have to do that. Step farther back. Include the art.

"When I look at *I Ching*, I see . . ."

No, step farther back.

"Lord, when I step way back, I see people living in a bounded, well-defined world, characterized by geographic and linguistic unity; a world in which they must yield to the elements, to the rise and fall of the rivers and the changing seasons; a world in which the organization of the whole determines whether the parts can function well (they must all function in concert, in harmony); a world that lives under the dome of Heaven, of an overarching natural order, within which people are living vis-à-vis one another in a similar order, harmony, and hierarchy, with rules of graciousness and deference essential to maintaining order and harmony, and either going with the flow or using stratagems to ride the flow successfully, while having an appreciation for the small objects and minute details resonating to the whole."

And now what does that tell you about Me?

"You are the whole to which the parts are resonating, to which they must yield (since stratagems do not work with You), who embodies the order they must replicate in their lives and social relations, who is seen in the beauty and order of nature."

And what does that tell you about what it is like to be God?

"You are that calm center, that framework of order, that creative source of beauty, and that inner impulse to relate to others well. Am I on track, Lord?"

As I told you, you might say that the Chinese sought Me, not Me them. Through the oracle bones, they sought to be in tune with Me. And I saw that My way of relating to humans need not be only through whispering and urging, but that people can respond directly to the physical, moral, and aesthetic order I present; that these are not separate, unrelated tasks for Me but are all of a piece and they are one way (that) I communicate to people and that people can respond to Me. This, again, is a step toward My integration as a "personality."

"So: The Chinese have an aesthetic appreciation of Nature and want to fit in harmoniously. But, in real life, there is always a plane of action. The Taoists are one-sided and neglectful of the demands of action. The Confucianists are one-sided in the opposite direction. They address action, but fail to fit it into a cosmic context. For them, it remains at a social level. But doesn't the *I Ching* combine the two?"

Exactly! You have been reading My mind, literally. *I Ching* is a kind of synthesis of the two emphases of Chinese thought—harmony in the natural and (in the) social orders. The first is larger, a frame for the second, and more open to Me, but the Taoists took it away from action. The Confucianists were preoccupied with action solely in the context of social harmony and not in accordance with My will. That is why they became stultified and concerned with petty rules and old texts and trivial matters.

In *I Ching* you see both, and that is why there are classic commentaries in both traditions. Both felt it was their book.

"And the book has been popular ever since."

Yes, the synthesis was more appealing to the common people than the two intellectual traditions. Common people know the necessity for action. They bear its brunt. And of course they want to know what will happen—hence, casting sticks to predict. But they also want guidance, good advice, and don't have the illusion of self-sufficiency the Taoists and Confucianists have.

Polytheism, Egypt, Confucius, the Tao, the *I Ching*—I now knew something about the pieces of the puzzle, but hadn't a clue how they were supposed to fit together. Was there a big picture?

I tell different cultures what they are prepared to hear

27

"Lord, I have prayed about various cultures, and I don't see how they fit together."

Look at the broad sweep for a moment. What do you see?

"From prehistoric times, You are dealing with people through nature and their own intuitions, aesthetic appreciation, emerging moral sense . . ."

Yes.

". . . and perhaps through each person's own development, and self-awareness and awareness of the other."

Yes.

"That starts getting articulated as the Way by the Chinese and as the cosmic order in Mesopotamia and perhaps in India in the idea of Rta (the primeval Indian term for right order)."

Yes.

"And You are seen in natural phenomena—in particular plants and animals, in geographical structures such as rivers and mountains, and in larger forces such as life and death and fate and famine. I gather these are all ways in which You are manifesting Yourself."

Not just manifesting Myself, but communicating through them.

"Communicating what, Lord?"

Go back to the Way. I communicated to the Chinese, who have an affinity for this, the sense of harmony. The "cosmic order" can

mean many things, including a Newtonian rational system, or a moral order enforced by the gods or by Divine Justice. Because of the Chinese affinity, I communicated the fine sense of balance and harmony and right proportions, not as weighing things on a scale, which is how the Greeks heard Me, but in something like a moral aesthetic sense—aesthetic in a larger sense that then encompasses the moral and spiritual—that right balance and sense of center and working with the natural flow and understanding oneself rightly in order to contribute correctly to the larger social and natural harmony, and understanding each thing by its right name and nature and place in the scheme of things.

Since, in a sense, an ontologically rich sense, all nature is Me, this communication to the Chinese was crucial, and is something people in other cultures can learn from. It is an essential part of My total story.

"Why is it important to You personally?"

The universe is something like My body, but it has ethereal as well as gross aspects (just as the human body does). If people misbehave and throw it out of balance—and I am not just talking about ecology here, but more subtle ways of acting out of harmony with the natural order or the Way—then you might say that I get a stomach upset. I am, among other things, the source of cosmic order, both physical and more than physical. I need people to help. The world is better because people are in it, since they actualize higher possibilities and are able to articulate the moral order in action, the natural order in intellection, the aesthetic order in appreciation, and so on. They are My partners in this effort.

"I gather that You developed Yourself, moving from rather vague appreciations and understandings during the prehistoric period and to the more articulated Chinese understanding."

That is correct. I have inspired them, but learned in turn as they articulated those inspirations. To some extent, human beings are My pen and pencil, or ink brush, as you are.

"But I still don't understand why You reveal one set of ideas to one people, another set to another, and they all contradict one another."

The contradictions are more apparent than real. Nevertheless, your observation that they differ from one another is correct. There are several reasons for this difference.

The first is that, just as when I communicate with you, it is in your own voice and in your own language and in your own vocabulary, using your own knowledge and concepts. That is how I communicate with all people.

The second follows from the first. Each culture has, at a particular time, certain human, institutional, and conceptual resources. Each also has certain traits or talents that I work with. Just as the writing instructor might tell one young writer to write more simply and another to complexify, I tell different cultures what they are prepared to hear and to understand and to act on.

Third, the total revelation would be more than any single individual or culture could bear or well act on. So there is a kind of division of labor. For example, I told the ancient people of Israel to act in history and to keep My covenant and abide by a set of religious and moral rules. That was task enough for them. I told the ancient people of India to develop the inner life and to get in touch with the transcendental Atman, the Self beyond the Self. Both were and remain valid tasks.

One reason I am telling My story now is that today it is time for mankind to begin to sort out what is true and not so true in the various religions and other sources of insight, and to piece them together into something more adequate.

I would like to stress that I have communicated over the millennia with human beings and other creatures in myriad ways. Do not attend only to the canonical revelations enshrined by the different religions. I have communicated through the many myths and stories and legends that have been collected. Some are directly from Me, some are invented by men (people), most are a mix of the two. All are communicated in terms of the capacity and vocabulary of the listeners.

I communicate through prayer, through dreams, through insights that seem like one's own thoughts, through hunches and intimations and intuitions. I am present in the human heart and speak to people directly. Directly does not mean simply or literally or in a loud voice.

People must learn to listen, to heed. That requires openness of heart and sensitive attunement to My voice, to My urgings.

Telling My story involves what it is like to be a Being who communicates with those whom I love and whose actions mean everything to Me and (what it is like) to do so in this indirect and typically unheard or unheeded way. That is what My revelation to the ancient Jews is about.

I am a God who whispers. It is not difficult to hear Me. It is not, as some say, that I am hidden. Far from it. I am not in hiding. I am everywhere, right in front of their eyes. But they have to choose to see, to hear, to heed. Men's (people's) hearts are usually closed. The Old Testament, for example, is replete with cases of individuals resisting hearing My word, My instructions.

Can you imagine the anguish, the suffering in such a God? If I did not care about human beings, it would be nothing to Me that they do not listen. If I were the detached, "perfect," self-sufficient God many theologians write about, it would not matter to Me. But I am not such a God. I care about human beings, I care about each and every human being infinitely, in a direct and total way you can only begin to imagine. I care what human beings do. And I am sorrowful when they do wrong, when they do not meet their historical moment in the right way. I long to be close to human beings, for them to be in harmony and attunement with Me. It would be wrong of Me to be close to them on any other, more false, terms.

I am a suffering God. If you miss that, you miss everything. Suffering is at the heart of the universe. It is not incidental. An accident. Something preventable. It is at the core of what it is to relate to an Other in a loving way. Otherness requires separateness, distance, alienation, independence, freedom, a certain amount of friction. It is not (only) creatures who are imperfect. I am too. I need this development in order to become more perfect, more fulfilled. I need it and human beings do as well.

In all these different ways of communication, My experience is one of love, of reaching out, of trying to catch a person's attention, of satisfaction when heard—because I and the Cosmos are then moving forward—and of frustration, endless, unrelenting, bitter frustration when not heard, of acute pain when not heeded, of anger when double-crossed, and of tremendous suffering, like the suffering of a mother or father who watches a son or daughter go bad. There is no anguish like it.

Here I Am

Why shouldn't that be the whole story of creation?

28

What is the point of it all? My intellectual curiosity was being satisfied, as God was answering questions about the Creation and how He has related to various cultures. For a philosopher, that goes a long way. But I had a deeper yearning that was profoundly unsatisfied. What, I wanted to know, is the point? *Is* there a point? Or does God preside over a world that lacks discernible meaning?

"Lord, what is the meaning or purpose of life—and of the world?"

The meaning of the universe is not exactly a teleology, though this is not a bad concept. In other words, it is not a beginning-to-an-ending narrative of progress, with a single, simple outcome, such as reuniting with God. The meaning that encompasses (the entire story) is a total holistic meaning: they (various moments) are all bearers of this total meaning simultaneously and, in a sense, all the time. Think of the meaning of a body of work, such as Beethoven's symphonies. Their meaning does not depend on the Ninth being better than the First.

"Lord, I can understand a story-like meaning that goes from lower to higher, or worse to better. And I can understand a rather formal meaning in a single work, its patterns and structures and the like. But, frankly, I don't see that the collected symphonies have any overall meaning. What do You mean by meaning?"

I can see this will take some time. You will come up with an analogy that works for you if you keep searching. You surely understand that a single symphony has a meaning—it certainly has a meaningful structure and sequence—yet "the purpose of a song is not to get to the end." The purpose is in the doing of it. Ask yourself, what is the doing of a life? (Of) a universe?

"Much of it is a struggle to achieve certain ideals—achieving justice, right versus wrong, and so forth."

Exactly, but that is not all. There is insight, understanding, beauty, love itself.

"Well, I meant ideals in a broader sense than just ethical values."

That is right.

"So we are supposed to achieve those things worth achieving?"

It is for God to achieve them as well, for God to grow and develop.

"And purpose does not require a sequential, progressive pattern with a climactic ending?"

That is correct. Beginning and end are much closer (to each other) than you imagine.

"Then You are working with individuals, both for their own growth and for the social and cosmic order?"

Yes, though that does not sound as intimate as it is. One lover doesn't say of the other, "I am trying to call her into being, and trying to create a harmonious, well-ordered household." That is immensely too sterile. You are living in and through one another, enjoying each other's growth, feeling the pain of each other's heartbreak, and trying to create a life together that has value and reflects a range of values. But you falsify all that if you make it too means-ends, too instrumental in conception. It starts from an intimate core, just you and her and making a life together.

Why shouldn't the universe be like that? Why shouldn't that be the whole story of creation? You do not say about the love, oh, it's meaningless because it lacks a larger purpose. If you say that, it's not love. The universe is one great act of love. That is what it means to "call into being." The cosmic order reflects and promotes that. Analogously, the social order.

"So I should conceive of telling Your story as telling a love story, not so much the external drama of it (boy meets girl) as the intimate life of it."

Exactly. That is what Maritain meant when he talked about getting to know the mind of God.

Catholic philosopher Jacques Maritain wrote, in *A Preface to Metaphysics*, that ontological knowledge "seeks to discover . . . the secrets of Being, . . . of love, of purely spiritual realities . . . above all, of God's interior life."

It is just as how you want to get inside the mind and heart of someone you love. You want to understand them from the inside out, you might say. I want you to understand Me from the inside out and, in those terms, how I have related to Abraham, Buddha, and others.

Don't worry whether Noah or Abraham is historical, or (about) historical controversies over Moses, Zoroaster, and others. Assume that the spiritual texts and historical records give you a good glimpse of what they were like and what they were up to and what they thought and said. In some cases, like Noah, it will not matter if there was exactly a Noah—he certainly represents a kind of man of an early time that I related to in an intimate way. Just take it on its own terms. If something is so wildly unhistorical that it actually contradicts My experience with mankind, I will tell you.

Abraham is a perfectly good place to start.

I started reading the Old Testament. I had already received a vision of Creation and answers about the Garden of Eden. Noah and the Flood comes next, but just before that is the strange Genesis 6, which reports (in the Everett Fox translation) that the "divine beings saw how beautiful the human women were, so they took themselves wives, whomever they chose." The divine beings "came in to the human woman" and they bore them children.

Yes, that is important. It shows the erotic draw of the material world. It expresses My craving for the physical . . .

"Oh, I'm getting upset again, Lord. This does not fit my idea of God at all!"

Just relax and hear Me out, and don't let your preconceptions get in the way. I love the world. It is Me and yet not Me. It spun out of Me like a spider's web—is that part of the spider or different from the spider? And I care for it like a mother for a newborn, or not yet born, babe. But there is a desire in such love for physical union that is erotic in nature. By erotic, I don't mean just sexual, but an object of fundamental desire. We desire many things, but they are not (all) fundamental, not all central to our purpose, our telos. That union that is central to our purpose is erotic, and the sexual is a part of that.

Hence the story, which is really about Me, or about aspects of Me, hence "godlings." I told you how I resented—I can only use human language here—Adam's cavorting with Eve, and of course he was wrong to place her above Me, but it was a natural mistake. The erotic draw of the physical is so strong that the sexual can easily displace the overall telos—the part can displace the whole. I feel this erotic draw, both as a metaphysical fact about Me and the world (which) I created and (which) is an extension of Me, and as a more intimate fact about My particular interest in and communication with men and women.

"I have sometimes felt Your presence as Abigail and I were making love." Sometimes I want to say, "Butt out, I'm doing this!"

Of course, why would I not be present there, as I am in other experiences. I am a participant, and both your higher draw (toward love of the other for her own sake) and lower draw (sexual desire) are manifestations of My nature as well.

This is about erotic power and its perversions. I did not, of course, "take wives," or lust after individual women (or men) in the human sense, but there is a draw that is "lower" for Me also, and part of the development of Myself was to pull back here, as I did earlier in the Garden of Eden, and to accept the appropriate way, you might say, for a god to relate to a world.

"You saw that, instead of relating intimately to You, people were being seduced by the material world?"

Exactly. The material world—the senses, ego, and so forth—is deceptively powerful. It is easy for it to seem like the only thing that matters, in fact like the only thing that is really real.

"And You actually regretted having created the world?"

No, I felt sadness, infinite sadness. Of course, I understand—understood enough even then—not to regret the world and the people in it. This is the necessary drama of Creation, and I am part of it, with My best and worst sides, and so are human beings. But I love them—love you all—in a way that causes boundless suffering.

This answer moved my heart. Rather than a perfect Being ruling over an imperfect world, where all the imperfections are all our fault, we and God are in the same boat. God too has "best and worst" sides and feels responsible for causing "boundless suffering." If I cause suffering, or have a "worst-side" day, I certainly regret it, but then, I don't expect to be perfect. For God to face suffering caused by His "worst sides" is sadder still. It is odd to want to console God, but that was what I felt.

"Well, then, what is the next thing that is important?"

The most important part of the entire Old Testament is the Abraham story.

"What should I understand about Abraham?"

He is, as I told you earlier, the first man who truly heard My voice—and recognized it as My voice. Although I appear in many ways, an important part of My nature is that I am One. I am a Person, and I am One. Polytheism is all good and well, but it utterly fails to grasp that fact, and as a result, it not only has an inadequate (partial) picture of the whole but it cannot be a sufficient guide to life or basis for interacting with Me.

As you can see, none of the other modes of revelation achieves that. The Eastern (the Chinese) relates to Me through an aestheticized nature, fine but incomplete. It is in error insofar as it takes the natural order to be fixed, impersonal, eternal, unchanging, regular, law-like. But I am a Person, willful, interested, engaged, unpredictable—I surprise even Myself—and that is essential not only to My story—you might just think, "Well, God isn't all He's cracked up to be"—but to the true nature of the Cosmos, the total reality.

In spite of its apparent polytheism, Egyptian religion is an important step toward monotheism, because it has a sense that God is personal and that the various gods are manifestations of a single God—not fully articulated except in the odd case of Akhenaten, but quite presupposed. The Egyptian God is, however, inadequate for guiding action.

And hence the importance of the contrast between Israel and Egypt, and the story or experience of Moses.

"Didn't the people of Israel experience You as acting in history, fighting battles for them, and the like?"

Do not get carried away with that aspect. The chief thing was the divine encounter. They encountered Me as a self. I revealed Myself and I gave them a law.

"And monotheism?"

I also revealed Myself as One God who demanded allegiance.

Scholars say that, in the earliest textual stratum, the God of Israel does not dispute the validity of the gods worshipped by other peoples. "Lord, at the beginning, it seems, You were understood as just one god among many."

But always (as one) who demanded absolute obedience. The rest (the monotheism) flows from that.

"Why was revealing Yourself as a Person important, Lord?"

First, because I am, among other things, a Person. Second, it was the first step to personal guidance—once interiorized (as) a God personal to each individual, loving and guiding, not just in the abstract but a partner in each individual's life.

"Was Abraham a real historical person, Lord? Was Moses?"

I know those are important questions in one way, but for our purposes, now at least, they are not. The stories reveal a truth. In the case of Moses, they reveal the truth of the inadequacy of the Egyptian revelation. Read these texts again and you will see Moses responding to the fully personal, fully One God, and seeing the inadequacy of the Egyptian lack of full articulation and realization of this. Confronted with the One God, their gods become false. The same is true of polytheism. Their gods are real—they are real manifestations of Me—but they are not final, not adequate.

"Well, is the idea of the One God final or adequate?"

That is not the question for now, but you know the answer: of course it is not complete, and in that sense, a fuller, more adequate conception is needed. But for that, one has to relax some of the logical constraints that make it difficult to accept that God can be both One and many, a Person and much more than a person, immanent in nature and yet not reducible to nature.

I wanted to put God in a conceptual box. He wouldn't let me do it.

He responded immediately, like a soldier reporting for duty

29

I found that most people had turned from God. I have always communicated with people, whispered in their ears, you might say, given them signs. But most do not listen. They pay no attention—because they do not want to. They are enjoying the pleasures I have given them, or using the pains as an excuse for self-pity. But Abraham was a remarkable man. When I whispered to him, he responded immediately, like a soldier reporting for duty, "Here I am."

In Genesis 12, the Lord speaks to Abram (Abraham's original name) out of the blue. "And the Lord said to Abram, 'Go forth from your land and your birthplace and your father's house to the land I will show you. . . .' And Abram went forth as the Lord had spoken to him"—no questions asked.

The most famous story occurs years later. The Lord gave the aged couple a son.

> And it happened after these things that God tested Abraham. And He said to him, "Abraham!" and he said, "Here I am." And He said, "Take, pray, your son, your only one, whom you love, Isaac, and go forth to the land of Moriah and offer him up as a burnt offering on one of the mountains which I shall say to you." And Abraham rose early in the morning and saddled his donkey and took his two lads with him, and Isaac his son, and he split wood

for the offering, and rose and went to the place that God had said to him. . . . [They arrive at the place and set up the altar and Isaac is placed on it.] And Abraham reached out his hand and took the cleaver to slaughter his son.

We don't breathe until we reach the ending.

And the Lord's messenger called out to him from the heavens and said, "Abraham, Abraham!" and he said, "Here I am." And he said to him, "Do not reach out your hand against the lad, and do nothing to him, for now I know that you fear God and you have not held back your son, your only one, from Me."

I always want to know what really happened and couldn't resist asking again, "Was there a real Abraham and did these things really happen to him?"

The story is true to My experience with mankind, and there was, in a sense, a first man (person) who heard My voice in this particular way.

"What particular way?"

The absolute authority I hold. He heard it, did not question it, and acted on it—promptly.

"The lesson is obedience to God?"

Yes, that is the obvious lesson and it is the correct lesson.

"It must have been an important step in humankind's relation to You. Was it also an important step for You?"

Let's pause for a moment over the first part of that.

"Why it was an important step for people?"

Yes, exactly. Every human response to Me had understood that My voice had special standing, hence the early division into the sacred and the profane. The Near Eastern empires had articulated this explicitly as the capstone of an imperial order. But My commands are more than sacred and more than those of a king. They are absolute, one almost wants to say absolutely absolute, not absolute in this or that context or up to a certain point, the way

you have to follow a court order unless it is overturned by a higher court. Even Supreme Court decisions and kings' orders can be questioned and criticized. That is within human competence to do. Not with My commands. They are beyond human understanding, not because they are in principle ineffable or bizarre, as if I had some really bizarre reasons, but because the structure of the world and of the spiritual development of the world requires absolute obedience, total yielding.

You see, it is a matter of principle. Anything held back, even for the best of reasons, is a sacrilege, a defiant act, a claiming to possess things or a right to things or an authority over oneself that one does not have, hence an illegitimate act. You are not only, in a respect, Me; you are Mine. And that is not because I am some petty, or vast, tyrant, but because yielding what is Mine is essential to the spiritual development of the universe, and of you and Me.

"But kill my son? If You told me to do that, I would not believe it was Your voice."

Don't get hung up on the details. Of course, I would not command such a thing. But only the extreme example is sufficient to drive home the point of obedience and of divine dominion being total. That does not mean you should believe every voice you hear or do whatever some would-be prophet tells you to do.

"But You gave Abraham an extraordinary command, and he obeyed immediately."

That is right, and that is the correct standard of obedience.

The Abraham who, without a murmur, takes his son to the mountain to be slain reacts very differently when, in Genesis 18, God is determined to destroy the wicked city of Sodom. Over his own son, he does not argue, but over strangers in Sodom, he will not be silent.

Will You really wipe out the innocent with the guilty? Perhaps there may be fifty innocent within the city. Will You really wipe out the place and not spare it for the sake of the fifty innocent within it? Far be it from You to do such a thing, to put to death the

innocent with the guilty, making innocent and guilty the same.
Far be it from You! Will not the Judge of all the earth do justice?"

Abraham accuses God of not living up to His job description, and God gives in! "Should I find in Sodom fifty innocent within the city, I will forgive the whole place for their sake." Abraham argues Him down to ten, and God concedes, "I will not destroy for the sake of the ten."

God actually seemed to be learning how to be a better divine judge. "Lord, Job also argues with You, prophets object to their assignments, and Lamentations laments. Do they teach God?"

Not "teach" exactly. But I learn from the interaction. I am growing, learning what it is like to deal with autonomous others. I am learning the difference between Self and Other.

I had two objections. "But, Lord, first, You have understood that all along—in dealing with animals, for example."

Yes, but there are degrees and differences of kind as well. As we discussed regarding the Garden of Eden, at first I was not sufficiently distant. They were like playthings, as you as an infant were for your mother.

"And, second, You *are* everything."

Yes, but in a very complex sense. Remember these categories of identity and difference are inadequate here.

This kind of talk was making me very edgy. At stake is whether God is really God, the God we have placed on a pedestal, or is He something less than that, perhaps much less? "Lord, it sounds as if You were unfinished, imperfect, and perhaps inconsistent."

Yes.

"So You are developing, discovering Yourself, and becoming fuller?"

Yes.

I suppose all this was already implicit in the idea of a developing God, but something that you can accept in the abstract is much harder when you get down to cases. Was God turning out to be profoundly disappointing, or was I missing something?

My essence for human beings is that I will *be there*

30

Let's go to Moses.

Saturday mornings Abigail goes to Torah study at the temple nearby. Afterwards, she and I have brunch, and she reads the passage and tells me what everybody said. They were making their way through Exodus.

When the story begins, the people of Israel are in bondage in Egypt. The Pharoah "who knew not Joseph" is concerned about the threat posed by their growing numbers. He makes their lives "bitter with hard bondage" and orders their male infants drowned. To save her child, one mother hides him in the reeds, where he is found by Pharoah's daughter. She names him Moses, "for from the water I drew him out." She has him suckled by a nursemaid, who turns out to be Moses' real mother, and raises him as her own son.

We hear nothing else about Moses until he is a young man, who sees how his people are treated. "And he saw an Egyptian man striking a Hebrew man of his brothers . . . and he struck down the Egyptian and buried him there in the sand." But he had been seen. "And Pharoah heard of this thing and he sought to kill Moses, and Moses fled from Pharoah's presence and dwelled in the land of Midian . . ." There he agrees to herd sheep for a man who becomes his father-in-law.

Meanwhile, the Israelites "groaned from the bondage and cried out, and their plea from the bondage went up to God. And God heard their moaning, and God remembered [literally, took to heart] His covenant with Abraham, with Isaac, and with Jacob. And God saw the Israelites, and God knew."

"Lord, do people have to cry out to You before You respond? Wouldn't You know they were in trouble and come to their aid whether or not they called for help?"

People must cry out to Me, not because I have to be courted, but because I have to be communicated with. People must let Me know what their condition is and what they would like Me to do. So they cried out and, of course, I heard them.

"And You 'took to heart' the covenant with Abraham, Isaac, and Jacob?"

Yes, there is always a context or background to any communication. That was the context here. And remember that I love individuals and peoples, not just mankind generically. We have a history together, as any persons do. So that was part of the background of My responding.

"'And God saw the Israelites, and God knew.' What did You know?"

What I needed to do.

"And what was that?"

Read the next chapter.

"It's about Moses encountering the burning bush."

Yes, I had to get his attention. Often I have to put something in people's paths to get their attention.

And the Lord's messenger appeared to him in a flame of fire from the midst of the bush, and he saw, and look, the bush was burning with fire and the bush was not consumed. And Moses thought, "Let me, pray, turn aside that I may see this great sight, why the bush does not burn up." And the Lord saw that he had turned aside to see, and God called to him from the midst of the bush and said, "Moses, Moses!" And he said, "Here I am."

"Like Abraham, he reports for duty, 'Here I am.'"

Moses had the capacity to listen to Me and to obey.

God gives Moses his mission. "And now, go that I may send you to Pharaoh, and bring My people the Israelites out of Egypt." But Moses lacks standing. "Who am I that I should go to Pharoah and that I should bring out the Israelites from Egypt?" However, Moses will not be on his own: "For I will be with you." Moses protests. "Look, when I come to the Israelites and say to them, 'The God of your fathers has sent me to you,' and they say to me, 'What is His name?', what shall I say to them?"

"Lord, asked Your name, You say, 'I-Will-Be-Who-I-Will-Be' (Robert Alter translation) or 'I will be-there howsoever I will be-there' (Everett Fox). And in Fox, You say that Moses should tell them 'I will be-there' sent me. There are other translations as well. What does this mean, Lord?"

Several things are going on in that name. I did disclose it and they got it essentially right. Self-disclosure is part of it. Presence is part of it. The fact that I am seen all the time, that I am ever-present to people, communicating with them *sotto voce* all the time. It is also reassurance, because I am there to help. When you need Me, I will be there. It also has something to do with the quality of presence, that I am fully and authentically and immediately and intimately present, as when you say that one person is "more present" than another.

It means that My essence for human beings is that I will *be there*, be present, that I am a companion and friend and ally; that My very presence is the heart of Me, and is what (the what of Me) human beings need to know, (the what of Me) that matters.

I will be there for you, by your side, in the fight or in the suffering or in the love. I will be a participant and a partner. That is My essence for human beings.

This is the heart-string, the axis of the universe

31

It is often said that the Old Testament gave the world, not only a law, which Hammurabi had done, but an ethical code, which was unique.

"Is that right, Lord?"

Well, the ethical content was certainly there, but it was not unique. There is ethical content, overt or covert, in virtually all My large-scale communications (let's call them). It was more explicit and more dramatic in the case of the Jews, and that was valuable, and helped to shape the world.

"Confucian thought is certainly ethical."

But ethical in a different sense. For Israel, ethics was a set of divine commands—commandments from a personal being, from God Himself. For the Chinese, ethics is the way to fit into Nature, into the natural harmony of things. That is a profound understanding, and it is right, but it is different.

"Is it more right than Israel?"

No, of course not. The two are compatible. I am both Nature and a Person. What I command as a Person will also prepare you to fit in with the right order of things. But if, like prehistoric people, you are sensitive to the spiritual side of Nature, including human nature, and listen, you will learn how to fit into the normative order.

There are advantages to each. Divine commandments come from a Person, which are compelling as a communication and (as) motivation. They are very precisely directive, and therefore particularly good for things that are black-and-white, matters of right and wrong. They have the sense of ultimacy, of imperative necessity, that you absolutely must do this or you will be in disobedience and at odds with God.

The Confucian approach is sensitive, reasonable, contextual, not too much, not too little. It does promote harmony. It would also teach one to tell the truth, honor one's parents, be faithful to one's wife, not to covet, and so forth, but that will be in the context of all of life's adjustments. The ethical and the practical fade into one another seamlessly. So the ethical loses some of its edge, and that may be a loss, but in real life the two do fade into one another. One's duties include being practical. It keeps one from being fanatical, rigid, rule-bound, or literalistic.

"You gave the people of Israel, not just an ethical code, but myriad rules and rituals for worshipping You."

Maintaining the clarity of monotheism and the faithfulness to Me was important. The expression of that faithfulness in rituals, temple life, and so forth, is totally appropriate, as it is, in other forms, for other religions. Do not discount "arbitrary" rituals, as "mere" behavior. Outward observance, when it reflects inner yielding, is useful and appropriate. You may be grateful to a person and he or she may know it, but sending a thank-you card is still appropriate and even necessary.

"I still don't understand, Lord. Why do You need to be worshipped?"

Because that is the appropriate response to Me. And because it helps move men and Me forward.

I am divine spirit who represents the telos of the universe. I am not perfect but man owes Me deference and obeisance, just as you would owe courtesy and deference to a president or judge or priest or lady. It is wrong for this proper relationship to be violated or ignored.

Worshipping Me is also a way of putting man in alignment with Me and My purposes. It requires deference and recognition of divine authority. Why do you think you obey Me? It is because you are rightly attuned to the reality of Who I Am and what My role is.

"If we are just supposed to obey God, no matter what He asks of us, why does He need to be making promises (offering us a *quid pro quo*) in return? He doesn't owe us anything, does He?"

Yes, He does—I do. Remember that I need people, just as they need Me. It is a reciprocal relationship. I am not an Oriental potentate, puffing smoke, and demanding that My slaves cater to My every wish. I am a Person, and when people give to Me, including the gift of belief, I give something back. It is not a *quid pro quo*; it is an appropriate reciprocity. One can always denigrate friendship relations, as one friend helps another, as a kind of self-interested trade-off, but that is not quite adequate to the "one good turn deserves another" idea. A proper and harmonious relationship is created such that certain behavior that is constructive and helpful is appropriate to it. When people or peoples treat Me with respect, then I treat them with respect and fondness. A relationship is established. The Jews are not My only people. In theory, everyone can be one of My people.

"Lord, what were You doing between biblical times and rabbinic Judaism centuries later?" (Later, when I read this prayer again, I received further comments I have put inside brackets.)

Think back to where the story leaves off. I have revealed Myself as a Personal God to the people of Israel—forget the rest of the story for now. This idea of monotheism is powerful for redirecting people's spiritual attention. Instead of rivers and lakes as deities, as expressions or presences of the Divine, they look for, try to find, to contact, the one true God, who speaks to man and has an active interest in what human beings *do*.

Take the history of Israel seriously—not as a "period" in the "history of religion." Take the story told in the Old Testament seriously—people relating to Me as a people, (at least) in part, then falling away. It is, as you say, not a success story, but then again, it is. I have reached people, reached them in a very powerful way, opened up their souls, shaped their consciousness and their conscience, and taught them to be uncompromising in the worship of Me, which is to say, to place their relation to God over everything else, to understand that, compared to being in harmony with Me, all else pales.

[Remember how satisfying this was to Me. How I yearned for human contact, interaction, understanding, how My own nature could not grow and expand and develop without a significant other. And remember also that this is not just a "personal desire" of Mine, but this is what life, the universe is all about. There is serious work to be done, the heart of which is the relation of nature (including people) to Me. We work together for the great telos which, in a sense, I embody and define. This is the heart-string, the axis of the universe.]

And they learn to fight for Me, to resist superstition and magic—the attempt to manipulate Me, to satisfy their desires by illicit means.

They are carrying this forward as a people, not just as disparate individuals.

How is monotheism, this special and fragile relationship to a personal God, to survive?

[No, this is not quite right. My motive was not to ensure the survival of monotheism. That is in a sense their motive—I reach the person as an individual, that person is a leader of a people, that person learns to put Me first, then teaches his people to do so, then tries to lead them in the path of righteousness for My name's sake. While I obviously prefer that monotheism survive—that the force of Moses' relating to Me personally not simply evaporate—that is not in any way the meaning or motive of My relationship to Moses. That (meaning or motive) is completely and intensely personal. It is then a matter, you might say, of mundane morality that Moses is then obliged to make sure that the force of this special relationship not simply die out, that it survive. But even in the case of Moses, his motive was that the people of Israel have the right relationship to God, not that monotheism survive. He was, however, acutely aware—as any religious person is—that Israel was an island of faith in a faithless world, and that its survival was also the survival of this special relationship of man to God.]

"Lord, the historical books are mainly about Saul and David. Why are they important?"

I rely on human beings. There is no spiritual story in the universe without this partnership (between God and human beings).

The essence of Saul and David is that they were *fighters*. My truth does not survive without people willing to fight for it, both as individuals in their own lives and as peoples in the world at large. There are always evil impulses and evil forces and contingencies that can make all go wrong, all be lost.

David is all too human, but understands power, has ample personal skills, and is willing to fight. And he feels the pull of the Lord. That is his challenge, not to indulge himself (and) appropriate his talent and opportunities solely for himself, but to use them for Me. He does not always succeed.

"Lord, why is there a covenant?"

Why a covenant? I demand commitment from people—not just tune in, tune out at will, as one feels, by whim. I demand that this relationship be put before all other things. If relation to a woman requires commitment, then how much more must relation to God require a commitment?

Look, I make a deep commitment to those to whom I relate (and to everyone else as well). I care about nothing more than the spiritual fate of their souls. If they are in tune with Me, they feel the same. They know that this is the ultimate relationship. A covenant is merely an external expression of that. I don't "demand" it. Moses felt the need of it, and it became in biblical history an expression of the cluster of truths I outlined above as well as the sense of Moses and others that the covenant was a vehicle for uniting the people in the right relationship to Me and (for) the survival of this people, not just for ethnic reasons, though those are obviously present as well. People don't just relate to Me as pure spirits. They have to make their way through the world. They have to hold together, to pull together, and to survive.

32

It is an earnest
pledge of love

I dreaded the assignment—all that ranting and raving about the scourge of God on a wanton people. I had been told to revisit the Prophets.

Here is Jeremiah (23:19-20):

> Behold, the storm of the Lord!
> Wrath has gone forth . . .
> It will burst upon the head of the wicked. . . .

And Isaiah (63:3-4, 6):

> I trod them in my anger
> And trampled them in my wrath;
> Their juice splattered on my garments,
> And stained all my robes.
> For the day of vengeance was in my heart.

Such passages abound. But it seems I had missed the point.
Can't you see what Isaiah and Jeremiah are about?
Then it came to me, either by my thinking it or by God prompting the thought . . .
The latter . . .

. . . that these are love letters. They are love letters from God to the people of Israel.

Now my eye dwelt more on passages such as Jeremiah 31:3.

> With everlasting love have I loved you,
> Therefore I have continued My faithfulness to you.

"Lord, You even use the image of the bride and bridegroom in Jeremiah 2:1."

> I remember the devotion of your youth,
> Your love as a bride . . .

That's right.

"Lord, You look in vain for an explanation: What have I done, or where have I failed, such that I am not pleasing to you (Jeremiah 2:4-5)? You are trying to get people to respond to Your love, to live right, as anyone who loves someone wants them to do. And so You punish and chastise them to get them to change (Isaiah 58:6-7, 9). But You are willing to forgive them. You stand ready to do so. You report for duty *to them* (Isaiah 58:9)."

> Then you shall call, and the Lord will answer;
> you shall cry for help, and he will say, "Here I am."

"And again in Isaiah 65:1-2, 12."

> I was ready to be sought out by those who did not ask,
> To be found by those who did not seek me.
> I said, "Here I am, here I am."

"And You take them back lovingly in Isaiah 62:2-5."

> For as a young man marries a young woman,
> So shall your builder marry you;

And as the bridegroom rejoices over the bride,
So shall your God rejoice over you.

"Yes, I see, Lord, these are like love letters."

Yes, that is right. It is an earnest pledge of love and invitation for them to love Me back.

Can't you see already the trend (theme)? Love—not just from a distant God but from One who is arriving.

"Why, then, all the wrathful judgment and chastisement?"

It is love, passionate concern for the state of people's souls. Obedience (to My law) is one side of that coin. My loving grace and salvation is the other. Obedience is one side of that coin; loving acceptance (yielding) is the other.

External obedience, commanded obedience is one step, but no one (no leader such as Moses) ever thought that was all. The crucial thing about obedience is circumcision of the body as symbolic yielding, yes, especially one's erotic and creative power and assertive force; and of the mind or heart, in yielding to God His own. Hence (the importance of) sacrifice—not making oneself miserable but yielding to God a small portion of what is His own—that requires, much like (the understanding in) the East, overcoming one's desire and ego (one's desire for self-assertion and dominion) in order to yield up to God one's material resources and, ultimately, oneself.

"Isn't this also about the sovereignty of God?"

And, yes, the sovereignty of God, which is another way of saying the necessity of yielding to God. And that is the same as happiness.

God's covenant with Israel is not a covenant of commands (only); it is a covenant of love. "These are the chosen people" is like "This is the girl of my dreams," the one I have fallen in love with.

"But commands and obedience are central. You have told me so Yourself."

Yes, of course, that too. We have discussed the proper role of obedience and even abiding by arbitrary commands. But that is not the be-all and end-all. There is a larger context—of love. Love is the basic force in the universe. I enter the world out of love. The world yearns for Me, and turns to Me, out of love. Love forms the bond between man and woman, one neighbor and another, and the orders of nature. It is love that pulls all of nature upward, and heals the soul and repairs the breaches in the world. Even on the level of physics, it is love that holds the world together, and provides its energy.

I felt anxiety rising, even before praying, an agitated foreboding. I told myself: Avoid surprises. Just review the route already taken.

"Lord, am I supposed to trace what You are trying to communicate to each culture?"

That, and My total development. The material on early man is important, detailed, and up front because it reveals My development in very stark terms.

"Maybe I should start with Your message and then go over Your personal development?"

No, they can't be separated in that way. Look at what I told you about the Garden of Eden—it is equally a story of My development.

Take Zoroaster, for example. I wasn't trying to communicate My dual nature. I was just being Me, and it is an aspect of Me that he picked up on and articulated very sharply, perhaps too sharply. But that interaction (of Me and Zoroaster) was a growth experience for Me as well as for him and mankind. I came to see My other side more clearly.

Okay, this was it: His *other* side? Take a deep breath and keep walking. "What is that, Lord?"

I am limited and incomplete—in a sense, not all-powerful; in a sense, not-all-knowing; in a sense, not all-good. I am searching for My own fullness, and since I am also the World—the totality—I–the world–mankind are all seeking fulfillment (fullness) together, in partnership.

God continued to ride roughshod over my lifelong understanding of what God, if He existed, would have to be like.

My Other Side

33

The world is a sacrifice

Before Moses, before Akhenaten, before Zoroaster himself, there was what was known simply as the Old Religion. From roughly the fourth millennium B.C.E., it was practiced by people living on the south Russian steppes.

The Old Religion affirmed a cosmic order, later called Asha by the Persians and Rta by the Indians, that ensures the regularity of the stars and the seasons and orderly existence for the community. The human order is part of this cosmic order. Virtue—especially truth, honesty, loyalty, and courage—sustains the natural order; vice disrupts it. Prayer and sacrifice support Asha or Rta, which is also upheld by the highest god, Ahura Mazda—literally, the Lord Wisdom—who submits to it as well. In this effort, he is aided by six lesser gods, the Holy Immortals—Good Purpose, Best Righteousness, Holy Devotion, Desirable Dominion, Health, and Long Life.

Yes, they perceived the order of the cosmos, which is physical, spiritual, (and) moral. Worship and sacrifice are rightful parts of that order. Without them, man is not in his proper place and I cannot be in Mine—in part because there is a hierarchy, and I am the source of order in the soul and telos for man and nature, and in part because I deserve respect, so that "something is rotten in Denmark" when I am not paid respect and man (a person) ignores Me or snubs Me or insults Me and glorifies himself (or herself). The individual soul, the family, the community, and I are all thrown out of kilter, distorted, put awry, by such actions and attitudes. Worship and sacrifice put things in their proper order. They orient the soul to Me, and they allow Me to enter into the person and provide guidance and safety.

The cosmogony of the Old Religion starts with the sky and water and earth, not unlike Genesis. But then the gods create the three prototypical creatures—one plant, one animal, and one man—reminiscent of Plato's forms, which are not universals (such as humanity) but models (such as the perfect man or perfect justice).

Yes, very similar, and not inapt. What is it for there to be a thing? For the thing to have a particular character or item-hood, there must be a prototype, something like the standard meter (that defines a meter) or a canonical color sample that defines forest green. Otherwise, what would you have created? Doesn't creation always begin with, "I'm going to make an X"?

"Then the gods offered a triple sacrifice, killing the man, the animal, and the plant. All life springs from this sacrifice, and as the Zoroastrian scholar Mary Boyce puts it, 'the cycle of being is thus set in motion.'"

Yes, there is a deep truth here. The world is a sacrifice. By that I mean the act of creation is a sacrifice and ongoing existence is a sacrifice. It is a sacrifice for Me, more precisely for the God beyond God, to enter the world. And the world itself is a sacrificial offering. It is a place of struggle and suffering, not just for living creatures, but for Me as well. But, like a sacrifice, it is a struggle that makes sacred, that makes holy, that honors and submits to the ultimate divine ordering. I submit to that and the world must submit to that.

"But I don't understand why it is necessary to create a world at all, if it entails such suffering?"

But, you see, holiness unto itself is nothing. Pure bland eternal perfection is nothing. It is not even perfection—it has not been mediated as Hegel would say—it has no internal complexity, no development, no achievement. It has the perfection of a blank sheet of paper or a lump of clay not yet shaped into a figure. For the soul, including My soul, there must be spiritual growth, not just a placid acceptance of untested consciousness, a self that does not yet know itself to be a self, a goodness that has not yet fought evil and temptation (the greatest evil is always within). Even the plenitude-of-being idea is not without merit."

This is the idea that the best world would be one brimming with as much being as possible, and so God created a world filled with every gradation of being, from the most perfect down to the least perfect.

Would one think it more perfect if the universe consisted of a single, unchanging hydrogen atom (rather) than a flailing, mortal organism?

"Boyce explains that, each day, rituals reenacted the original sacrifice."

Of course, all (each of) our lives reenacts—is engaged in—the sacrifice at every moment.

"What about the Old Religion's views on death and the hereafter?"

It has to do with the meaning of life. Death is always about the meaning of life. Afterlife is always about the assessment or judgment of life.

Central to this religion was the sanctity of oaths, contracts, and treaties—stable elements in a violent world—protected by the high god Mithra.

"Lord, isn't this emphasis on oaths overdone?"

Good question. Man's (a person's) word is sacred. What is the basic bond between people that expresses the I and the Thou, that respects the Thou and the selfhood of the other person? It is speaking truthfully and giving one's word, backed by one's honor and integrity and personhood, for agreements made. They were very right to fix on the sacredness of one's word.

"According to Boyce, 'A power was felt to be latent in the spoken pledge, and this power came to be recognized as a divinity.'"

Of course. Think about it. What miracle permits man to speak— to speak truthfully of things—with all that implies for the referential capacity of language, for the ability of experience and other evidence

to reach the truth of things, not to mention higher truths, or mathematical or conceptual or metaphysical or cosmogonic truths?

In a sense, all knowledge reaching out to things, consciousness reaching out beyond itself, is a divine act, is in-spired, filled with My spirit. What do you think is the tie that connects the mind to the object? Just light rays and the like? But you know how little that explains. It doesn't even explain how you know light rays.

Now think of the further act, the promise. It is made to a person. That requires a further miracle, the recognition of the other as other. Even recognizing objects as other, as not merely parts of one's own stream of consciousness—(David Hume's) "impressions and ideas"—is a kind of miracle. And (so is recognizing someone else) not only as another object, but as another person, another center of subjectivity and action, will and purpose, of goodness and the potential for evil, of spiritual striving and participation in the Divine.

Now think of how it is possible for one such center, not only to communicate ideas and intentions to another, but to make a commitment. What is a commitment? It is a moral fact. It creates an ethical relationship between you and the promise that did not previously exist. This is a reality, but not of a physical type.

Nor is it adequate to call it an "institutional" fact, as if it were simply a shorthand for describing customs or conventions. It is a real fact. An obligation now exists. Among the things a complete account of the universe would have to include are obligations created by promises. Institutions do not explain promises but more the other way around. Institutions are, in part, complex ethical facts, created by various commitments and other relationships of an ethical sort, such as parent and child.

If you leave out the ethical phenomenon, and describe these merely as social patterns, as sociologists and anthropologists do, there is no miracle here, but such descriptions are not complete and therefore, however accurate, not really adequate.

How are ethical facts, nonphysical and also not just states of consciousness, possible? Because of Me. Ethical facts are spiritual facts. There is a spiritual relationship between people that occurs only within the spiritual matrix that is My presence in the world. In living the ethical life, people are participating in Me, whatever their self-interpretation of their own ethical lives.

It was this fine old religion that Zoroaster was to throw into disarray and rage.

34

To look evil
in the face
is a spiritual act

Zoroaster had a great yearning for the truth and for knowing Me, and great discipline in seeking the way of truth, as a priest and in other roles. He sought to understand not just the forms and procedures, but the meaning. Of course, some of his teachers were wise and also in touch with Me. But he was more persistent, more open, and had a more flexible and creative mind, so he could take in more.

He was My first really great prophet.

"He spent years wandering in search of truth?"

Yes, this is what made him remarkable. Most people, even most spiritually attuned people, are not really seekers after the truth. They mainly have some truths that they nourish and try to apply to their own lives or to the lives of others (to help others).

The ancient religion was already quite good, but Zoroaster sensed that there was something more, both in terms of understanding it all and in terms of living a spiritual life. So he did seek out all the great teachers and seers of his day, and he prayed and meditated and listened with an open ear.

So one day I came to him. I had whispered in his ear many times and these whisperings were not unheeded—they led him on in his search—but on this occasion he actually saw Me, in several of My aspects, and My message came through to him in a totally articulate manner.

Zoroaster was seeking the truth. The Lord Wisdom was looking for a messenger. They were searching for each other. Then, one morning, as Zoroaster was purifying himself in the river, he beheld on the bank, a "shining being" who revealed himself as Good Purpose. The priest was brought into the presence of the Lord Wisdom and five other figures so radiant "he did not see his own shadow upon the earth, owing to their great light."

In the collection of hymns known as the *Gathas*, Zoroaster reports addressing the Lord Wisdom.

"Then as holy I have recognized Thee, the Lord Wisdom, when he [the Holy Spirit] attended me with Good Purpose, and asked me: 'Who art thou? Whose art thou?' Then I said to him first: 'I am Zarathustra. Were I able, I should be a true foe to the Deceiver, but a strong support to the Just One.'"

This encounter began a series of visions, revealing a single God who "created everything that was created" including the other divine beings, who could also be seen as aspects or manifestations of Himself. For it is written that they are "of one mind, one voice, one act."

Yes, we have talked about My manifestations and why it is apt to call them gods. Of course, they emanate from Me by My spirit.

"Then Ahura Mazda, the Lord Wisdom, is also You?"

Yes, that is Me. Notice that he is the third god (in an older text) but claims authority over the others, as your text says, "whose actions and directions he rules." There was in fact a struggle. Go back to the cosmogonic accounts I have told you. I am "exploding"—both I as the universe am exploding and I as the mind and telos of the universe am struggling to create order and purpose and direction. All the parts of the universe, including all the spiritual parts or aspects of Me, are expanding, at work, involved in creating and directing things, both physical and spiritual.

These parts or aspects of Me are not always well integrated, any more than they are in a human personality. Just as your desires or temperament sometimes seem to have a life of their own, so some of My aspects have life of their own. Among the things I must order and provide direction to are My own aspects. I do this through

Wisdom, My own calm center that purviews (views or oversees) all, assesses all, weighs it in the balance, placates (pacifies) disturbances. There is, of course, an analogue for human beings, but this story is not just metaphor. This was really Me, struggling to supersede other aspects of Myself, and to be worshipped in My highest manifestation, not in My separate and sometimes truculent parts.

Zoroaster beheld not one god but two, one good and one his evil twin. The Lord Wisdom was the embodiment of goodness and wisdom. Angra Mainyu—literally, the Hostile Spirit—was the personification of pure evil. The world had two presiding gods at odds with each other.

Yes, he (Zoroaster) had the full experience of evil and he took it in and did not dismiss it or discount it. This is one of My most important communications. The experience of evil is a spiritual experience. It comes from Me. You would not be able to see it for evil otherwise. People would see it as bad luck or "just one of those things" or a character disorder or a bad personality trait. To look evil in the face is a spiritual act and it requires being in touch with Me and looking, as it were, through My eyes.

Evil is indeed a demonic force. It is not just privation or bad upbringing. It is a force on its own, spiritual in nature, not just physical—what else would it be?—and it works outside and within, and it works in Me as well and in all of nature. It is not just a phenomenon of decay or entropy or mortality. It is worse than death or nothingness. It is distortion, warping, perversion, twisting of things from their rightful nature to their wrong "nature," to something that is less and different from their nature, like a malignant cancer.

So the question is how to communicate that fact. How to give Zoroaster a vision that lives up to his own experience—the phenomenon of evil that he has seen through My eyes. I did it by showing him both sides of Myself as two gods. They are of course not equally powerful. I am very much more the positive than the negative side, as most people are. And there is no question that the positive will "win" in the end.

But, for people, for all of us, evil is very powerful, and it is wrong to underestimate it or sweep it under the rug, psychically, metaphysically. It is a force to be reckoned with. And, as powerful as its outer dimension is, its inner dimension is much more powerful. The two-gods vision represents both.

I revealed Myself as two gods in mortal combat. A limitation of the ancient religion was that it venerated and therefore understood only the good aspects of Me and the world. But to understand that is to miss the whole story of what life on this plane is about. It is about the inner and outer ethical and spiritual struggle—in the end, you cannot separate the two. I taught Zoroaster about this aspect of things in the most vivid way possible.

So I showed My other side to him (Zoroaster) as a separate god, the Hostile Spirit, that works to undermine the divine order.

"He beheld the original struggle?"

Yes, just as I have given you visual as well as verbal and visceral reenactments of cosmogonic events, I gave him a vision of an original struggle.

The scripture records: "Truly there are two primal Spirits, twins, renowned to be in conflict. In thought and word and act they are two, the good and the bad. . . . And when these two Spirits first encountered, they created life and not-life. . . . At the end the worst existence shall be for the followers of falsehood [Druj], but the best dwelling for those who possess righteousness [Asha]. Of the two Spirits, the one who follows falsehood chose doing the worst things, [and] the Holiest Spirit, clad in the strongest stone, chose righteousness, and (so shall they all) who will satisfy the Lord Wisdom continually with just actions."

Yes, very precise, accurate. Notice the language. The two gods are twins, a tip-off that they are two sides of the same being. Who doesn't have two sides? Life and not-life are obvious placeholders for order and disorder, or right order and wrong order. The "at the end" part we will need to discuss at a future time, but it is obvious that if you want to have a good life, you pursue Asha (righteousness), and if you don't, you will have a bad life. The generative role of falsehood is explicit here—that the source of evil is falsehood, not living in truth—which is why postmodernism and views like it through all times are morally dangerous and subversive of a good life. It is implied that the Holiest Spirit is stronger, clad in stone.

The Lord Wisdom foresaw that, if he were to create the world, the Hostile Spirit would attack it precisely because it was good. The world would become a battleground. He knew that in the end he would win, but he would need our help, for we too must choose sides, "so shall we all."

It is inevitable that evil attacks good precisely because it is good. It is goodness that evil must stamp out or pervert or turn against itself.

At first, the Hostile Spirit did not know about the Lord Wisdom, but the Lord Wisdom knew about his evil twin, "what he plotted in his enviousness to do, how he would commingle, what the beginning, what the end." After a lengthy era of peace, the Hostile Spirit "arose from the deep" and "beheld the light" of the Lord Wisdom's domain. And prompted by "his lust of smite and his envious nature," he "immediately attacked it," only to encounter "valour and supremacy greater than his own," as the divine beings rallied their forces.

Note that the divine beings do not attack but respond to an attack. The good are always on the defensive, with evil attacking them. There are constructive steps to promote and actualize goodness in its many forms and venues, but no aggressive war against evil is possible.

The Hostile Spirit needed help. "He crawled back to darkness" and recruited Daevas, devils, "frightful and putrid and evil," to fight on his side. The ancient text goes on: "The Daevas chose not rightly, because the Deceiver came upon them as they consulted, so that they chose the worst purpose. Then together they betook themselves to Wrath, through whom they afflicted the life of man."

My aspects have, to some extent, a life of their own and go wayward. One reason is simply their functional autonomy. Just as the stomach wants to just do its job, even if it is doing it in a way counterproductive sometimes for the organism. Or in a society, the lawyers are just doing their job, even (when) it causes larger harm. They

are living out their distinctive "virtues," but that is not always adequate from the point of view of the whole.

The other reason is more perverse, and that comes from My own incomplete and undeveloped nature. Just as a nice person occasionally feels like irritating others or takes pleasure in schadenfreude or deflects in behavior to avoid facing a certain truth. That is the Deceiver, the element of Lie in all of us. Even the first type of counterproductive behavior is a kind of Lie, since it consists in confusing the good of the part with the good of the whole—a Lie because it is often done quite knowingly. People take refuge, like Eichmann, in (saying) "I was only doing my job," or they avoid confronting evil by saying, in effect, "It's not my job."

Having rallied the Daevas, the Hostile Spirit "rose for battle."

35

This world,
this plane of existence,
is a battleground

The Lord Wisdom knew what the outcome would be. The Hostile Spirit did not.

Nevertheless, the Lord Wisdom generously offered peace. "Evil Spirit! Aid my creatures, and give praise, so that in recompense for that you may be immortal." To which, the Hostile Spirit snarled, "I shall not aid your creatures and I shall not give praise, but shall destroy you and your creatures for ever and ever. And I shall persuade all your creatures to hate you and to love me."

The Lord Wisdom knew that a battle would have to be fought. Otherwise, the Hostile Spirit would make perpetual strife "and a state of mixture [of good and evil] for my creatures. And in the Mixture he will be able to lead my creatures astray and make them his own."

Once the Evil Spirit agreed to fight, the Lord Wisdom revealed the final outcome: "His own final victory, and the powerlessness of the Evil Spirit, and the destruction of the [devils], and also the resurrection of the future body, and the freedom of creation from the Assault for ever and ever."

"Lord, it also led to the idea of a final judgment and hence of reward and punishment."

All inapt. Judgment occurs at every moment, and it is internal to the situation, not external. In other words, if one does wrong, one by that fact suffers wrongness—it does not have to be pronounced by a divine judge, then or later. And it has its reward intrinsic to it.

It is crummy to be a bad person. No good person would want that.

The trick of evil is to convince the person, or for the person to convince himself (or herself) that he (or she) can do this bad thing without becoming bad—like an alcoholic who thinks he (or she) can have just one drink, or that a little cheating is okay, or that since everybody takes bribes, that is just how business is done here.

"Were the Holy Immortals 'brought into existence for this one end, namely the utter defeat of evil,' as Boyce says?"

No, that is incorrect, even on its face. Good Purpose is not just about battling evil, it is about telos, direction, fulfillment, development. There is more to life and to the universe than just battling evil. Victory over evil in particular circumstances is the precondition of other fulfillments, but they have their own telos and role in the scheme of things. Love, beauty, and so forth are positive goods and actualize creation. They would still need to be done, to be pursued, even if there were no evil.

The ancient Pahlavi version has a fascinating twist on the creation myth. First the Lord Wisdom brought all things into being in a disembodied state, called in Pahlavi "menog," that is, spiritual or immaterial. Then he gave it material or "getig" existence. This gives things substantial and sentient form. The second step, Boyce explains, sets the "field for the battle with evil" since the world is now "vulnerable to assault." The Evil Spirit immediately attacks.

This is an accurate communication. The idea of a thing must come before the thing. There is a sense in which, as Plato saw, the prototypes exist first and then come into three- or four-dimensional being. You can say they exist in the mind of God if you like, but you see that that way of speaking does not fit naturally with the "self-created" nature of God—that is, we all come into being together—and, before that, the God of this world, namely Me, was not sitting around with ideas in His mind. It is more accurate if it refers to the God beyond God, which of course is also Me, but not the Me existent in this world. What the God beyond God is, is not easy to describe, but we can come back to that at some point, since it involves a whole story.

But you might say that the idea or potential for all things resides in the God beyond God "beforehand" or in another dimension. It is true that, in that mode or dimension, evil cannot strike. There is no evil in the "world" of the God beyond God. But there is no fight with evil, no goodness, no beauty, no virtues either. It is quite a different enterprise.

The main point of the contrast is not to focus on how things existed before material creation but how they exist in this world and for what purpose. As you sense, there is a big story here—the sheer need for "friction," for grit, for traction, for obstacles for spirit to grow and develop, but also to fulfill goods that cannot be fulfilled only in the mind's eye. Why does the artist, who may have (already) envisioned the final result, have to make it in material? Why does the composer (have to have an imperfect orchestra actually play the perfect symphony he hears in his head)? Why does the mathematician want to write down his equations? There is a deep truth here about the nature of reality. Reality wants to be embodied. In this respect, philosophical traditions that derive from Plato, Aristotle, Plotinus get it wrong. The material object does not "fall beneath" the "perfect" form; it actualizes it. The form may be "perfect," but like Kant's (imaginary) one hundred thalers (dollars), it doesn't exist! Or, if you want to say it exists in some sense, it doesn't exist in the sense that counts. It is not in the world; it is not instantiated; it has no instances. So it should not be hard to understand that.

But there is a deeper meaning here that also relates to why there is suffering. To be fully real, a thing has to exist in material form. We are not talking about materialism versus spiritual reality in this context, but simply existence in this world. That (material existence) does subject it to limitations—hence the sense of a "fall from grace"—which includes erosion, destruction, and in more complex forms, disease, dysfunction, and in human beings, death, suffering, and evil.

This may or may not be the best of all possible worlds (as Leibniz thought), but any possible world—that is, any world that can be actual—must have death, suffering, and evil. Those are conditions of its being real. Do not get off into ideas like the omnipotence of

God—those are inventions, logical devices that confuse rather than clarify. They are simply not apt. In other words (it is) not helpful to say either that God is omnipotent or that his power is limited. Those contrasts do not apply meaningfully or aptly in this context.

According to the ancient scriptures, the creation of the world occurs during the course of a sacrifice that the Lord Wisdom is conducting. During the sacrifice he actually consults with human beings or, more precisely, their *fravahrs*, their inner selves or souls. First he gives them "the wisdom of all knowledge," and then he lets them decide. They can either stay in their ideal nonmaterial existence until the battle is over or go into the material world now, risking all in order to defeat evil. They choose to fight.

Yes, this world, this plane of existence, is a battleground. That is not all it is. Do not make the mistake of reducing all human life to one long moral struggle. That is a feature of all existence, but it is not the totality of it.

"What is the rest?"

Well, that is too long to recount. But start with love. The world is also pervaded by love, from the physical level on up. It is pervaded by beauty, by rational order, by purpose, by many other things. Evil attacks these things, but it is not going to win.

The Old Testament story is an answer to Zoroaster

36

"Lord, I don't see how *Your* story develops."

Let Me tell you how it is from My side. All these things are happening simultaneously. The Chinese are casting oracle bones and I am communicating with them. At the same time I am instilling in those who are receptive the truth of Heaven (*T'ien*), of their membership in a cosmos, an ordered natural reality.

"With which they must be in tune . . ."

Yes. At the same time, I am presenting a very different vision to Zoroaster. I am revealing the two sides of My nature, presented as two forces contending. This is not as evil as it sounds. The negative side is mainly the side of incompleteness that motivates the whole story.

The Old Testament story is, in a sense, an answer to Zoroaster. It brings out the developmental side. The Old Testament narrative is the story of My development.

"So You are developing through all this?"

Yes, good question: What is the impact of all this on My development? Isn't it clear? Relating to man harmoniously (in My presence to the Chinese) actualizes the harmonious in Me. I "satisfy" the recognized order—like being an aesthetic object that has to be seen (by a sensitive observer) to come into its own.

The revelation to Zoroaster is a self-disclosure that involves a self-discovery. I articulate much more clearly My own divided nature—

the orderly part and the disorderly part. And that clear separateness is the first step to overcoming it. It points the way to overcoming it.

I had thought the idea of a divided or incomplete God was alien to the Judeo-Christian tradition until I read Jewish scholar Jon Levenson's *Creation and the Persistence of Evil*. It is an arresting account of a central theme in the Hebrew Testament that one does not readily notice: the ongoing struggle for order to triumph over chaos. Chaos is symbolized by images related to water—oceans, floods, and sea-monsters such as Leviathan. The opening of Genesis in which the waters are separated from the earth is an essential step in the creation of divine order.

Levenson explains that God's task is the "confinement" of chaos, not its elimination. Chaos, symbolized by unruly waters, remains a constant threat and "the survival of ordered reality hangs only upon God's vigilance in ensuring that those cosmic dikes do not fail." That vigilance is assured by God's covenant with humankind in Genesis 9 never to flood the world again. In fact, it was not so much God who decided to flood the world as it was evil that opened the dikes.

Yes!

The world, Levenson explains, "is inherently unsafe." "Creation endures because God has pledged in an eternal covenant that it shall endure and because he has, also in an eternal covenant, compelled the obeisance of the great adversary." Thus the world contains an "ancient and enduring opposition to the full realization of God's mastery," which is destined to be eliminated in the end. There is both an "optimistic element in this theology, which is the faith in God's ultimate triumph," and a "pessimistic element, which is the tacit acknowledgment that God is not yet God."

This was just what I had been told: God develops—comes into His fullness as God—only over time and only through interaction with human beings and other elements of creation.

"Our cup of salvation will indeed run over, but it is now only half full—and half empty," explains Levenson. "Life is a continual war against the Evil Impulse, a war that does not see a definitive victory in present reality, but in which battles can be won." The Evil

Impulse—the unruly erotic, darker, aggressive side of our nature—is an "innate impediment to reality as God, the potentially omnipotent, wishes it to be." In one midrash, a Rabbinic elaboration on the Bible, "the projection [of the Evil Impulse] goes as far as the inner being of God himself."

Yes.

"This is a theology with absolute faith in God's *ultimate* goodness," Levenson says, "but a rather qualified faith in his *proximate* goodness." Nevertheless, that ultimate triumph of God's goodness is in some ways *present today*: "The partial present availability of eschatological [final] reality is . . ."

Yes.

". . . in various ways and degrees, a conviction characteristic of many communities in the spectrum of ancient Judaic culture—Qumranian, Rabbinic, early Christian, and perhaps others."

Specifically, Levenson says, it is "in moments of obedience to God's commandments, that the ultimately real becomes available in the present order."

Yes.

Levinson concludes:

> It is in those elusive but ever available moments that the deeply flawed present is forced to yield to the perfect future. And it is in this idea of a multileveled act of unification—unification in God, in creation, and in the human self—that we find the deep root of the profound theology of the *mitzvah* [good deed] as a theurgic [activation of the Divine] which flowers a millennium later in Spanish Qabbalah [Kabbalah]. It is the *mitzvah* that effects integrity throughout all tiers of reality and enables the life-enhancing divine energy to flow freely and without inhibitions.

"Then, Lord, human effort completes creation, understood as God's order and sovereignty?"

Yes.

I had come across a similar idea about mitzvot (the plural of mitzvah) in *The Thirteen Petalled Rose* by Adin Steinsaltz, the greatest living Kabbalist, and had been told,

Mitzvot are central. They construct the world.

"Lord, is it true that a mitzvah is a 'spiritual act, sacred in itself'?"

Yes, (they are) sacred points of God shining through.

So the Old Testament can be seen as a response to Zoroaster's vision of "twin" gods, one good and one evil. Instead, it presents one God who is contending against evil, including His own incompleteness, and defeating it with our help, not only in the end-time but right now.

Zoroaster was just one offshoot of the Old Religion. The other was carried by invaders across the Khyber Pass into India.

The Self

There are two trajectories, East and West

37

Four thousand years ago, the same terror that had swept into the Persia of Zoroaster's youth thundered through the mountain passes of northwestern India. The quiet lives of farmers and herders of prehistoric India were, says archaeologist Stuart Piggott, "rudely and ruthlessly interrupted." The invaders were, an ancient scribe writes, "a host whose onslaught was like a hurricane, a people who had never known a city." They knew something more powerful—the warhorse.

They were called Aryans because they came through Iran (Aryan), and they swept all before them, not only into India, but as far south as Mesopotamia and as far west as Greece. These warriors were not literate, but they brought a rich oral tradition, an offshoot of the Old Religion of Zoroaster's day. Their scriptures, the Vedas, are still sacred for Hindus today.

Be quiet and listen. There are two trajectories, East and West. The West is from prehistoric (primitive) polytheism, a sense as we have discussed of the awe of nature and something like a Buberian I-Thou with animals and the like. It moves from that to the ancient empires understanding Me as the Ruler of the Universe and trying to line their order up with Mine. This involves, not just awe, but understanding that I am normative, set the standard. Notice how that is both same and different with (the) Chinese, for whom it is not a vertical relation but a horizontal one—for them, I am normative in the sense of being the order in which they are already immersed and must just get in swing with. Back to the West, I revealed Myself to Israel in a dramatic fashion.

Presumably, this referred to the revelation to Moses. Some scholars believe that, originally, the Jews in Egypt were unfamiliar with the stories of Abraham, Isaac, and Jacob. Those stories belonged to other loosely related tribes. Later, the tribes came into contact and put the stories together. "If so, Lord, were they right to do that?"

Yes, of course, they were right to "read backward" that the God speaking to Moses was the same God as had spoken to Abraham.

When you read more Hindu materials, you will start seeing that I had a development there that is parallel (or analogous) to My Old Testament development, as different as they may seem on the surface.

But also look to pre-Aryan religion. Remember the remarkable "guru" figure in (prehistoric) Mohendo-jaro (that looks like a yogi in meditation). That was already a very spiritually receptive phase.

One thing the Vedas understood was the nature of sacrifice. This is another way of recognizing, and deferring to, the order of the world, the divine hierarchy. When you read the strange tales of the gods, listen for My voice and then ask Me about it.

The Upanishads show a radical turn inward and also a kind of monotheism. Here the Atman was born. I revealed Myself as the Brahman who is identical with the Atman. This is a very complex relation and its relation to the God of Israel is complex.

The Hindu revelation is very old, very profound. Do not assume that other revelations fit into the Hebrew framework. They all fit into a larger framework. None is primary, the master narrative, though some are more adequate than others.

In the Vedic tradition, the god of victory of the Old Religion was replaced by Indra, an amoral warrior-god, said to be "bountiful to his followers, valiant in combat, reckless, drinking deep of soma," the intoxicating elixir of the gods. He fights his supplicants' battles, demands lavish offerings in return, and rewards them with riches.

In one of the Vedic stories, great demons, led by the monstrous dragon Vitra, attack the gods and threaten to destroy them. The young Indra, "the thunder-bolt wielder," takes them on alone. Indra prevails and, from the body of the slain monster, fashions the world.

"That is suggestive, Lord. I get the impression of You . . ."

Yes.

". . . young, heady, taming the chaos . . ."

Yes.

". . . establishing Dike, the Way, Rta (Greek, Taoist, and Vedic terms for cosmic order)."

Yes.

"And this elemental resistance to the Divine is what the world *is*."

Yes, yes.

"It requires a battle."

Yes.

"And we are partners in this ongoing battle."

Yes.

There are three streams of Hindu religious life. The Vedas taught proper ritual, a tradition transmitted through priests, the Brahmins. Closely related was the dharma of social role. This was the way of Action. The Upanishads teach spiritual liberation through meditation and other spiritual exercises. This is the way of Knowledge. The Puranas, stories of gods such as Vishnu and Shiva, inspire a more personal relation to the gods. This is the way of Devotion.

"Are all three ways aspects of Your message?"

Yes.

"So all three are true?"

Yes, in some (important) respect.

"I get the sense that ritual is important as a sacrifice, a setting aside something for God, a dedication of one's life to God."

Correct.

"And what about the Puranas?"

The Puranas are important, not (so much) for their specific content, as for their understanding of Me as personal.

"Personal in what sense? Aren't they all merely myths, not reports of actual encounters with God?"

They look like that but they are not. They have the glimmer of Me as really a Person. Since I did not have (for them) the dramatic presentation of My revelation to Israel, they didn't have a "real history" view of Me, but they did have an intimate, personal relation to Me. They understood that I was a god they could call on for help, relate to, (and) personally worship, as we see in (the scene in the Mahabharata about) Draupadi's sari.

When the rightful king gambled away his beautiful wife, the wicked victor ordered that she be disrobed in public. Hearing her cries, the divine Krishna ensured that, like a magician's handkerchiefs being drawn out of his sleeve, the unwrapping of her sari never came to an end.

Devotion to a particular god primarily takes the form of *darshan*—seeing the god and being seen by him or her. Not every Hindu icon carries the presence of a god, but those in properly dedicated temples do.

In addition, in times of trouble, an avatar—a god in human form—appears. When Gandhi studied Christianity, he found it quite incredible that Christians believe in only one incarnation. Hindus believe there have been many.

"It seems that Hindus have no problem accepting Jesus. They simply regard him as another avatar."

I send individuals from time to time to "heal the world." But that is not "God made (become) flesh." All people are, in a sense, God made flesh. People come into the world for their own purposes (their own mission or task in life), but (the) goal of all mankind is, in a sense, to heal the world.

"That means none are especially divine?"

No, that concept (classifying them as divine or not) does not work well.

"What is 'healing the world'?"

This is a big topic. Briefly, every individual has a destiny that has to be worked through. As we have explored, this includes Me. And we work through our destinies in tandem, in company, (in) interaction with one another. "Saving," "healing," "descent," "ascent" are not quite right. There is a general unfolding. Every individual has an important, a crucial role to play.

"Are Jesus, Krishna, and Ramakrishna (a nineteenth-century Indian sage) all avatars?"

That is not a useful question. There is no category of avatar.

"Lord, Swami Prabhavananda, who considers Jesus to be an avatar, quotes Krishna: 'I am the goal of the wise man and I am the way.' That sounds like Jesus: 'I am the way, the truth, and the light.'"

There is a Way, and it is exemplified in great individuals, great souls. Since there is in a sense One way, the language is apt.

"Why the egocentric formulation—'*I* am the way'?"

That comes from the individual's feeling so merged with Me, or so identical with the Way, that the language feels natural.

The way of the good man (person) *is* the Way.

38

I am the Ur-consciousness of each individual's consciousness

An "incomparable book," Schopenhauer said of the Upanishads, "the highest of human wisdom . . . almost supernatural in conception." To this day, philosophers, writers, and even scientists have echoed that praise. The central theme of these ancient Hindu scriptures is the unity of all things. Their central insight is that the Atman is the Brahman. There is a deeper Self behind the self or personality as we ordinarily experience it, and this deeper Self is identical with the One Reality that transcends all categories.

The Indian relates to Me through an aspect of the Self that relates to, or is identical with, Me in My total form. It is, or at least feels, quite impersonal.

In the summer after these prayers began, long before I had read the Upanishads, Abigail and I were spending a quiet week on the Maine coast. In their later years, her parents had owned a house on the bay, and she still has good friends there. The view can be seen in Abigail's paintings on our living room wall.

I was relaxing in our bayside cottage, when the voice spoke. I was told to suspend external perception and dwell on the inner flow of consciousness. I had studied phenomenology, which teaches a method for doing just that, so this was not an unfamiliar assignment.

Dwelling just on my sensory experience, I could feel the weight of my body on the chair, the air on the surface of my skin, my breathing, and, more vaguely, my internal organs.

The next instruction went beyond anything I had been taught. I was now to step behind the flow of internal experiences. I did not know how to do that, but I was told to try.

I found myself in a still center "behind" my inner and outer feelings, even "behind" my thoughts. It was as if I could "look out" and see that those things were taking place, but at this tier of consciousness, I was not "myself" feeling and thinking those things.

I did not understand why I had been led to this experience until I started praying about India, and was told,

I gave those people a very different side of Myself—not more profound or real, just different (from the side presented to the people of Israel or other peoples). This fit their culture and their capacity.

The people of India received more truly and clearly than anyone that the way to reach Me is through the inside, that I am the Ur-consciousness of each individual's consciousness.

"The way to reach inside is through meditation?"

Yes, the denial of the world, the shutting out of the world, the withdrawal to inner peace. Theirs is not the whole of the story, but it is an essential—in some ways, *the* essential—part of the story, the heart of the story.

"So the Self, the Atman, is identical with You?"

At that point, it gets tricky. In one sense (or respect), I am everything. And yet you are a center of subjectivity opposite Mine. And, in (still) another way, you know that I am inside you, and you are— or can be—inside Me.

I was moved deeply into the inner relationship to God. "Lord, my self feels like an articulation of God. But it doesn't feel as if it is via the Atman. It feels like my normally experienced self."

Yes.

"If that's true, then the Atman seems like a fifth wheel."

No.

"And I always feel that there are two distinct actions—sometimes God enters me, sometimes I enter God."

Yes.

Later I recorded a different experience. "This Self behind the self, the witness Self, seems much closer to God than my ordinary or empirical self—not just close but something in the direction of identity. This Self behind the self relates to my desires, worries, and the various states of my empirical self, much as God relates to me. My Self sees my empirical self with a loving tolerance and concern, sees the desires as weaknesses but also as just facts to be lived with, sees the worries in perspective, much like an idealized loving parent."

That's right. Your Self is My vicar on earth.

The inner connection to God was okay, but "Atman is Brahman" implied more—that the individual person is less real than the indescribable One. In fact, that it isn't real at all.

Personally, I had no desire to give up my separate self, and in any case, it did not seem logical to say that different people were all identical with one impersonal unity. My protest was rejected.

This is a very important doctrine (insight) and it is basically true. Again, you will need to relax and not push your substance and identity categories here. Spiritual reality does not work by those rules. You all have elements of the Divine, of Me, in you.

The goal—one way to describe the goal—is to be "at one with God, the God of All." At bottom, the Soul's will *is* the will of God. The Soul *is* "at one" with God. The Atman language is a bit off target, a bit misleading.

With people in India, I sought and achieved an intimate personal relationship—more with a few seers than the average people, but that is always the case—by meditation, Atman awareness, sense of unity with the Divine.

"Then the Indian seers got it right?"

There were ups and downs, glitches and failures in that tradition as there were in Israel. At times, they have drawn themselves too inward, and some of the metaphysical edifice is mistaken. I mentioned already the misinterpretation of maya (regarding the world as not much more than an illusion), and some of the mistakes have led to untold suffering.

I regret that but it seems to be one of the hazards of revelation.

What detachment does is to put you on My side of the great divide

39

"So, Lord, the physical world, the world of our desires, is not as important as it seems to be."

Yes, that is central.

"That is more about us than about You. How is that *Your* story?"

Don't worry about what is and is not My story. It *is* about man's relation to Me. What is the chief draw of unbelief? It is the conviction that physical objects are the end of the story. And desire is the chief excuse for not following My will.

The issue of the metaphysics of real versus unreal is not important. It is a rather silly question, actually, since the fundamental structures of reality are so far from what this framework imagines.

What *is* important is that man lives on more than a physical plane, and that the fulfilled life befitting a human being is a life in concert with God, and a high-minded life, not unduly attached to physical things and desires.

"Unduly attached? Some attachment is okay?"

There is nothing wrong with desire. I put beauty in the world and of course men (people) desire to look at it. The world is full of potential sensory delights. You should enjoy them all.

But you should not become too attached to them, as if they were the most important thing. Given all the things of higher value and of more transcendent reality, they pale in importance, delightful as they are.

"Don't all religions say that?"

No. They all assert that there are things more important than desire, but they do not preach detachment *per se*.

"But, since they do direct one's attention to higher things, why is detachment itself so important?"

What detachment does is to put you on My side of the great lines (the great divide). There is a physical reality and you can identify with that, and there is a divine reality and you can identify with that—if you detach from things first.

You cannot do your full work in conjunction with Me without detachment.

One of the Upanishads, "The Forest of Wisdom," tells how all the seers of the kingdom were called together. King Janaka announced, "Venerable Brahmins, these [thousand] cows are for the wisest one among you."

Flaunting their humility, none of the seers dared to step forward. But Yajnavalkya, a seer who often appears in the Upanishads, did not hesitate. He stepped forward and claimed the prize.

The other seers were furious at his presumption. "Do you really think you are the wisest?"

We can see Yajnavalkya smiling as he replied simply, "I wanted the cows."

"Lord, this story . . ."

This is much more on track. There is nothing wrong with desires *per se*; **it is only excessive attachment to them that deflects the soul from its journey. He was right to win the contest because he was the wisest. "None of the other Brahmins dared to speak." This was not holiness. It was concern for how they would appear to others.**

Someone who is honestly aware of his (or her) desires and of other factors in a situation, and proceeds realistically and ingenuously, is capable of meeting the real challenges in life, of being My partner in human history.

Detachment came up in a completely different context. I was asking about the doctrine of maya as a rejection of beliefs about the physical world. The answer focused not so much on the reality of the world as on the nature of beliefs.

Beliefs are an attachment to the physical world, which is not ultimate . . .

Interesting, I thought, it is not only desires that form undue attachment to the world; beliefs do also.

. . . That makes them (beliefs) a wall to the Atman, which is a spirit beyond that world. You have to get the furniture, the stuffed chairs, out of the way so the spirit can enter and move about freely. The Atman is not about having beliefs. It sees, as it were, phenomena. It does not worry whether the phenomena are "real" or this or that, it just sees them for what they are, clearly.

"Lord, I wonder if my obsession with the ultimate goal is itself a desire I need to detach from . . ."

Yes!

". . . and I should just let things be, and do my own job."

Yes.

Our beliefs, whether religious or nonreligious, tend to be held with a high degree of attachment. They are not just understandings of the world, but passionate convictions that form our self-conceptions. Anything that challenges deeply held beliefs threatens a person's identity. People certainly need to have convictions and a sense of who they are, but I was told, these should not be held with excessive attachment. We have to find the right balance.

I wondered if the Upanishads weren't a bit over the top: "Nothing other than the Imperishable [another name for the Brahman] can see, hear, think, or know." "Lord, that can't be right."

(This is) basically on target. While the "nothing else thinks" claim is too broad and fails to represent empirical particularity (of individual human beings), it is also true that all are in a sense thinking through My mind—or, put it the other way around, that it is My mind that radiates through and energizes all minds.

"Union of the personal self with the Divine Self is presented in the image of lovers. 'A man in the arms of his beloved . . . so a person in union with the Self.' In this union, 'there is neither thief nor slayer, neither low caste nor high, neither monk nor ascetic. The Self is beyond good and evil, beyond all the suffering of the human heart.'"

A wonderful example of truth gone wrong. It is true, in a sense, that the Self beyond the self is beyond good and evil and human suffering, but that is not where good and evil count, and where suffering both occurs and has a role. The real action is with the (personal) self, and its struggle with good and evil, and its sacrifice and suffering. To try to escape that, or to rise above it, is to default on one's duty, on the meaning of life, like a great actress who never played a part (in order) to avoid good and bad reviews.

"The stress is on oneness with the Divine: 'Where there is unity, one without a second, that is the world of Brahman. This is the supreme goal of life. . . .'"

So wrongheaded, almost the opposite. It would be truer to say that the goal is precisely to encounter another—even for Me, as we have discussed—and to love or fight or whatever is called for.

"There is then a striking image: 'The senses, while that man lies dying, gather around and mourn the Self's departure.'"

Yes, that is apt. There is no harm in death, though there is suffering. The senses' attachment clings to life, cannot imagine anything beyond this life. The craving for an afterlife is not higher—as if to long for happiness in heaven were more noble than to long for it on earth. It is simply the desires wanting to go on as before, but in a less troubled realm.

The Upanishad had said that the Self is "beyond good and evil." Instead of a moral law based on God's commandments and His judgment, there was no clear God, no commandments, no judgment, and not much of a code of right and wrong beyond one's social roles. Action was chained to the never-ending wheel of karma, and history was nothing more than endless cycles of renewal and decline, leaving a residue, it seemed to me, of amoralism, resignation, listlessness, and near-nihilism.

"Lord, there is an absence of God and no idea of doing His will."

That is not right. I am present in each, to each, under different names. People relate to Me, take Me in, in different ways. They feel

My presence, and it affects their attitudes to life, which they then express. Do not look for the "God of Israel" in a different guise in these religions. Remember I am much more than a personal God. Be open to the other aspects and learn from that.

Your point about moral relativism (and) nihilism is not quite right, but it does point up the fact that, as people relate to Me differently, they draw different lessons and lifestyles from that relating. But don't think of that as error, any more than the lack of Taoist insight is an Old Testament error. They got a different part of the story. Put them all together, and you have the whole story.

40

I did not feel ineffable

We have clarified the ways in which I grew and things I learned from (My encounter with) Zoroaster, polytheism, and so forth. Now the question is how did I grow and what did I learn from interacting with Vedic and Upanishadic sages.

It was different (from other encounters). There had been vaguely mystical experiences of Me before, but these seers were highly spiritual, highly developed, and made much more of the encounter. It was like the difference between being swept away by a sunset and having an experience of mystical union with God—a qualitative leap.

"How did this affect You?"

Before, I had mainly whispered to people—as conscience, aesthetic awareness, and of course presented Myself in nature. I had, you might say, realized Myself in all these ways.

Now people were coming to Me—not in limited ways, praying and offering sacrifices and so forth—but in a kind of merger. I was not just "extending My limbs" as physical nature or being the quiet advisor and guide, but they were entering into Me, and I was receiving them. That was a new experience.

"And it made You understand or develop a new aspect of Yourself?"

It is hard to explain. It's like suddenly finding that you are the natural home for these creatures, as they return to the cosmic womb.

And I became (or actualized this aspect of My nature) the bosom or womb or home or ocean that all return to. That is no more important a part of My nature than others we have discussed, but it is important, and was both a new development and a new side of Me.

And then another thing happened. Much more than before, these sages began to ponder My nature and (to) try to articulate their understanding of it. Look at those early Upanishads and compare them to the early documents of other traditions and you will see the difference.

And two changes occurred as a result. First, for the first time, I was an *object* to be defined and analyzed. It is like your first experience with a psychologist who has a lot of boxes to put you in (introverted, repressed, etc.). As God, I had not pondered My own "nature." I had no need to "define" Myself, but the effort of others to do so had an impact, as it does when someone assigns to you a personality type. If the description is apt, you think about yourself in a different way. But, most of all, it came clearer that I was an object to others, a source of puzzlement, even mystery, to them. In fact, they would say that My nature was ineffable, beyond all language, all logical categories. They would describe Me in paradoxes—neither existent nor nonexistent, and so forth.

And this has an impact. I did not feel ineffable. To be sure, I am hard to describe and human concepts are not adequate, but that is true of the physical universe as well.

"Is that a problem?"

It puts a barrier between Me and My creatures. How can they approach the ineffable? And even that mystical aspect leads them to regard Me as a pea soup they want to dive into.

As you know, I am a Person, though I am also much more than a Person. But even the God beyond God is not ineffable—just very, very removed from normal human categories.

"That is ironic. The effort at a mystical union actually creates more distance."

Well, there is a great deal that is valid in Vedic and Upanishadic understandings and practice, but it did leave Me with a problem:

how to break through the fog of mystical union. Part of the history of God is the effort to correct people's misunderstandings. I did that, with mixed success, in the Mahabharata.

"Lord, does doing one's duty fit in here?"

Not exactly. Suffering and sacrifice are more essential. The essence of sacrifice is the denial of desire. The full sacrifice is being equally willing to have desires satisfied or not, depending on the will of God.

"Yes, Lord, I have experienced that." I was thinking about that early training in obedience, in which I was given arbitrary commands. Sometimes what was commanded was subsequently withdrawn, but only after I had become quite as willing to do it as not to do it. "Lord, does setting aside desire in this way relate to reincarnation?"

Indirectly, since the Atman *is* detached and "successful" reincarnation involves detachment. The aim of each life is to meets its particular challenges, and that requires detachment—a total willingness to forgo other pleasures.

"Then the inner relation to God, mystical union, is not important on its own. What matters is to live the life you're assigned, not to relate your Atman to the Brahman?"

Yes!

"So the idea that the Atman is Brahman poses a danger. It can pull people out of the real world, make them smug and complacent, and neglectful of ordinary life, as they waft off into a misty-eyed union with the One. The Mahabharata seems to constantly undercut that idea at the same time that it honors and expounds it."

Yes, this is right! The Mahabharata is a corrective.

Action

Passivity is not called for, action is

41

In the Old Testament, the truth of the One God is precarious in a polytheistic world. "Lord, why is survival of the truth a big issue in Israel but not in India?"

It is an issue in India, but the threat to the truth, (to My) communication, is different. There was no possibility that Vedic piety would disappear. It was in no way dependent on the survival of a regime or a specific people. The threat (in India) to My communication was the loss of grip on reality.

"Not so much a threat that the message would be lost, but that it would be understood in some flabby way, hence misunderstood?"

Yes. And that is what happened. Look at Shankara.

Shankara is considered the greatest of all Hindu thinkers. Writing in the ninth century, he articulated a nondualist or Advaita Vedanta based on the Upanishads. In this view, All is One. The appearance of a plurality of selves and objects is something like an illusion. Spiritual liberation is achieved by removing this ignorance and realizing the Self's identity with the Brahman.

The dominant school is radical idealist monism. All tension is lost. Don't get Me wrong. Shankara was a great man and understood in great depth what he understood, but what he understood was extremely one-sided.

The outer world is not unreal, not in any sense other than being less important—for example, the desires are not as important as they

seem to be, hence pleasure and material wealth must rank much lower. But the outer world is also Me, and I am also real and present in this form. Life on earth is not just play-acting, an unwelcome pause between stops in heaven. Passivity is not called for, action is.

I was surprised when I was first told to read the Mahabharata. It is perhaps the world's greatest epic, but it is barely scripture at all.

"Lord, is it a revelation?"

The Mahabharata is a compendium of many stories. Some are "revelations" written by men of spiritual openness. Others are imaginative fiction. There are degrees of revelation—an insight or moral impulse can be a revelation in part. Just read without worry, and I will let you know which parts to pray over. Also, remember that these are the reflections of the religious life of a people over a millennium.

The Mahabharata presents a sustained tribute to dharma, the norm of proper action. The rules of dharma are usually stated in an uncompromising form, such as: Always tell the truth. Always grant the wishes of a Brahmin. Heroes are praised for their constancy in upholding dharma. However, the Mahabharata also contains a powerful countertheme—the limits, or even the trap, of dharma. Piety prevents saying this outright. It is expressed as well as masked by the dictum "Dharma is subtle."

More myth and legend than history, the Mahabharata tells a story of dynastic struggle within the royal family of the northern Indian kingdom of Bharata, a name that still appears on Indian currency. The good King Samtanu, the epic reports, "knew dharma" and was "upright, true to his word." His son and heir was "of like conduct, like behavior, like learning" as well as "mighty in strength."

While hunting, the king sees a "divinely beautiful maiden" and falls in love. He seeks her hand in marriage, but her father, who is "king of the fishermen," insists on one condition: the son born to his daughter must inherit the throne, not Samtanu's current heir. It is an impossible demand. Heartbroken, the king drags through his days in brooding silence.

Distressed at the king's unhappiness, his son agrees to renounce the throne. "And for your progeny as well," demands the fisherman.

He will have no kingdom, no wife, and no children to pray for him in the afterlife. "Agreed." It is an extraordinary oath, and the son is showered by flowers from the gods, who proclaim his new name: "He is Bhishma, the Awesome One!"

The king's marriage results in two possible heirs, the blind Dhritarashtra and Pandu. Since kings are also warriors, Dhritarashtra's lack of sight disqualifies him. Pandu and his line take precedence. However, Pandu is killed while his eldest son, Yudhisthira (Yudi for short) is next in line but is still a minor. Dhritarashtra serves as interim king. But his son, Duryodhana (Dury for short), lusts for the succession for himself.

Yudi embodies all the virtues. Like George Washington, he cannot tell a lie. The ruthless Dury, by contrast, connives at Yudi's destruction. After efforts to kill Yudi and his brothers have failed, Dury, who is able to cheat, challenges Yudi to a game of dice. Round after round, Yudi bets all and loses all—his wealth, his kingdom, even his brothers, himself, and finally his exquisite wife, Draupadi.

In a shocking scene, the wicked Dury has the now-enslaved queen brought before the gathered throng and orders her to be disrobed in public view. Krishna, who is both a character in the story and, unbeknownst to others, the god of the universe, intervenes. As Dury's henchman unwraps her sari to reveal her naked body, more sari appears without end. Anguished by the scene, Dury's father, the interim king, cancels the results of the gambling.

To make peace, Yudi offers to share the kingdom. Dury, unyielding, refuses to give the rightful heir even a token domain, "not the land equal to the head of pin." The matter must be settled on the battlefield.

Thus begins the Great Bharata war, which gives its name to the epic. It is a battle between good and evil, as the world spirals downward in the cycle of time. The eve of the first battle is the occasion for the most famous part of the epic, the Bhagavad-Gita, which Gandhi called "an infallible guide of conduct."

Yudi's younger brother Arjuna is the most dazzling warrior on his side. Arjuna's friend Krishna declines to fight but agrees to steer his chariot. Both sides draw up for battle. The fate of the cosmos hangs in the balance. At that critical moment, Arjuna becomes paralyzed with doubt. Isn't it a violation of dharma to fight against his own relatives and teachers?

All is lost unless Krishna can persuade Arjuna to fight. Drawing on every facet of Hindu thought, he presents one argument after another, to no avail. Finally, he plays his trump card. Transforming himself before our very eyes, he shows himself as the awesome god of the universe. That does it. Arjuna fights.

That scene is typical of the tension in the epic. Good characters like Bhishma and Yudi are said over and over to be the perfect embodiment of dharma. Yet it is just this obsessive fidelity that results in calamity. It is Bhishma's stubborn vow of celibacy that breaks the legitimate line of succession and causes the war. It is Yudi's punctilious sense of honor that leads to his gambling everything away, including his wife. Having served at the court of the blind interim king, Bhishma feels obliged to fight for the side he knows to be in the wrong. It is Arjuna's reluctance to fight against his "grandsire," the esteemed Bhishma, that causes his failure of will.

The great battle is waged day after day and, finally, is on the verge of being lost. The only way for good to prevail is to deceive an indestructible warrior on the other side. Yudi is the only one he will believe. But Yudi refuses to lie! Once again, Krishna himself intervenes, persuades Yudi, and saves the day.

There is, however, a cost. Before the lie, Yudi's chariot glides over the earth, its wheels never quite touching.

Now they sink to the ground.

What is morally imperfect is morally required

42

"Lord, was there something You were trying to get across with the Mahabharata?"

I am trying to shake people out of their (moral) sloth—taking the easy answers of piety or penance or caste duties. I am trying to problematize not only dharma but "spiritual liberation" as well, but they are resistant.

Spiritual liberation (moksha) is considered the aim of meditation and other yogic practices.

Their common sense tells them that "dharma is subtle," that transcendence of worldly concerns is not a practical or realistic answer, but they want to flee to those easy pieties.

In fact, Yudi, who loves to converse with the Brahmins, is accused of trying to be a saint instead of a king, of wandering off into the spiritual instead of attending to his real-life duties.

The point of life on the material plane is to "engage the demons"—to confront the real challenge of "sin," adverse forces, material difficulties, mortality, suffering, and so forth—not escape (through yoga) or conventional conformism (dharma). These can be elements of a spiritually fulfilled life, but are not the whole story.

"That is how the epic has been striking me."

Yes, but you are not emphasizing My side. The Hindus got the main drift, the nub (as in the Upanishads), the deep spiritual connection to Me, but they went off the deep end and there are serious

dangers there. Dharma devolves into caste rigidity and mindless, meaningless conformity, like the problem with all ritual. Spiritual liberation devolves into escapism, lack of responsibility, an addlepated mindlessness and disregard of life's duties and challenges. It even tries to denigrate suffering, as though it didn't matter. It matters greatly and that is why it is central. It is not sufficient to say, "Oh well, another fine ascetism notched in my belt."

"So Your voice is one of hectoring, agitating?"

Yes, and one of the authors heard Me well, and repeatedly puts in the dilemmas, the reprimand of Yudi not to "wander off" and such, but as you have observed, this (counterpoint) has little resonance in Hindu official theology or ethics.

"Am I right, Lord, about the trap of dharma?"

The moral life is ambiguous. That is because you live on the material plane. Arrangements of matter cannot be made perfect, cannot be put into perfect conformity with (pure) moral rules. Matter is by its very nature resistant.

"That seems too abstract, Lord. I know we can't make a frictionless plane. But that doesn't explain why, for example, Yudi has to lie."

Yes, it does. Yudi has to deal with people who are themselves embodiments of particular desires. Among these desires are evil purposes. And they can be defeated only by using their set of embodied beliefs and desires. This is what Yudi does. It is the only way to prevent evil in this case. So what is morally imperfect is morally required.

The point is not to refute or subvert dharma. Dharma is essential. When you commit a moral imperfection, it is important that (you) know it. You are left somewhat compromised, and it is important to know that also. But you also need to understand the necessity of this morally imperfect act.

"How does all this relate to being material?"

By that I mean the whole person—the Self—is embodied in the world, with a physiology, a psychology, ego, and such. And, as you know, in a sense that is the only way to *be*. Otherwise, you are only the "idea" of a person.

"But the Self behind the self would still be there."

Yes, but as we have discussed, it would be a Self without a life—without a full life and all that entails. It would be the permanent possibility of a life. Life is lived on the material plane. That is where it is all enacted. And the material plane involves these ambiguities that lead to morally imperfect decisions in situations that call for them.

"What should I understand about the epic's message?"

I have already told you—the corrective to the high-flying tendencies of Hindu thought, the tendency to lose contact with the ground through yoga or asceticism or various doctrines (such as monistic idealism).

The discovery of the Atman and the Brahman—a particularly important discovery for people with a Valhalla-style pantheon—was so heady that it was natural of them to skip a beat and try to leap right into (the) Brahman. But, while the discoveries of Atman (and) Brahman are valid, that escape is not the purpose of life.

Competition between seers was a central part of certain sacred rituals. The contests were called battles, which reflected the struggles and conflicts in real life. The victor represented the triumph over the dark forces. "Lord, could the Mahabharata be such a competition or battle?"

Yes!

"So a ritual sacrifice is a battle. And a battle, and the life of action in general, is a sacrifice."

The creation of the universe is a sacrifice.

"What do You mean by 'sacrifice'?"

Don't stop Me now. Just listen. The creation is a sacrifice. A sacrifice also involved battle. The Mahabharata is about a war that is a sacrifice.

In fact, the battle takes place on a field used for sacrifices. And the setting for the telling of the story is a sacrifice that runs over several days.

That action part corresponds to David (in the Old Testament). The challenge of the world of action is that it cannot be pure. Human beings are fallible (weak and such) and circumstances are murky, multivalent, not clear-cut. So the Mahabharata tells a complex story, both praising dharma and yet recognizing its purities are counter-productive in real life.

There is a struggle against forces of evil or disorder. The struggle occurs in the messy plane of real life, and therefore dharma—rules that would govern in an ideal world—can do damage.

The battle must be fought with tools that work.

"Arjuna and Yudi even more are too otherworldly and must be pulled downward."

Yes. The (ancient) Indians—while in real life, gut fighters like everyone else—developed a religious consciousness that was very high-minded, that sublimated the desires and veered toward the idea that action in this world was an illusion. So they needed desperately to be brought back to earth.

The (brahminic) focus on the ritual (of sacrifice) was misplaced. It (sacrifice) is a metaphor for the world of action. So just doing the right things in the ceremony, letter perfect and all, is not karma (as ritual was regarded), (it is not) effective action.

The root meaning of *karma* is action.

The message should have been the reverse—not that (ritual) sacrifice is the spiritually relevant action, but that action is a sacrifice, should be seen as a sacrifice that maintains the order of the world, and makes it sacred, and is an act of proper worship, and, yes, (in Aurobindo's four aspects) an act of worship, of fitting homage and honoring Me.

Sri Aurobindo, the greatest Indian thinker of the last hundred years, writes in *Vedic Symbolism*, "The sacrifice was represented at once as a giving and worship, a battle, and a journey." It is a giving because it involves an inner yielding. It is worship because it was the centerpiece of Vedic ritual. It is a battle between the gods and their human allies against "the powers of falsehood, division, darkness." And it is a journey because "the sacrifice traveled from earth to the gods" and "involved the path by which man himself traveled to the Home of the Truth."

The purpose of an activity is to *become*

43

"After death, do we review our lives, what we did right and what we did wrong?"

The Atman does not die. It "returns to Me." It is assessing all the time. Most people do not contact the Atman often enough to be aware of that.

"You have often told me just to note objectively where I went wrong and why, and not to indulge in guilt. This assessment is a benign, objective review?"

Yes.

"What, if anything, happens differently at death?"

At death, you also reconcile with others. You are in fact reunited.

"This reminds me of the dream in which I died and ended up in an afterlife with two women who seemed to love me."

This is correct. It is not just an amorphous reunion with God. People (as Self behind the self) are distinct individuals, even though they are incarnated as individual personalities. So they (as Selves) are not the same merely as their empirical personalities, but they are aware of those personalities, remember them as you remember your youth (which is) also, to some extent, a different self. And they appraise . . .

"And regret what they did wrong?"

No, regret is not part of it. That is an earthly emotion. It is much more detached, objective . . .

"The way I assess a historical character or some inevitable error I don't blame myself for but see more as a learning experience?"

Exactly. Heaven is not a place for rewards or punishment. The rewards come on earth, and the sinful, as you have quoted, are punished *by* their sins.

"So virtue is its own reward?"

Yes, but there is also the overall project of the Atman, of the universe, of Me, and a good life contributes to that.

"So the aim is not merely to stack up virtues but to contribute to that project. And what is that project, Lord?"

What is the goal of anything, of any activity?

"To produce a result?"

No, that is (true only for) a narrow range of activities. The purpose of an activity is to *become*, to increase one's being in a certain respect.

"But we build a fire to get warm, we work for a paycheck to pay the rent . . ."

Yes, but why do you do those things? It is for self-fulfillment, self-actualization, becoming a fuller partner with nature, with being, with Me, a fuller actuality in the community of being.

"But don't we do it for pleasure and the avoidance of pain?"

Yes, of course. That is the grit, the material reality of the world, and of man's (people's) life in it. But a life only of that (pursuing pleasure) is a life of despair.

"Hedonists say that life doesn't have any overall meaning, so we should just enjoy ourselves."

Of course someone can say (and believe) life is meaningless and (that) he (or she) lives for pleasure, but that is not the reality of his (or her) life. His (or her) whole life-force is aiming at something higher—health (moral and mental and well as physical), not just pleasure—goals and goods that are worth the pain. Why do talented artists struggle for their art when they could make good money on commercial design?

But it doesn't stop there. It is not just that some people have a particular passion for art or whatever, but that their very life-force is a force toward (their) total actualization in the community of being.

That is true of social life, of family life, of biological life, of planetary "life," and so on.

"In the ecosphere?"

Yes. That is the dynamic of the universe. And remember that I *am* also all of this.

"I keep looking for a purpose that is more like an ultimate wonderful outcome—some kind of sublime union with God, an ultimate merging of all into one."

You are already part of Me, but in a way that is unfulfilled, incomplete. Actualizing yourself in all these ways is to participate more fully in Me. So is being in touch with your Atman. A mystical merging that destroyed all individuality would be a diminution, not a gain.

"Well, some kind of perfect bliss, eternal life at the end of it all . . ."

See how superficial that is—like a Club Med in the sky. Get real.

"Is the actualization something like climbing up the levels of being in a Neoplatonic way or an evolutionary process in which the world, both human and natural, progresses toward an ultimate spiritual fulfillment, like Teilard's Omega point?"

In a sense, but you never leave behind the physical and biological and psychological "levels." Every "level" is being actualized all the time.

"Another kind of satisfying outcome would be a development that is progressive and culminates in a final synthesis, like Hegel's Absolute."

No, each thing is actualized in its own right, in its own day. It does not have to be a stepping-stone to something else.

"What is the purpose of death?"

(Life without death) would be like endlessly expanding your first novel.

"If the Atman is assessing all the time, is that where reflective insight and ethical consciousness come from?"

Yes. The Atman is normative, objective, sets high standards, but is understanding. It's like Rousseau's Legislator.

In Jean-Jacques Rousseau's *The Social Contract*, the Legislator is the ideal constitution-maker, "a superior intelligence beholding all the passions of men without experiencing any of them," his happiness independent of ours, "yet ready to occupy itself with ours."

44

Each life is a kind of test

Early in my adventure with God, Abigail and I were vacationing in Maine, staying in a cottage by the bay, a quiet place for reading and reflection. I felt that God wanted to tell me something, so I got very still. But nothing came. However, after a time, I was guided to look at the first page of the book I had brought along, Marcel Proust's *Remembrance of Things Past*. Describing how a dream, at first clearly remembered, fades into incoherence, Proust comments, "Then it would begin to seem unintelligible, as the thoughts of a previous existence must be after reincarnation."

This should be explored, I thought. I always like to trace an idea to its source. The first mention of reincarnation I could find was in the Brihadaranyaka Upanishad. The seer Yajnavalkya (the same guy who won all the cows) explains, "As a caterpillar, having come to the end of one blade of grass, draws itself together and reaches out for the next, so the Self, having come to the end of one life and dispelled all ignorance, gathers in his faculties and reaches out from the old body to a new."

I had never been attracted to the idea of coming back as somebody else. What could that person possibly be to me? But my disliking an idea didn't prevent it from being true, so I asked, "Lord, is reincarnation true?"

Yes. And it was part of My revelation to the people of Israel (not just India). But many found the idea frightening and had reason

to do away with it. I say this to reassure you. Reincarnation is not incompatible with anything in the Bible. Continue to pray to the Lord thy God and continue to read the Bible.

"Why is there reincarnation? What is its use?"

I know you are reluctant (to accept reincarnation) because it seems inauthentic (and illogical) to you. But it (the standard view) is about right.

You are right to come to beliefs on your own, on the basis of what seems to you to be evidence, (but) open your mind and rethink your concepts. Many people who believe these things, as with spiritual truths generally, are working with inadequate concepts, as if they were trying to describe the Einsteinian universe with Newtonian concepts.

"Lord, what is reincarnation?"

There is a prior question—what is the soul? *What* is reincarnated?

"Okay, what is reincarnated? The Atman?"

The Atman is instantiated (not reincarnated), but the What of reincarnation refers to the continuity of the self from one life to the next.

"Yes, I see the difference. That each life is an incarnation of the Atman does not really provide a contentful link between one life and the next."

Be still a minute.

I quieted myself. "Lord, I get an image of cleansing."

Yes, that's right. It's like dipping something into a cleaning fluid, rinsing, and repeating. Or like dipping a wick in tallow over and over to make a candle. Or firing steel several times.

"So it is a way to improve the soul, maybe to purify it?"

That's okay for now. Each life is a kind of test. Your sense of that is accurate. Each life meets a new kind of test, and that is a reason for many lives.

Each life needs to be purified, sanctified, made more a part of Me. Each life is faced with a struggle to do this. The struggle is carried on through successive lives.

"And our personal selves, are they carried on too?"

Yes, (though they) differ from one time to the next.

"Is the series of lives cumulative or sequential or progressive?"

Cumulative—in the sense that the previous "dips" add up—but not sequential in the sense of first base before second base.

"Therefore, not progressive?"

Progressive in the sense of cumulative, not in the sense of moving up a ladder of success.

"Well, what I'm getting at is whether you move from a low-life, even subhuman, to a higher life, a Brahmin or king or something like that?"

No, you don't. So it is not right to say that, if you are poor or sickly or low-born, it is a punishment for a past life.

"So the doctrine of karma is wrong?"

Not entirely. Whether you succeeded in a previous life determines both how purified you have been and whether you have "punched that particular ticket."

"If you are getting purer, how could you could be a saint in one life and come back as a pirate?"

Your soul is purer even if you are now a pirate or hot-tempered or weak-willed. In other words, you will not be able to tell in this life, at least from those traits, how purified you have become.

"But you can tell by other traits or in other ways?"

Yes, by contacting your Atman.

"Now I am also puzzled whether there is one Atman or many."

Many, so it might be better to talk about your Soul in caps—the Soul behind the soul.

So Jill's Atman or Soul is not the same as Jack's. We each have our own Soul.

45

Life is for a purpose and the purpose is not just entertainment

Ask about karma.

"Now I understand karma as less a matter of making up for past wrongs and more a matter of which challenges a person needs next."

No, that is not right! Karma is a matter of "righting the balance" after the imbalances of your previous life. Remember how I have told you: Don't feel guilt, just note the consequences.

I took this to mean that we should not wallow in self-recrimination. We should just note what temptation led us astray and in what way that made our life worse.

Every act (action) has consequences, and these play out over more than a single lifetime.

"And they result in unpaid balances on wrongs that have to be righted in the next life?"

Yes, but (the correct concept is) less (a matter of) good and evil, right and wrong, less moralistic, and more (like) "these are the consequences."

"Like the Newtonian law that for every action there is an equal and opposite reaction?"

Yes.

"How does this relate to dharma?"

Dharma is the balance within a life.

"Relative to one's social roles?"

That part was overdone because of the Hindu social structure. It is balance in all respects, including the emotional harmonies within the individual, the relation between one's past conduct and one's present attitudes, (one's) relations to others . . .

"And to nature?"

Yes.

"And to You?"

Of course.

"Are You striving for balance too?"

Yes. My job is to orchestrate the whole. You (people) can help or hinder that effort.

"What about the Hindu goal of liberation from rebirth? My own sense of life is that it is a blessing more than a burden, not something to be liberated from."

Life is for a purpose and the purpose is not just entertainment. It is to achieve a result.

"To achieve balance?"

That's okay for now. When you achieve balance, there is no reason to be born again.

"Then spiritual liberation *is* the goal?"

No, balance is. "Liberation"—misnamed—is the result. It is a karmic consequence of a life "balanced out."

About this time, I was stricken with a serious pneumonia which, with repeated relapses, lasted for the greater part of a year. When I returned to prayer, I had lost the thread.

"Lord, I don't recall where we left off. There seem to be several ideas, related to one another, all a bit unclear to me: First, the Atman is the Brahman . . ."

Stop there. I have told you before that these (human) notions of identity and nonidentity, sameness and difference, are inadequate. That is why I always say, "I am you and you are Me, *in a sense*." We have not paused to explicate that sense, and it would not be productive to do so.

"Lord, it is still not clear what is reincarnated. I could say the soul or self or 'essence of who you are,' but these are just labels for the mystery. The problem begins with the fact that, in the ordinary sense of person, the reincarnated person, Jerry 2, is a different person from the source-person, Jerry 1. They lived at different times, spoke different languages, had different occupations, personalities, and tastes, and they share no memories. So if I am Jerry 1, what is Jerry 2 to me, and vice versa?"

But you know the answer already. The Atman or Soul of Jerry 1 and Jerry 2 are the same. And I have told you that the Atman, while it lacks many of your personal characteristics, is not just a generic self. It is distinctively you and has a history as you and a concern for you. Think of an actress or an avatar (or character) in a computer game. The same actress or player goes from role to role or game to game.

"So the Self is to each reincarnated self as an actress is to each role or a player to each game character. Does my Atman—or Self behind the self . . ."

Yes, that is a better formulation.

"Does it continue to have a continuous awareness, as the actress does, and remember the various roles or reincarnations?"

Well, remember that time is not what you think it is, and so "memory" is not exactly apt, but awareness is. And the answer is yes, it does.

"Thinking about things that You've said, it sounds as if time may be like a long novel such as a family saga. The story is clearly chronological—the grandmother comes before the granddaughter. But the reader stands outside the chronology internal to the book and can open it in the middle or toward the end."

Yes, that is apt if you don't try to build anything too literal from the analogy.

"In a movie, a woman steps into a mirror and finds herself in a different period of history. Theoretically, she could step into or observe any time."

That is an okay analogy.

"One might call it the simultaneity of times."

Okay.

(It is) necessary for humankind to experience the range of "truths"

46

The key to karma is dharma. Dharma is your duty in your situation.

"Lord, is this You talking or me?"

It's Me. Your duty in your situation is your assignment in this life.

"So your duty follows from your assignment?"

Yes.

"What if you fail?"

You come back again.

"You mean otherwise you don't?"

No, that is not the point. The point is that your task is unfulfilled. It still has to be done in the next life, though the same task may take a new form.

"Do You mean if you fail in courage in this life, courage will be a key part of your assignment in the next life?"

Something like that.

"For how long a period of time do you keep reincarnating?"

Forever. I know that is disturbing to your beginning-to-end mentality, but that (mentality) is a very narrow view of reality. When you understand time better, it won't be so disturbing.

"And between lives you review how you did?"

As I explained before, that view of time is inadequate. There is no "between" lives. You—your Atman—is viewing your life all along.

"Surely there must be some way of gaining lessons."

The lessons are through the living itself, and they are not a means to an end. The living, the fighting, the doing of your duty, your work with Me, is (you might say) an end in itself—though the means-ends dichotomies are not very helpful.

"So you learn the lessons of life simultaneously with living that life. Is this related to the simultaneity of times, like a book you can step into at any point in the plot?"

Yes, that's fine. It is all in a sense "seen" "at once," but that does not mean that time in the sense of one thing happening first and then another thing is "unreal." It is perfectly real and adequate as an understanding, but it is not the whole picture.

"And I gather that outside this world or plane of existence, it is not applicable."

That's right.

"And that means that the lives would not really be in a sequence?"

The lives are in a kind of sequence—though that's not the final frame of reference—but the worlds are not.

At some point I had been told that, just as there are multiple lives, there are multiple worlds. Evidently, one world cannot be said to come "before" or "after" another world. "Perhaps chronological time is internal to a world."

Yes.

"If the lives are in a kind of sequence, then is there progress or retrogression or cumulative learning through successive lives?"

No, no, and yes. You are not moving forward or backward, but you are learning, adding to your store of wisdom.

"So it is not that Jerry Martin now knows more than his earlier incarnation but less than a later one. It is that the Atman, which is continuous across lives (and perhaps even outside our time system), is learning."

Yes, that is correct.

"Are we adding to our sum of achievements as well as of wisdom? You have said that our tasks are not just tests. They are work that really needs to be done, that You need to have done."

This is a complicated subject, but yes, I have work for you to do and it has to be done, and I need help to do it and you can help Me. You enter the world to take on necessary tasks.

"It sounds like the first missions given to rookie soldiers, which need to be done but also provide valuable training. In fact, it reminds me of the quests mythical heroes are given."

Yes, the latter is especially apt.

"So life is a quest."

Let's not get overly literal. It's just a metaphor.

"But an apt one?"

Yes.

Discussing reincarnation in *Philosophies of India*, Heinrich Zimmer writes, "It is by doing things that one becomes transformed. . . . Actually living through, to the very limit, a particular role, one comes to realize the truth inherent in the role. Suffering its consequences, one fathoms and exhausts its contents. Knowledge is to be attained, in other words, not through inaction . . . but through a bold and advertent living of life."

Whether virtuous or criminal, human or animal, one is to live one's life fully, to its absolute limit, "until there is finally no space left within him for any darker, inauspicious karmic force."

That is right. Each life must be lived to the fullest. Each is an exploration, an experiment.

"Each life has a truth and has limits?"

Yes, and that—those—can be discovered only by living them out.

"For the individual or for mankind?"

Both. The individual must test these through many lives; that also enriches and educates the total spiritual life of a culture and of mankind. This is also the secret of the diversity of cultures, and the diversity of revelations. The multiplicity of cultures is not just a conditioning or limiting factor on revelations—it is itself a necessary diversity for mankind to experience the range of lives, the range of "truths."

"I assume this applies also to the varieties of spiritual guidance. Some advise the inactive or quiet life of withdrawal from the world, others active lives of various kinds."

Yes, the "inactive" life is one of the lives that must be explored and has truth—and limits.

"How does this relate to Your story, Lord?"

My story is that I live in and through each of these stories, these individual lives. I am intimately connected with them, as a helper, as a vicarious partner. My own "fate" or "day" waxes or wanes with each individual setback or triumph. This is not just the drama of individuals' lives; it is the drama of My life as well. It is *the* big drama of it all.

"Zimmer speaks of the truth inherent in each role or life."

Yes, every role or life task-challenge-mission has a truth and has a falsity, in the sense of limitations. But "truth" here is elliptical for its own inner meaning or sense, its distinctive thrust, just as each work of music or poetry, or each athletic event, has its own mission, obstacles, keys to success, tendencies to failure, to overreaching or underreaching, facing or failing to face the truth of that mission. Succeed or fail, one learns something, and the universe learns something. Another piece of the puzzle is put in place. Like marking off towns you have visited on a trip, another life possibility can be checked off, but more than that, it is added to the ontological quotient or quantum of the universe, of all Being.

And individuals do not do this alone. I am with them whether they know it or not. I am deeply involved and deeply concerned. I help when called upon and, as best I can, when not called upon.

The word *truth* is appropriate here because there is a truth about the situation in each life. And part of the challenge, almost the whole challenge, is to recognize that truth for what it is, to face it, pleasant or unpleasant. It may be the truth of being the child of an alcoholic or of being retarded or disfigured or a weakling or (of having) this or that temperament, intelligence or set of aptitudes, physical features, etc. One has to face it front on and deal with it. If you succeed, the world moves forward. I move forward.

The (central) question (for the person) is: What is my project? Why am I doing what I am doing?

"And Your role in all this?"

I *relate* to people (and things). I share their adventures, their loves and losses. A parent is not just a teacher of lessons, but lives (in a relationship with the children) and suffers and is a nurturer and so forth.

I live through each individual life—inspiring, guiding, being blocked, whispering, coaching, feeling joy, and suffering.

"So one dimension of Your story is the personal copartnering."

Not just one dimension—the crucial dimension.

47

Without love,
the normative
is useless

He was to become the Buddha, the Awakened or Enlightened One, but he was born Siddhartha Gautama, a prince and member of the warrior class. In the oldest collection of Buddhist scriptures, the Pali Canon, he tells his story.

> I was tenderly cared for, supremely so, infinitely so. At my father's home lotus pools were made for me—in one place for the blue lotus flowers, in one place for white lotus flowers, and in one place for red lotus flowers—blossoming for my sake. Of Benares fabric were my three robes. Day and night a white umbrella was held over me, so that I might not be troubled by cold, heat, dust, chaff, or dew. I dwelt in three palaces: in one for the cold, in one for the summer, and in one for the rainy season.

Eventually, the pampered Gautama ventured beyond the palace gates and was shocked by what he saw: an aged man with twisted body, another afflicted by illness, and finally a corpse surrounded by mourners. He asked his driver to explain what he had seen and learned, to his horror, that we all are subject to age, illness, and death.

> And he, going to his rooms, sat brooding sorrowful and depressed thinking: Shame then verily be upon this thing called birth, since to one born the decay of life . . . shows itself like that!

The next time Gautama went out, he saw "a shaven-headed man, a recluse, wearing the yellow robe and [was] told, 'He is one who has gone forth.'" What does this mean?

"To have gone forth, my lord, means being thorough in the religious life, thorough in the peaceful life, thorough in good actions, thorough in meritorious conduct, thorough in harmlessness, thorough in kindness to all creatures."

The prince returned to his rooms and, "there and then cutting off his hair and donning the yellow robe, went forth from the house into the homeless state."

In an intense effort to achieve spiritual illumination, he engaged in increasingly severe ascetic practices.

I determined to take food only in small amounts, as much as my hollowed palm would hold. My body became extremely lean. The mark of my seat was like a camel's footprint. The bones of my spine when bent and straightened were like a row of spindles. . . . But by this severe mortification I do not attain superhuman, truly noble knowledge and insight. Perhaps there is another way. . . .

In this frame of mind, Gautama came upon "a delightful spot with a pleasant grove" and sat down under a sacred tree and meditated for days. Finally, enlightenment came. He promptly went to the holy city of Varanasi (Banaras) and preached his first sermon, "The Four Noble Truths," to five fellow ascetics.

"There are two ends not to be served," he explained. "The pursuit of desires and of the pleasure that springs from desire, which is base, common, leading to rebirth, ignoble, and unprofitable; and the pursuit of pain and hardship, which is grievous, ignoble, and unprofitable." Avoiding both indulgence and extreme asceticism "brings clear vision, it makes for wisdom, and leads to peace, insight, enlightenment, and Nirvana [escape from the chains of existence]." He preached "the Noble Eightfold Path—Right Views, Right Resolve, Right Speech, Right Conduct, Right Livelihood,

Right Effort, Right Mindfulness, and Right Concentration. This is the Middle Way."

Before I had read about the Buddha, I was praying about Indian ascetic practices. "Lord, is severe self-denial a way to worship You?"

That was wrong and is wrong everywhere (more or less). That is why (one reason) I sent Buddha. The rest (of Buddha's teaching) is mainly consistent with My revelation to the Indians.

"But You sent him a special message."

No, I had sent the same message, against asceticism, to many. But they ignored it, or they accepted it but did not have the impact on others (that) Buddha had.

However, I was also told,

Buddha is a special case. Not so much a big revelation or development of Myself, (but more) a perceptive distillation of one part of what it is to be human, of kindness. That is precious, delightful, but not a major spiritual step. It has given rise to more error than truth.

"Perhaps the error is found, not so much in Buddha, as in later doctrines in the Buddhist tradition."

Yes.

India, like Israel, is a birthplace of religions. Abigail and I went to northern India to visit major sites of Hindu, Moslem, and Buddhist culture. Since these prayers began, I have found myself spiritually sensitive. As I travel, I sometimes stop in places of worship, either to pray or just to take a look. On one occasion, I was in downtown Seattle and stopped in at a mainline Protestant church—I don't remember the denomination. Almost immediately, I felt I was suffocating and raced to escape from the building. At the opposite extreme, I attended a bar mitzvah at a Conservative Jewish temple. As soon as I stepped into the sanctuary, it was like coming in from the cold and being hit in the face by a wall of hot air. Except, in this case, it was the dense presence of God. So palpable that I looked around, expecting others to be reeling as I was. But, no, they were just chatting.

As we visited the sacred sites of India, I expected my inner seismograph to be way up on the spiritual Richter scale. We saw Hindu temples with figures of Vishnu and other gods, a Moslem mosque as the men were gathering for prayer, evening rituals conducted by young Brahmins, funeral fires on the banks of the sacred river Ganges, the revered cows wandering in the middle of traffic, even a holy man walking the streets naked. But my spiritual sensors registered only once—at the place where the Buddha gave his first sermon. We approached the monument marking the site amidst a crowd of devotees and tourists. We could hear the chants of Buddhist priests in the distance. We had not yet seen anything, just stepped onto the grounds, when the deepest sadness came over me. It was not my sadness, but the sadness of the Enlightened One, as if he were feeling, "Oh, no, no, they are coming here to worship me. I am not a god. That was not my message at all. I was a complete failure."

According to the Buddhist scriptures, the Enlightened One now understood the "chain of causation" that results in suffering. He saw that, "from the organs of sense comes contact; from contact comes feeling; from feeling, craving; from craving, clinging to existence; from clinging to existence, the desire of becoming; from the desire of becoming, rebirth; from rebirth, old age and death, grief, lamentation, pain, sorrow, and despair."

"Such," he concluded, "is the origin of the whole mass of suffering."

That seemed extreme to me. "Wasn't Buddha overreacting? Giving up all desires to avoid suffering seems like putting out your eyes to avoid ever seeing anything ugly."

Don't dismiss him on that account. There is wisdom here.

"Is his reaction to suffering less central than it seems, or what?"

The main theme is his compassion. It is not that *he* will grow old, get sick, and such, but he is a very sensitive soul who reacts very strongly to, feels, the suffering of *others*.

"But we suffer and You suffer for a reason, don't we?"

Yes, but the first step is to fully acknowledge the horror of suffering, not just to dismiss it as "shit happens" or transmute it into "growth." Suffering is the pits. It has all the "evil" (that) those who turn against God on account of it believe it has.

As Buddha's story goes on, death is described as permanent separation from family. "But, if there is reincarnation, that is not the real story of death, is it, Lord?"

Yes, in a sense, it is. Something goes on (and is reincarnated), but it is not Fred and Jane. Death is final (in that respect). So the loss of death is ultimate.

As I read more, I could see Buddha's virtues. "Lord, Buddha is impressive for his boundless compassion as well as his reasonableness and moderation."

Buddha was an extraordinary person. There was such sensitivity to his nature—no membrane (no filter)—that he felt the sufferings of others to an extraordinary extent. He almost literally felt *their* pain, sometimes more than they did in the midst of (their own) deflections.

It is not so much that he listened to Me—hence, there is no God in his preaching—as that I was present in and permeated his sensorium, his sensitivity to others. That is how *I* relate to human suffering, as does Jesus. I both hold My own suffering (disappointments, anger, and so forth) but also everyone else's. Buddha was like that with regard to those with whom he came into contact.

"But isn't Buddha's message very limited?"

All messages are limited. There is nothing wrong with his message. It is the pure truth on those things he spoke about.

"But Buddha sees life only as a trail of tears. He does not seem to appreciate the joy of existence, the gift of life."

Yes and no. You have had a good life so far; many have not. Nothing guarantees that your life will continue to be good. Look at most people in human history.

Don't cover up the horror of death, the burden of life.

"So Your communication with Buddha was successful?"

Yes, this was the only case of pure, total communication. Culture did not interfere, since the Hindu culture is an appropriate context for these revelations.

"Does Buddha eclipse the Vedic tradition?"

Of course not.

"Life is a wonderful gift. Isn't it a mistake to want to escape rebirth?"

No, not in the way he meant it. "Birth" really means "attachment to life." You are right that there is nothing wrong with being born. If there were, why would Buddha and Jesus be born? It is indeed a blessing. Buddha's comments were taken literally and he was not unhappy with this rendering, since it helped communicate the truth he was trying to get across.

"But if birth and rebirth really just mean attachment to life, then the whole idea of giving up attachment in order to prevent rebirth no longer makes sense."

No, it (the chain of causation) is still a logical pyramid. Buddha was correct. This literalism has done little or no harm.

"Oh, I see, one does not so much eliminate birth and death as transcend them."

Yes.

I was told to quiet myself and become receptive. I felt God merging into me, then me into God, and was told not to think but just linger there without thinking. It was like the Brahman or God beyond God perhaps. It didn't feel personal but not impersonal either, and it seemed to have a magnetic pull as an object of desire. It felt encompassing not just of me but of everything, not like a matrix, but like a nest or envelope, perhaps something similar to the Void of the Buddhists—I thought I heard a "yes" but then "not quite that"—a place that offered rest and integrity (in the literal sense of having one's disparate aspects settle into a coherent unity).

Buddha went directly to the heart of the spiritual life. He understood that that is a life of personal fulfillment (bliss) that overflows to others.

Notice the extent to which love runs through so much of My revelation to mankind. Without love, the normative is useless. No one always does right. We are all in need of grace, which is to say, love.

48

Love is important
but so is compassion

Release from this travail of woes requires spiritual enlightenment. So Buddhism teaches. Transcending all desires and beliefs takes many lifetimes. Only then does one enter Nirvana, the blessed Void in which the chains of birth and rebirth are broken. Avalokiteśvara achieved the ultimate goal. He was a Buddhist saint or Bodhisattva, a Buddha-in-becoming. He was ready for Nirvana. But, hearing the sounds of a suffering world, he returned to the world, and will return again and again until every last person has been released.

"Lord, with the ideal of the Bodhisattva, were You trying to communicate something special to mankind?"

Yes, I love every individual "infinitely." That unbounded love that popular religion often attributes to God is exactly right. It is like a mother for a child. It is not enough that I relate one-on-one to individuals. That is truncated. Human beings need not just individual friends, but families, social groups, and communities. You relate to individual friends in the context of these groups—not just with them (these social groups) in the background, but they help define (and) produce the concepts and values reflected in the particular friendship.

The same is true for Me. I do not just relate to Jacob, but to Jacob as husband of . . . , and father of . . . , and of course to the people of Israel and to the nations. I can have an extraordinary relation to a single individual, such as a monk or mystic, but that is not the only dimension of spirituality, and the world's spirituality—and Mine—is weaker if not shared.

It is shared in many ways—in congregations, religious traditions, ethnicity that is imbued with religious feeling, in mores, and so forth. But a very important way is in the religious mission to save mankind, to bring all people to Me. To take the word to the nations is part of relating to Me.

In the Buddhist mode, this is reflected in the sacrificial life of the Bodhisattva. It is obviously relevant to Jesus as well. Love for Me, love for one's wife, family, friends, love for mankind, love for nature, for Being are all intimately related to one another.

The Bodhisattva's vow is sometimes described as world-redemptive. "What does that mean, Lord?"

Not like the Jewish repairing the world, as in the Kabbalistic text (the Zohar), which is repairing an ontological rift, but more like saving everyone from a burning building—getting each person out of the illusions of maya and into an enlightened state.

The Buddhist goal is Nirvana, pure emptiness.

The doctrine of the Void is without merit. Later elaborations of Buddhism that emphasize the illusory nature or nonreality of the world are metaphysical nonsense. They are not helpful; are indeed harmful. The world is quite real, even though it is not the most important thing, and there is more to it certainly than natural science or common sense reveals.

According to Heinrich Zimmer, "The Bodhisattva assumes the various forms in which he appears for the salvation of beings in the phenomenal realm. He assumes, for example, the divine forms of Vishnu for those who worship Vishnu and of Shiva for those who worship Shiva."

"Is this what You do, Lord, assume these forms?"

No, I am not to be confused with a Bodhisattva and the analogy is not right. I appear as Myself to everyone and they hear Me as best they can and express what they hear in whatever language (symbols and such) is available to them. But I certainly do not think,

"These folks believe in Santa Claus, so I will appear as Santa Claus to them." I would prefer that everyone see Me as I am and hear My message as I intend it.

"Buddha is called the Compassionate One, but You have said that Jesus is the essence of love."

Compassion is not the same thing as love. Don't rush to boil everything down to a single principle. Love is important, but so is compassion. No human being loves everyone, but can feel compassion—fellow-feeling—with all human suffering.

"What about Krishna and the Lord of Love of the Upanishads?"

The Lord of Love does not refer to an actual person, any more than Indra (and the other gods do). It is the Vedic (Upanishadic) version of My love for all mankind.

This is a problem for Hindu thought. The "Olympian" (Vedic) gods are mythic or legendary, and are not appropriate vehicles for My love, or (for) the love that is a force in the universe. The Brahman is abstract and generic and not a person.

Krishna, Vishnu, and the others, are the Indian efforts to capture the loving aspect of the divine reality, the personal. It is primarily persons who love. But Krishna is just a personification of Me.

"By the same token, couldn't it be said that the God of the Bible is just a personification of Krishna?"

No, I am Me. Tales about Krishna capture aspects of the divine reality, of Me, but they are in the class of legends or tales. There are no actual records of Krishna's talking to someone, for example.

"So the Bible is the only record of the real You?"

No, the Hindu scriptures capture other fundamental aspects of divine reality, of Me, mainly the nonpersonal aspects. Those aspects are not sources of love, except for the love that is a metaphysical reality in the universe.

"You have put Jesus at the top. He is the only one who is the ontological essence of love—love that continues today and is available to everyone who 'believes in him.'"

Yes, he has that special niche, but that is not to say that his role is more important than the other religions.

You relate to Me personally, and see the other revelations as glosses on that experience. But they could just as well see your relation to a personal God as a gloss on Brahman or Buddha or the Tao.

"Let's see if I understand that. The Hindu could say the Brahman is the fundamental reality and God is a manifestation of that divine reality. They already have avatars, which would fit Jesus, and he could be a unique avatar. Buddha is not providing an inventory of the divine reality, and his message would stand regardless of whether there is a God. If there are gods, they would need to become enlightened. The Taoist could say that one way to tune in to the Tao is to hear it as the voice of a divine Person, but it would be one who went with the flow, not much like the Old Testament God. We started with love, but I felt You wanted me to pray about the big picture."

You have been. But take a step back and look at it all—the whole story, My story.

"One part of the big picture is the revelation of various aspects of Your nature."

No, not that.

"Oh, You mean Your story, the story of Your development?"

Yes, that. What do you see?

"I see a God emerging, struggling, ordering, interacting with nature, animals, people, revealing Himself and aspects of divine reality to various peoples, each with their own particular concepts and types of receptivity."

And then . . .

"You are suffering through it all, out of love, and moving everything forward toward some unspecified purpose. Is that the gist, Lord?"

Back up again, (step) farther back, what do you see?

"An emerging God who orders and guides the world and urges humans along as partners in that effort."

Now step really far back.

"I see a God who goes from incarnation to incarnation, world to world, doing the same task (or whatever) in each . . . to whatever end."

Look at that.

"I don't know how to get a handle on that, Lord."

Look at the Hindus, also the Bodhisattvas, for an account.

"You are a kind of Bodhisattva?"

Yes.

"Lord, that answer seems to contradict what You told me before. (When answers seem to contradict each other, I include both.) Perhaps it is just an analogy or the context was different."

Yes.

Connection

The heart of reality is transformational

49

It is one thing to hear, or think you hear, the voice of God. It is another to encounter Jesus or at least his image. That also happened to me, very early, even before I was asked to be a "new Elijah" and "tell God's story."

As unusual an experience as it was, it did not actually feel strange. I was driving home from work, stopped at a red light, and a somewhat transparent image appeared beyond the windshield. It was the face of a man, thirtyish and, oddly enough, fair (shouldn't he have been darker?) and clean-shaven (shouldn't he have had a beard?). He had extraordinarily kind eyes. Somehow I seemed to know who he was. I asked (not out loud), "You are Jesus?"

Yes.

"You are God?"

Yes.

"You want something of me?"

I want you to believe in me.

I felt surrounded by the presence of love and asked, "What does that involve?"

Having faith in me.

"To do what?"

To heal, to touch, to save, to love.

He looked very sweet, almost feminine. "Are you androgynous?"

Yes, you might say so. I combine the elements of my Father and the elements of my divine Mother.

"Mary?"

No, my divine mother, the feminine aspect of the Godhead.

He would not have shown up, I thought, unless there was something he wanted of me. "Is there something you want me to do?"

Yes, I will tell you later. That's all for now. But I give you my healing grace.

When I got home, I asked God, "Lord, did You send Jesus to me?"

Yes.

"Why?"

Isn't it obvious? You need to know him. He can help you in your work and in your life. He is the pure embodiment of love, a great resource and treasure for mankind, for all who believe in him—including the Jews, if they will but make use of him.

They don't need to give up their Jewishness, their traditions, their historicity, to do this! Or their rejection of Christian and other persecutions or their honoring of those persecuted.

God seemed to be responding to my anxiety about upsetting my Jewish wife.

A few days later, Jesus appeared again. I guess I didn't recognize him because I asked, "Who are you?"

I am Jesus of Nazareth.

"Are you God?"

Yes.

"Are you the only one who's God?"

Yes.

"Why are you in this world?"

I have a face. You can see it. God is too distant. It leads to great misunderstandings. He cannot appear directly to people. I can.

"You said 'He' as if God were other."

He is both other and me. You need to revamp your concepts. They are not adequate to the facts.

"What else do you want to tell me?"

Keep looking at me. What do you see?

"You look soft, gentle, loving, slightly feminine."

Yes, I am love. I have a combined nature of God the Father and my Mother, the Healing Force of the Universe.

"You also look sad, a heavy look."

I carry many burdens and I care about those who suffer.

"Did the crucifixion hurt?"

Of course.

"Do you 'carry the suffering of the world'?"

Yes.

"What does that mean?"

Think about it. I suffer for all mankind. I carry the burden of the fallenness of the world, of its rending, its being torn. I would like to heal it, but I can't do it alone. I need your help, the help of all mankind.

"What caused 'the Fall'?"

Sin. Men and women are quite extraordinary, beautiful creatures. They reflect the glorious handiwork of God. And we love them deeply. But they are also terribly flawed. That was a disappointment. We did not realize the implications of their finitude—that these magnificent energies could lead them into such error and neglect of God. The will is both their strength and their weakness. The terrible force of sexuality is both God's greatest blessing and greatest curse, because it leads to such troubles.

The mending will lie in my erotic power, which is the power of union, the power to make whole, to create connections where they are now frayed. But it is not easy because people enjoy not being whole, not being healed and connected to God. They constantly work both toward and away from God. That is their privilege and their curse.

"How do you help?"

By love. I love mankind, as does my Father, but I love them visibly, in the flesh, as one human being to others. I have literally felt their pains, suffered their wounds, felt the sorrow of separation from them.

"Does that mean that people must 'believe in you' or they cannot be 'saved'?"

That is nonsense. They can believe in God and relate to Him directly, or indirectly in many ways. But they can get the benefit of my love only if they are open to it.

I knew I was not open to it. Jesus represented the maudlin, bloody, unconvincing Christ of my childhood. I had left that Jesus far behind and had no interest in returning. But when I prayed again to God, I was told,

Listen to Jesus. He can help you. Do not forget his abiding, healing presence. You need what he has to offer, radiant love. Talk to him now.

"Jesus, please give me your love, and Abigail and my family as well. What would you have of me, Jesus?"

Have peace in your soul. All will be revealed. Everything is unfolding according to God's plan. You are worried about me, about Abigail's reaction, but also from feelings lingering from your childhood. Do not be afraid. Abigail is a special friend of mine. She understands me as few do.

Abigail is Jewish, and loves the people of Israel and the Hebrew Bible, but also loves country gospel, the New Testament, and Jesus— not to mention Gandhi.

Your own childhood experience (of religion) was crude and fragmentary. Do not cling to it (in your rejection of it). Start anew in your understanding of me. Abigail will guide you. Talk to her about me.

I am no threat to Jews. I fulfill part of God's promise to them. The fact that my own followers have persecuted them is no sign of my lack of love of them. I am a Jew and their Messiah. It is all right with me if they do not accept that. I do not hold it against them. They are doing their best and they—the religious ones—are keeping their covenant with God. The others are no better—and a bit more fallen—than other secular people. They had more to lose, a precious gift they are throwing away. But my heart remains open, and after many wounds are healed, their hearts will open too.

Do not neglect my story as Messiah. It is a key part of the over-all picture you are being guided toward. There are many sources of inspiration, but I—my love—is central to them all.

Praying to God again, I asked, "Lord, what is the meaning of this emphasis on Jesus and on letting him into my heart?"

You can't write about his message and role without experiencing it, any more than you could have (written about) the Atman (without experiencing it). The task, this subject matter is transformational, not just a third-party look at the structure of the universe. The heart of reality is transformational, is the task of transformation—just as the eye is to see, the universe is to heal.

At this early stage, I was still uncomfortable with anything that sounded weird. "Lord, I am feeling resistant. How can I go about opening my heart?"

You know how. Relax and practice and give it time. Keep at it.

I turned to address Jesus. "Jesus—gosh, what I feel when I address you!—almost tearful. What would you suggest?"

Just relax. Remember that I am in your heart already.

Then I went back to God. "Lord, I feel my inner recesses opening up, as if my heart were building more conduits. My soul's inner arteries or membranes are filling up with Your spirit or love. Connecting with the Atman seems to take one out of oneself (a withdrawal) whereas Jesus' love brings something in: we have to flow into God and let God flow into us, East and West combined."

Yes.

50

Love is always the love of something incomplete

"Should I address you as 'Lord'?"

"Jesus" will do.

"Jesus, please come into my heart."

I am in your heart already. You just have to let yourself feel it.

"How do I do that, Lord?"

Sit and let down your defenses. You know how to do that.

"Yes, it's like relaxing a defensive stance, standing down."

Exactly.

"And letting the soft inner core of my personality, which is normally shielded, take you in."

Exactly.

"Jesus, the message of love is hard for me to take in. Well, love is hard for me to take in."

The more you take in my love, the more you'll understand my message.

Some days later, the face of Jesus appeared again, just looking at me. It was a bit unnerving.

"Why are you looking at me, Jesus?"

Don't you know?

"I feel scrutinized."

What is the meaning of that?

"I feel inspected, as if you are trying to see who I am, what I'm made of."

That's right.

"Why does looking help?"

How else would I see you?

"Okay, so you need to look at me, but why do I need to see your face?"

I *need for you to see* my *face.*

"I want to look away."

But you don't.

"No, I know I need you. God has told me so."

I am also God. But you haven't accepted that. I am going to keep looking at you until you see me, (until you) see me for Who I Am, God and the Son of God, as well as the Son of Man and Messiah of the people of Israel, of my people.

"Why does your presence seem threatening?"

Because you are afraid of me. You are still afraid of love—of full, unreserved, unremitting (unrelenting) love—love that knows all, demands all, conquers all. That is too much for you. You have trouble accepting it from Abigail. You have more trouble accepting it from me. You need to explore why you are blocking it. Why are you afraid of love?

I thought about that for a while. "Well, I do not feel worthy of love."

That is your mistake. Everyone is "worthy" of love. Love is not something to be earned or deserved. It comes to you in virtue of the kind of being you are, one of God's creatures. You feel you have secrets, that if God knew what was in your heart or your libido, He would not love you. But everything in you was put there by God. Nothing is shameful. (Feeling) that (shame) is a legacy from your childhood. You have no secrets and need none. Everything about you, even your sins, is blessed in my eyes.

In a sense, it is only sinners I love. I do not love people in spite of their sins but for them. It is their hurts, their wounds, their incompleteness that calls forth my love. Love, even the love of God, is always the love of something incomplete, something in the process of fulfillment, of moving to completion.

At the time, I thought he meant to say "love from God," but that was before I learned that God is also incomplete.

You do not have any desires that I have not myself felt. Remember that I took the sins of all on myself. That does not just mean carrying them; it means actually feeling them. I have personally felt all human sins.

"Still . . ."

Do not deny me the right to love you. Love yourself as I do, flaws and all, and you will serve me and our Father all the better. I love you, Jerry. That is a direct, personal love—not generic or abstract or empty—and I know all there is to know about you. And Abigail loves you almost as much as I do, and she is not blind to your "faults" either. Accept our love and become more whole, and better able to do Our Service.

I am looking at you, searching your face, for an invitation to let me into your heart. I will not stop until I succeed, and I will not stop then either.

Ponder this—take it all seriously. Nothing is more important to you. Nothing is more important to Us, and to Abigail.

I thought about all the things I might feel shame about—ego, sex, overeating, and so on—but of course God already knows all those things. Then it occurred to me. My shame is about being looked at. So, of course, Jesus is looking at me—with love. It is especially about being looked at when I am expressing feelings, even feelings of joy or pleasure.

Since birth, I have had a stain on my forehead, a reddish-purple birthmark, like Gorbachev's but much larger. A mark of Cain. Everyone could see at a glance what an unworthy creature I was. That makes me uncomfortable even to be seen. Laser treatments have lightened it but childhood feelings leave a deep imprint.

Meanwhile, Jesus' image had appeared. He kissed me on the lips as a parent might kiss a child, and it did not feel strange, as a male kiss usually would. At the same time, he put his hands on my cheeks and, with the kindest eyes I had ever seen, looked lovingly into my eyes. A warm, affectionate, forgiving smile spread across his lips.

"It's okay for me to feel what I feel, to be me, to be seen—and to be seen being me and feeling these feelings?"

Yes, it is. Indeed it is.

What needed to be opened was not so much the recesses of my heart as the very surface of my skin and the feelings that move just beneath the surface—to turn my face toward him and receive his loving glow, like letting the sun bathe and caress your face on a summer day.

His smiling eyes continued to look at me, tracing the surface of my skin, including the stain, and loving it all, his fingers touching the trickle of feelings just beneath the surface. He was almost making love to me.

51

I *expressed*
Myself in him

The incarnation is reincarnation. That thought came to me, either on my own or perhaps a hint from higher up. I had not yet read the Upanishads or had my own experience of the Self behind the self, but I wondered if the incarnation of God in Jesus could be understood by analogy with the relation of your soul to your personal existence. It was Jesus who responded, speaking of himself in the third person.

That's right. God's soul was in Jesus: Jesus was God in this life. Just like the reincarnated baby. God had to be born, grow up, learn things, and was actually bounded by life circumstances, biology, and so forth. He was "just a man," as much as your soul is in this life.

Then God put it to me this way,

I *expressed* Myself in him. Remember that I'm evolving. What problem did I need to solve? The people of Israel were not obeying. They did not understand Me. There was no explicit recognition that I suffer. They knew I loved them but it was abstract and remote (to them). It needed to be made concrete. I had spoken through the Prophets but they failed (were not heeded).

"Are You talking about the 'new covenant, not of letters but of spirit' announced by Paul [2 Corinthians 3:6]?"

Not a supercessionist Christianity . . .

Supercessionism is the view that the covenant under Christ annuls or supercedes the Mosaic covenant.

. . . (which is) a human invention, but a new step in My relation to man (people). I *expressed* Myself *in* Jesus. He was My medium.

In the sense that an artist works in a medium such as oils or marble.

Jesus brought the personal aspect of relating to Me to a new level of intensity, of intimacy, of inwardness, not the vague inwardness of mystic meditation, but the inner place where the individual and I could meet and talk and pray together. When he says, in so many words, "I am God," he is reminding everyone of their direct identity with Me, and "people know God through me" offers him as a personal intermediary. No, an intermediary is not necessary, but people find God fearsome or awesome or distant. In many times and cultures they expect to relate to God through priests and officials. They are hesitant, shy, feel they do not know how to proceed or how to talk to God.

So Jesus as a human being comes before them, affirming his own identity with God, and offering to have the same relation to them that he has to Me. He opens his heart wide and offers it as a thoroughfare to Me, removing many obstacles that indeed can include the laws and the priesthood and rituals, which can create distance as well as drawing people closer, and offering a direct relationship with him and through him (to those who) desire relationship with Me. He aims to be a pure medium or conduit, one hundred percent conductivity, and he nearly succeeds.

Leaving aside the elaborations of later centuries and institutions, think how few obstacles, how little clutter, Jesus puts between believers and himself, not even guilt and moral rules, just "believe in me."

We will not now go into how Christianity as an organized religion developed from these seeds. For many it was also a question of the survival of My message, of this special relationship. It needed missionaries, congregations, therefore episcopacies, and creeds (to stifle the craziness), and so on from there.

As Abigail and I looked forward to our first Valentine's Day together, I wanted to give her something meaningful. I asked for guidance.

Ask Mary.

I had had enough strange experiences for a lifetime, and with a deep sigh I thought to myself, "Here we go again," but, as usual, did what I was told. "Mary, what should I do about Valentine's Day?"

Immediately I felt Mary's full presence, a presence that filled me with joy.

This won't be surprising to Catholics perhaps, who have a strong sense of the presence of the Mother of God, but I was raised Baptist. We did not believe in praying to Mary. Nevertheless . . .

I was showered in a breathtakingly luminous joy. For some minutes, I could only sit back, enraptured. Then I started to bow down to her, but she cautioned,

Do not bow to me.

"Why not?"

I am only mortal, like you. One should not bow down to idols.

"But you are so powerful."

That is because I am human, and feminine. I touch you as a man (person) even more than Jesus does. I also have a better disposition.

Her presence was accompanied by a fragrance of perfume and flowers and the glow of soft lights in an array of pastels—and of joy. "What is that?"

That is the healing power of love. I am not pure love as Jesus is, but I am a simple, direct, uncomplicated source of love—and of divine light, which is refracted through me.

Then she was gone. I had forgotten to get an answer about Valentine's Day. So I asked one of the French ladies at Abigail's favorite dress shop for a recommendation. She said that Abigail had been admiring a piece of jewelry which, luckily, was within my modest price range. It turned out to be just the right present.

One day, as I sat down to pray, I heard the voice of Jesus:

I am always with you. I love all of you, even the things shameful to you. I loved you when you turned against God at the age of five. I anguished over that.

When I was five years old, my baby brother, only eighteen weeks old, died in a terrible accident. I had resented this upstart and then he died. The finger of guilt pointed at me.

"I felt guilty as charged, but I was too young to have any thoughts about God."

You had a simple, natural faith (and) relationship to God before. You felt terribly abandoned, betrayed.

My mother was overwhelmed with sorrow and cried every day for years. In her grief, she could not reach out to me. Emotionally, I was on my own.

That (emotional neglect) was more a key (to your turning away from God) than "murdering your brother." The shame resulted mainly from abandonment, from lack of standing. Feeling abandoned, you abandoned God out of resentment.

"But, Lord, I was just five years old."

You are not just a five-year-old. You are also a (an older) soul. The soul is always present. It is you but it is bounded (and) influenced in this life by your biology, circumstances, personality, and so forth. It is limited or inhibited in its role, (in its) response. But the soul is present, making decisions, shaping your experiences, from a very young age, perhaps six months. The soul does not bring specific memories from past lives but it brings life experience, the kind of knowledge or deepening or character development you have from living through something.

In these early days, I was still worried about giving up my job to pursue a very strange project called "telling God's story." "Jesus, I'm not asking you to second-guess God, but please give me your perspective on all this."

What would you want someone you loved to do? I know you can trust God's promise. He will keep his covenant with you. You must keep yours with Him. It will not always be easy. That is not the promise. But it will work out fine. You will never regret doing what He wants of you.

Since Jesus had said I could get help from others, and remembering that historian Paul Johnson prays to Jane Austen, I called on Martin Buber and was told,

The life of faith involves risk. You must leap over the chasm. This is not a journey you can take by easy steps. You

will have to stretch yourself to the breaking point. Faith
demands that. Spiritual insight demands it. Do not be
afraid of the Abyss. The Lord's hands will be underneath
you. You will not slip. This is an opportunity to put your
intellectual training to work in the most important way
imaginable. Do not shrink back. Do not delay.

I asked Mary.

All I can say is that you will have my support and succor.
Go forward and all will be well.

"God, I feel the most love from Mary."

**Yes, Mary has a very accessible feminine, maternal love that is
very healing for you. You should contact her more often and in a qui-
eter, more sustained way.**

"Would it be okay to do that now?"

Of course.

I was eating some walnuts at the time. Mary appeared:

You believe those walnuts love you, but not that I and others
do. You need to wean yourself from that dependence. It is a form of
maya, an illusion of love and care and goodness. Then focus on the
real thing. Let down your guard and just soak up the love, like lying
in the sun.

"I feel the presence of God in all His power and glory but, Lord,
I still don't feel the love."

Relax and drop your defenses. You will.

"I feel too shameful to be loved."

**Shame is a burden, an obstacle you have fallen in love with. You
nourish it and keep it alive. Let it go. Give it to Jesus.**

I "gave it" to Jesus, as best I could. "Thank you, Jesus." I tried to
envision myself as someone who loves me might see me.

No, you (still) don't get it. You have a beautiful soul. It is your
soul, the real Jerry Martin we love. The empirical Jerry Martin is
okay too and should not feel shame. But we really cheer for, root for,
your soul to win its chariot race of spiritual development.

So I go back into my soul, into that "inner nothing" I had visited before, that I subsequently understood as my Atman or something like it. From that vantage point, my shame seems superficial,

like some debris that floats by on an ocean current. The shame is no longer an obstacle. But can the "empty nothing"—as I experience the Self behind the self—be loved? Oddly, yes. It seems as if it is made of love, or made of the same stuff love is made of, so that love flows right in and fills it.

52

As soon as a person opens his or her soul, his or her past is "forgiven"

The life of Jesus is told in the Gospel of Mark. Long after my early encounters, I was told to ask him his side of the story. I took on the assignment like a reporter sent to interview a notable about his memoirs. Notebook and New Testament in hand, I went off to a little café in Doylestown, a longish walk from our home.

I started with the day Jesus was baptized (Mark 1:9-11): "In those days Jesus came from Nazareth of Galilee and was baptized by John in the Jordan. And just as he was coming up out of the water, he saw the heavens torn apart and the Spirit descending like a dove on him. And a voice came from heaven, 'You are my Son, the Beloved; with you I am well pleased.'"

I am an ordinary boy growing up. I was dutiful but, other than that, not very different from other boys. As I became a man, I was not explicitly in relationship with God, but I did seem to have an integrity, an inner peace though sometimes an outer storm, a sense of faithfulness without its having a clear object, a kind of nobility as others saw it. I seemed a bit on a different plane, above it all, not bothered by the little things.

I did not have a great interest in women, wine, and the other vices. I gave them a sideways glance, as one would at some slightly embarrassing oddity. I couldn't quite see why one would be so powerfully drawn to them.

I had been interested in the scriptures from an early age. It seemed obvious and matter of fact to me that they were the most important thing in the world. I did not see why others did not share my interest. I thought about them, not in an effort to be learned or pious, but just taking them seriously and trying to figure out what this or that saying or story meant, what its lessons might be.

I would sometimes talk about these things, and others would seem to find my comments interesting or even arresting. I didn't see why, since my interpretations were all, it seemed to me, simple and plain.

About the age of thirty, I guess—I was not a stickler for dates—I heard about the preaching of John. While I did not feel myself a great sinner, in the sense of giving in to the temptations of the flesh and so forth, I was acutely aware of my finitude as a human being, my limitations, and the need to be sanctified. Based on my readings of scripture, it seemed right to be baptized, to ask for grace and divine guidance, and to commit oneself to the Lord, to living rightly and obediently to Him.

It was a beautiful day, or so I remember it, and a crowd was there. John was a powerful preacher—his words were God's word set on fire—and he had the ability to reach each listener's heart. He certainly reached mine. He had a much stronger sense of divine voice than I had at the time, and it was an awakening for me. I guess you could say I was John's convert.

Because I did feel a seizure of the spirit—suddenly, the presence of God was palpably real to me, as if I were infused with His spirit, and I went forward to be baptized. John took one look at me and his eyes widened, and then a huge smile spread across his face, and he took me in hand, and baptized me in the waters, and said a prayer and thanked the Lord.

I did not see clouds parting, a dove, or any of that, but I felt an openness of soul unlike anything I had ever felt before. It was as if I was totally open, nothing closed or hidden or held back. I was an empty vessel being filled by the Lord. What previously had been ordinary virtues like integrity and honesty and openness became divinely tinged, divinely charged. What I am saying is that in one sense I did not change. A lot of the traits I became known for later I had always had. But after that day they were divinely charged. I don't know if God spoke or, if He did, whether His words were audible, but I felt His total love and support but also a divine charge, an assigned task or mission, to live my life from that day on for His purpose.

"What did you take that purpose to be?"

I did not know. I just remained open, and prayed more often and more fully, and tried to follow the guidance I felt I received.

"Did you feel up to the task or, like Moses, a bit inadequate to it?"

Well, I did not know what the task was, but no, that kind of question did not occur to me.

"Mark, in the very next verse, says 'the Spirit immediately drove [you] out into the wilderness,' where you were 'tempted by Satan.'"

Well, that is overly dramatic and conflates different events. I was not "driven" into the wilderness, but I prayed, and I often withdrew to pray and I guess people thought that was odd. I guess I was rather intense about it, and maybe that is why they say I was "driven."

I was not especially tempted. Temptations had never been very powerful with me. Others have added that because it made sense to them, but (it) was not part of my experience.

"John was arrested and you began proclaiming 'the good news of God,' and saying, 'The time is fulfilled, and the Kingdom of God has come near; repent, and believe in the good news.'"

Yes, John had been arrested, and it came to me that I should carry on his message. This was the same message that John had been preaching—about the Kingdom of God, and that the time was near, and the need for repentance. That is what he was preaching about the day I was baptized.

"It is such a puzzling phrase to many of us—'the Kingdom of God.'"

It shouldn't be puzzling. It is perfectly plain—isn't it? The Kingdom of God is the presence of God in your heart. That is the fulfillment of His promise to you. That is the greatest gift, the great-

est riches, the greatest reward. And of course it was and is at hand,
within easy—or perhaps not so easy—grasp.

But I don't mean merely that the spirit of God is always avail-
able, though that is true, but this was an unusual time in the history
of the world. The preparation had been made, the table had been
set, for the next step in God's revelation. This message built on two
thousand years of Jewish religious experience, and it was another
piece in the pattern of God's revelations to people around the world.

"What do you mean, the table had been set?"

The Jews had been taught obedience, and they had been chas-
tised by the Prophets when they failed of obedience. The idea that
the right relationship to God is based on placing obedience to God
above all else, above all worldly concerns, is the prerequisite.

"What happens once the right relationship is established?"

God's love comes flooding in. Obedience establishes the conduit
for receiving and being filled with God's love. That was my message,
that was John's message, that remains an important message today.

"And the part about repentance?"

You cannot receive God's love—you cannot have it flood your
soul—until you put aside other attachments. Love is a two-way
street. If all your desires are toward possessions and material things,
and pleasures of the flesh and of the ego, then you are closed to God.
Obey the Lord and you will be filled with His spirit. That is what
the Jews had learned. John and I were simply putting the exclama-
tion point on the sentence.

"Mark says you saw Simon and his brother casting a net into the
sea and said to them, 'Follow me and I will make you fish for people
[fishers of men].' And then you called other followers."

Yes, that is right. Don't pay too much attention to the chronol-
ogy in these accounts. Nobody was keeping track in those days. But
one of the things you do as a preacher is to recruit adherents, people
who can help spread the message—and help with the myriad tasks
involved in traveling around and preaching to large crowds.

"Why these particular individuals?"

They were ready and open and willing. They were called.

"Is being called something very special?"

In a sense, yes, but anyone who is sufficiently open is, in effect, called.

"Mark next says that you went to Capernaum and taught in the synagogue 'as one having authority.'"

Yes, I was a traveling rabbi and what you do is stop at each synagogue along the way and preach and teach and answer questions.

"But you taught with authority, 'not as the scribes'?"

Yes, I did teach "with authority," with a firm, direct sense of what the scriptures meant and what God's message was. I taught simply, honestly, and forthrightly, and people responded to that. The typical scribe or scriptural scholar tended to know the words but not the music and perhaps to be pedantic or show-offy.

"What about the story about the man with an unclean spirit, and you cast out the spirit?"

Yes, people are often infected with an evil side to their nature, as if something has taken hold of them, like Jung's "shadow self." It is possible to force a spiritual opening, to suddenly turn them, jerk them toward God, so that the evil side is drained, loses its power, and shrinks or withdraws.

"Next is the story about Simon's mother-in-law, who had a fever, and you 'took her by the hand and lifted her up' and 'the fever left her.'"

Yes, mind and body are interrelated, and some diseases have a spiritual cause, and I can heal those. Virtually all diseases have a mental or spiritual component, and the right relation to God can help heal those or make people better able to cope with them.

"Then people started bringing 'all who were sick or possessed' and you 'cured many' and 'cast out many demons.'"

Yes, of course. In a way, that interfered with my ministry, since my mission was not to heal the sick but to open people's souls. But it also helped the ministry since it spread my fame.

"In the second chapter, Mark tells about the incident where you say to a paralytic, 'Son, your sins are forgiven.' The scribes think: 'This is blasphemy! Who can forgive sins but God alone?' You are quoted as saying that indeed 'the Son of Man has authority on earth to forgive sins.'"

Yes, that is a true incident. The man was presented to me for healing, but I saw that he was troubled by his sins and his (feeling of) guilt, which is itself among the sins, and that this was the more important matter, so I told him that his sins were forgiven.

"Did that mean that you had the power to forgive sins?"

No, the rest of the story isn't quite right. I told him, correctly, his sins were forgiven. The model of forgiveness is not quite right. Past sins do not have to be "forgiven." They have to be released, lifted.

If you wrong a man (person), only he (or she) can forgive that wrong. One would think that if you break one of God's commandments, only God can forgive. But two factors modify this equation. First, as soon as a person opens his (or her) soul, his (or her) past is "forgiven." It doesn't have to wait for an act of God or a word from me. All I was doing was reporting the fact to this unfortunate man.

Second, sins are not so much wrong actions to be forgiven as conditions of the soul that have to be healed or mended. If you used to be a drunk, for example, no one—not even God—has to forgive you for that. If, having given up drink, you feel guilty about having once been a drunk, that guilty feeling is a sin and needs to be expiated.

Some are addicted to the crime-and-punishment model of sin, and of course they were and are offended by my attitude.

"There was a complaint about you and your disciples not fasting."

The complaint that I and my disciples did not always keep traditional religious restrictions is true. There are many ways to be obedient to God. We were being obedient. We were not flouting religious rules out of disrespect, but simply because they were not part of our worship or mission. Sometimes we were celebrating our fellowship, not to satisfy fleshly desires, but to enjoy and honor one another in the context of doing God's work. That is why I answered with the analogy of the bridegroom at a wedding.

According to Mark, Jesus says, "The wedding guests cannot fast while the bridegroom is with them, can they?" And then, "The days will come when the bridegroom is taken away from them, and then they will fast on that day."

The bit about not being with them later was enhanced after my death. The other quotes about new cloth in old garments and new wine in old wineskins are from other occasions. I would use these simple images to make different points at different times, but roughly the message was that forms of worship must be responsive to one's current contact with God.

"Next your disciples are accused of violating the Sabbath. After citing a biblical precedent, you make the striking statement, 'The sabbath was made for humankind, and not humankind for the sabbath,' and conclude with the overreaching claim that 'the Son of Man is lord even of the sabbath.'"

Read more about this term, "Son of Man," and then we can discuss it. Meanwhile, just keep it in mind that this is one way of saying, 'a person who is in attunement with God.' Respecting the sabbath may be one way of being in attunement with God, but it is not the only way.

"Chapter 3 begins with another apparent violation of the holy day. Here you looked at your critics 'with anger' and were 'grieved at their hardness of heart.' I find it disturbing when you display these very human emotions, some of which, such as anger, we expect a spiritual person to rise above."

Remember that anger is not always a vice. Appropriate anger is a virtue. And, yes, I was a human being and certainly felt sensations such as hunger and emotions such as anger.

"Mark 3:28-29 quotes you as saying that 'whoever blasphemes against the Holy Spirit can never have forgiveness but is guilty of an eternal sin.' You said that sins do not have to be 'forgiven' but perhaps sins against the Holy Spirit are sins that keep God at bay."

Yes, that is correct.

We are all
afraid to be better
than we are

53

This is a different Jesus than I had ever heard about—a normal kid growing up, just a bit unlike the other kids, then being "converted" by John and trodding the countryside teaching and preaching— remarkable in being so unremarkable, devoid of a celestial light show. Jesus's life is simple, straightforward, and human, whatever other dimensions it may have had.

I asked about an incident I found disturbing. "In Mark [3:31-35], your mother and brothers arrive and call for you. You respond, 'Who are my mother and my brothers?' And, looking at those around you, 'Here are my mother and my brothers! Whoever does the will of God is my brother and sister and mother.' Why do you disrespect your own family?"

There is a context here. My family had listened to the rumors that I had gone mad and had, basically, come to take me away. At that moment, they were listening to the crowd, not to God. And they were, in effect, rejecting—disowning—me, the me I had become. I had to affirm my primary attachment, which was to God and God's people.

"Mark 4 is also disturbing. You say your teaching is only for the select few, some kind of elite: 'To you has been given the secret [or mystery] of the Kingdom of God, but for those outside, every- thing comes in parables; in order that they may indeed listen, but not understand; so that they may not turn again and be forgiven.'" You don't want them to understand!"

My disciples had been like fertile soil. They had absorbed my message, had opened their hearts, and received the word and spirit of the Lord. They had been given the secret or mystery of the Kingdom of God. Unfortunately, those outside often listened with a closed heart or clouded mind and heard but did not understand. I was not keeping anything from them. The condition of their souls, their lack of attentiveness, weak effort, and so forth kept them from understanding.

"Okay, I see. The next passage [4:23] seems to say this very thing: 'Let anyone with ears to hear listen!'"

Yes, you cannot force people to listen, to understand, to open their hearts, to turn from the things of this world toward God. All one can do is to proclaim the message.

As you can see from 4:26, this is what the Kingdom of God is: it is the spiritual "ripe harvest" of the seeds planted by the messenger of God. And, beginning at 4:30, the Kingdom of God is likened to a mustard seed—from this the tiniest of seeds the greatest bush rises.

"But, again, in 4:34, Mark reports that Jesus spoke only in parables to the public but 'explained everything in private to his disciples.'"

That just means that advanced pupils get advanced lessons. You speak in simple generalizations in a freshman lecture class. You dissect, qualify, and criticize those same generalizations in a graduate course. That does not mean that you are keeping a secret from the freshmen.

"Mark 6:30-44 tells the story of the loaves and fishes: 'How many loaves have you?' 'Five, and two fish.' Jesus 'looked up to heaven, and blessed and broke the loaves, and gave them to his disciples to set before the people. . . . And all ate and were filled.'" This time I was answered, not by Jesus, but by God.

The message to you, Jerry, personally, is that you have enough loaves and fishes. Whatever you have I will multiply, and it will reach a great audience, and you will be amazed. Jesus was just a man. How

many "loaves and fishes" do you think he had, and yet I blessed him, and look at how many people he reached and reaches still.

"What are You telling me?"

Don't doubt yourself. Don't feel anxiety every time you take up My work.

Of course, I felt anxious! Talking with God still seemed really weird to me, and the task I was given seemed completely beyond my capacity. I had no scholarly background in religion. I was reading all these world scriptures for the first time or, in the case of Mark, the second time. True insights require years of study in the original languages.

Get it deep into your soul that you are My quill and I am the author. You do not need to bring anything to the table more than what you are. Just do what I say and you will be fine. Do not worry about the final product. It will take care of itself.

Well, I would just have to trust that, but I well knew that I could barely ask good questions.

"Lord, I have the sense that I should focus on Jesus' message of love—and let it into my own heart. I need to set aside my uneasy feelings with 'washed in the blood' and other echoes of my childhood. Is that right, Lord?"

Both points are correct. Also, listen to Jesus' human voice. At this point, also bracket our earlier prayers, which were contaminated in various ways.

Apparently, earlier prayers, perhaps because I didn't yet know what questions to ask or how to understand the answers, were less authoritative and should be understood in the context of later prayers. Then Jesus spoke to me:

Don't be so worried about all this. Don't be too wedded to the scripture. This is not exegesis that we're doing. You know what I am about, which is the healing power of love. You cannot mend the world without love. It is the force that holds things together. I am the embodiment of love. I know that sounds strange to you, but it just means that I have an unusual capacity for selfless love, care, kindness, tenderness, compassion.

Nevertheless, reading through the record of my life is a good way to tune in to who I am and to hear my voice accurately. Just don't get fixated on the words. It is not helpful for me to "correct" the scriptures. That is not what we are about.

So I went on. "In Chapter 5, Mark tells the bizarre story of a man who 'lived among the tombs,' howling night and day. You commanded the unclean spirits to come out. They went into the swine instead, who then 'rushed down the steep bank' and were 'drowned in the sea.' When folks saw the man returned to 'his right mind,' they were 'afraid' and 'begged' you to leave."

Yes, there is a deeper level here. People are comfortable living with evil, with sin. A genuinely good person has enormous power. He (or she) holds up a mirror to them, and they are afraid. We are all afraid to be better than we are. (This is) a major reason it is so difficult. To eat less, drink less, give up womanizing or ambition is threatening to the individual and also to those around him (or her). People don't want to be called to a higher standard. So they will avoid the good person or send them away.

"A sick woman touched your cloak and was instantly healed. You felt that 'power had gone forth' from you, and you said to her, 'Daughter, your faith has made you well.' This whole business of miracles—loaves and fishes, walking on water, calming the sea, and healing people—is disturbing to us moderns. Are we to take these things literally?"

Miracles are not well understood because they are not investigated. They are outside your scientific paradigms. They are simply dismissed, even when there are reputable witnesses. Miracles are frequent occurrences. They happen within the laws of nature, but those laws are not well understood currently. A more comprehensive science may evolve.

"Are the miracles to be taken literally?"

Of course. As I say, they are not all that unusual, though remarkable enough that people noticed the ones I performed. But "performed" isn't the right word. A miracle is not (normally) a feat. It simply happens in virtue of one's presence—the way some people make you feel better by their very presence.

"Are some of these stories about you exaggerated in subsequent retelling?"

Of course, that is what such a story is. These were iconic moments that were told and retold, and simplified and made more dramatic in the retelling.

"In Mark 5:43 and elsewhere, when you have performed a miracle, you mysteriously tell people not to tell anyone, as if you are hiding your identity as the Son of God."

That was not the point. I was not there to be a miracle-doer. That was not my message. The real reason people noted my miracles, which were not alone of their kind . . .

Historians say there were other well-known miracle-workers at the time.

. . . is that my presence moved them and, whether they understood my message or not, they sensed its importance and gravity. They felt my love. But when they came to tell others about me, they could not communicate those intangibles, so they told about the miracles, which were easy to tell and easy to listen to.

"As you teach in the synagogue, people start asking, 'Where did this man get all this?' and belittling you—'Is not this the carpenter?'—and 'they took offense at him.'"

Yes, people want to reject a higher understanding, so they attack the messenger, try to discredit him (or her). There is an inequality created between two people when one has wisdom that the other lacks, and the inferior person chafes and rejects the wisdom and its messenger. Think of Socrates and his fate.

54

By participating in him, they can participate in Me

"Mark 6 reports that you start sending out apostles."

Yes, I wanted to spread the good word, and they were by then equipped to do that.

"Why the precise instructions to take nothing with them, 'no bread, no bag, no money in their belts'?"

The reason is not poverty and self-denial. It is to define their role. If they had money and were buying themselves around, they would seem like paid proselytizers and as if they were putting themselves up as religious hierarchs of some kind. They were to relate to people as ordinary people, to focus on the message alone, and to find which people were receptive and accept their hospitality. That is a good teaching tool—called buy-in. You are giving them wisdom, creating the inequality, but they are giving you hospitality, restoring reciprocity. It allows a single-minded focus on the mission and the message.

"The Pharisees attacked your disciples for not following the traditional practice of washing hands before eating. In response, you cited Isaiah's condemnation of 'teaching human precepts as doctrines.'"

No, that didn't happen. I sometimes objected to people obeying rules but not being faithful to God, but the broad theme of faith versus rules or ritualistic conformity was not a major theme of mine. That was developed by my followers as a critique of those

Jews who did not follow me. They (those Jews) were wrong not to do so, but ritualism was not their reason for failing to do so. I did preach a radical message. But it was a radical message of love.

"Why would that disturb people?"

It was love predicated on a powerful direct relationship to God, which is the source or empowerment of all love.

"You challenged the idea that some foods are unclean: 'There is nothing outside a person that by going in can defile, but the things that come out are what defile.'"

Yes, that was a message. The Kingdom of God is the presence of non-ego-based love, which requires detachment from desires. Rules restricting eating can be a means to detachment, surrender or sacrifice to God, or they can become attachments of their own. The message is (to focus on) what is inside, the attunement of the soul to God.

"Your message seems a lot like the Prophets, and no more 'anti-Jewish' than they were."

The Prophets were tremendous critics of Jewish custom, and they had a strong sense of the inner dimension, the transcendent dimension, of religion. They are instructive.

"Mark 8 says that you taught the disciples that the Son of Man must 'undergo great suffering . . . and be killed, and after three days rise again.'"

No, (but) I did talk about suffering. Suffering is sacrifice. It is our gift to God. But connecting this with my death was (done) after my death. I did not say these things.

"Why the threat: 'Those who are ashamed of me and of my words . . . of them the Son of Man will also be ashamed when he comes in the glory'?"

It is not a threat, though it may have been heard that way. It was a fact like karma: Here are the consequences of your decisions. When the glory comes—when human beings are in union with God—you'll be left out.

"Are we talking about the end of time?"

No, we are talking about in each person's life, right now.

"But isn't everything moving toward some end-time?"

There is a teleology, but it doesn't work that way. Your notion of time is faulty.

"Why make things so personal? Is it because people need a concrete person to believe in?"

No, think about why it could be.

"Well, you could actually be God."

Bingo. To believe in me is to believe in God. It is a transitive relationship.

"Jesus, what does it mean to believe 'in' you? Is it belief in the proposition that you are God?"

Yes and No. It is a practice that may presuppose a proposition. The practice is something like yoga, self-denial, identity with God, putting away things of this world, and the like. The presupposition may be belief that I am God.

"But why should belief in you mean a set of practices—or put it the other way, why should a set of practices be expressed as 'believing in you'?"

Think of those cases where you achieve a mental attitude by focusing on something concrete.

"I was told by a black belt in karate that the only way you can drive your hand through a pile of bricks is by believing in your guru. What he does, you do."

Believe in my message, believe in me totally, and surrender yourself to me and my way, and you will be saved (and) have eternal life.

"Why put it in terms of 'eternal life'?"

What one wants is emancipation from the sufferings of this life—not Nirvana in my message, but a sense of transcending this life into something timeless and permanent, which is accurate—the Self beyond the self.

I was disturbed by two things here. First, it was jarring to hear Jesus talking about the Self beyond the self, even though it seemed consistent with other things I had been told. Second, it sounded like the bait and switch I had earlier accused God of—appearing to promise things He doesn't deliver. The next passage is a perfect example.

"You told a crowd that included your disciples, 'Truly I tell you, there are some standing here who will not taste death until they see that the Kingdom of God has come with power.' This sounds like a promise of immortal life here on earth."

No, they understood me, at least the ones to whom this remark was addressed, better than that. Anyone fully enlightened does not "taste death." Death is no evil for them. They understand the fullness of life.

"What about the ordinary folks? Surely they thought you were promising them they would not die but would live on."

They do live on.

"Only after dying—whether they believe in you or not."

I can communicate only as much as I can communicate. I cannot be responsible for what they cannot understand.

This comment seemed like a petulant excuse, blaming the audience for his misleading them. I wondered if my receptors had skipped to the wrong frequency.

"That sounds harsh and elitist."

No, each person understands the amount, and in the way, he or she is capable of. That is okay. That is how it is supposed to be. Hence, my message is heard on many different levels, in different ways, and with different imports and implications. There is nothing wrong with that. It is how life works.

"And it goes on through the challenges and limits of successive lives?"

Yes.

I wasn't sure if that was a sufficient explanation but I went on. "On a high mountain with Peter, James, and John, you were 'transfigured before them' and your clothes were 'dazzling white.' Isn't this just a metaphor for the light of God shining through you?"

Gurus, saints, and so forth, can do miraculous things. Do not feel you have to give a demythologized account. All these things are possible.

"Then what does 'transfigured' mean?"

It means something like 'translucent,' dazzling, transparent, light shining through as a finely spun bulb. It is a physical phenomenon—energy and power are emitted.

"What are you communicating?"

Go back to Mark 9:1.

"Some of you 'will not taste death until they see that the Kingdom of God has come with power.'" Here God answered,

I am saying, through Jesus, a very perfect transmitter on this
occasion, that in their lives, they will find the Kingdom of God, the
transfiguring experience of the Divine.

"But, Lord, why put it as if they are not going to die?"

Look at the language again.

"Well, yes, it just says this will happen during their lifetimes. But
it sounds as if the Kingdom of God is a Second Coming, apocalypse,
or something like that."

No, it doesn't. You are reading that in. The Kingdom of God is
the reception into the soul of God's presence. It occurs to people during this lifetime, not afterwards and not at the end of history. They,
those select individuals to whom he was speaking, understood this.

A crucial part of this communication is that I am using Jesus
both as the messenger—he is an Elijah—and (as) an exemplar—he
is God. He is God, and I am saying through him that they *can* be
"God" and that he *is* God, and by participating in him, they can participate in Me.

"Why just reach a handful in this remote corner of empire?"

I didn't just reach a handful.

"But there was only an audience of three—Peter, James, and
John."

I was not just "amazing" them but sending them (spiritual)
power (energy, breath). I was, through him, filling their spirits.

"Why not just do it directly instead of through him?"

They were too simple. There have been a few individuals who
are extremely sensitive and accurate receivers and receptacles for My
energy. Others are too obtuse, opaque. I can reach them only in
glimmers and inklings. Jesus, by the power of his presence, could
reach ordinary people—in part through miracles, in part through
what you might call charisma. Through him, I could say to them, "I
am your God. I am here for you. You too can receive Me just as you
can see Jesus is doing."

"Mark goes on to say, that 'there appeared to them'—to Peter, James, and John—'Elijah with Moses, who were talking with Jesus.' What were You communicating there? Did this happen?"

Yes, not just the image, but the souls of Elijah (and) Moses. They were important for giving the viewers the sanction of the tradition they understood.

"Were they actually talking with Jesus?"

Yes, you can talk to them too. Dead souls are always available.

"Some time after these prayers began, my brother, who died in infancy, came to me in a dream and told me he was sorry for any suffering his death had caused. If one credits this kind of experience, the universe must be very complex and certainly not what common sense or current science would expect."

Well, it is simple enough in its own way, but (it is) not familiar to you. The presence of Moses and Elijah also reaffirms for the audience the transcendence of death that is indeed part of the message.

"Mark 9:7 reports: 'Then a cloud overshadowed them, and from the cloud there came a voice, "This is my Son, the Beloved; listen to him!"' That fits with what You've told me."

Yes, I'm telling them to pay attention, he represents Me.

55

This is what theologians call grace

"Lord, there was a boy who had been possessed with a bad spirit since childhood. The disciples tried to cast it out and failed. Jesus is asked to do it 'if you are able.' Jesus responds, 'If you are able!—All things can be done for the one who believes.'"

Nothing is beyond what your loving Father will give you. All is possible. The most amazing things are possible.

"As the hymn says, 'only believe'?"

You need to have the right relationship to God. It is not a matter of superficial belief or attachment. It is a matter of being deeply in conformity with His will.

"*His* will? To whom am I speaking? It sounds like God, not Jesus, but You said '*His* will.'"

Yes, it is Me.

"Lord, are You saying that, for the person in tune with You, healings and so forth are possible?"

I am saying they are not beyond what I would want to give. Whether a certain event is possible (and) called for (fitting) is a more complex matter, but there is certainly no obstacle in physical laws or the like.

"The boy's father then cries out, 'I believe; help my unbelief,' which sounds self-contradictory."

He has prayed the right prayer. He has sought help for connecting with God. This is the most important thing. It is not as contradictory as it appears. He affirms his connection with God, but he knows it is tenuous, fragile, vulnerable, and so he asks that it be strengthened, secured.

Sometimes I was told that certain scriptures were inaccurate—not a surprise to a biblical scholar perhaps, but certainly not what I was taught growing up. It always made me nervous. One instance is in Mark 9. "Lord, Jesus tells his disciples that he would be 'betrayed into human hands, and they will kill him, and three days after being killed, he will rise again.'"

No, this was invented after his death.

Invented? This is a central part of the official story. But I prayed on.

"Next the disciples are arguing about who is greatest. Jesus takes a child into his arms and says, 'Whoever welcomes one such child in my name welcomes me, and whoever welcomes me welcomes not me but the one who sent me.'"

Yes, this is when Jesus is My full representative, is exemplary. He stands for Me. I am fully present in him. I am communicating My love and the path of salvation in a concrete human being. If they follow him, and fully take in his message, they *ipso facto* relate to Me, and are of the Kingdom of God, and transcend death.

"A disciple alerts Jesus that someone who is not a disciple is casting out demons 'in your name.' Jesus responds, 'Do not stop him; for no one who does a deed of power in my name will be able soon afterward to speak evil of me.' This seems to imply that you don't have to be an official follower of Jesus to be in connection with God."

Yes. Anyone who is acting selflessly out of a connection with Me is already in the Kingdom of God.

I grew up hearing about hell, but it is rarely mentioned in the New Testament. However, Jesus warns that anyone who "put a stumbling block" in front of those who "believe in me" would be better off severing their own hand or plucking out their own eye than being "thrown into hell, where the worm never dies, and the fire is never quenched."

"Lord, this talk about hell is pretty grim stuff."

A metaphor, like cutting your hand off. What is hell? It is suffering. What is a life of sin? It is suffering and a deeper wound than suffering—it is the torture of your soul.

"Plucking out your eye because it is better to enter the Kingdom of God . . ."

. . . of Selfless Love.

". . . with one eye than to go to hell with two? Why does Jesus always talk in parables? That makes it so hard to understand."

Parables are a training. You have to work to understand them, and this itself opens and develops the soul. Why does a psychotherapist not just give you the answers? Why doesn't the Socratic teacher?

"A man asks Jesus, 'What must I do to inherit eternal life?' He has kept the commandments all his life. Jesus says there is one more thing he needs to do, 'sell what you own and give the money to the poor.' The man is shocked and goes away grieving, 'for he had many possessions.'"

This was indeed a good man, who kept the law and lived morally and decently, and Jesus loves this, as I do. It is sincere and faithful and rises above selfishness. But it is not enough. One must detach from all desires, and this is the point of Jesus telling him to give away his wealth. The fact that the man is dejected shows that he is in fact attached to his possessions.

"Hearing how hard it all is, the people say to one another, 'Then who can be saved?' Jesus replies, 'For mortals it is impossible, but not for God. For God, all things are possible.'"

Yes, this is not a case where one pulls oneself up by one's boot straps. It can only be done by union with God. Union with God is both the end and the means. This is what later theologians call grace. Humans need to reach out to Me, but I also reach out to them. They need only to let themselves "fall into" My hands.

"Then Jesus tells James and John they will have to 'be baptized with the baptism that I am baptized with'—that they will have to go through the spiritual process Jesus has gone through—'for the Son of Man came not to be served but to serve, and to give his life a ransom for many.'"

Yes, and "to give his life a ransom for many" merely meant to devote his life to the enlightenment of others, like a Bodhisattva.

"Like a Bodhisattva?"

Yes, Jesus is a Bodhisattva.

56

Sins are not
debts to be "paid"

I did not note the context, but much later I was apparently contrasting the New Testament message of love with the Old Testament message of obedience, law, and judgment.

Can't you see already the trend?

I had been reading Isaiah, Jeremiah, and Daniel.

(The theme is) love, not just from a distant God but from one who is arriving.

"Is this about God's sovereignty?"

And, yes, the sovereignty of God, which is another way of saying the necessity of yielding to God, and that is the same as happiness.

"But the judgment and chastisement?"

It is love, passionate concern for the state of people's souls. Obedience (to My law) is one side of that coin. My loving grace and salvation is the other.

External obedience, commanded obedience is one step, but no one (no leader such as Moses) ever thought that was all. The crucial thing about obedience is circumcision of the body as symbolic yielding, yes, especially (of) one's erotic and creative power and assertive force; and of the mind or heart, in yielding to God His own. Hence sacrifice—not making oneself miserable but yielding to God a small portion of what is His own—requires, much like the East, overcoming one's desire and ego (desire for self-assertion and dominion) in order to yield up to God one's material resources and, ultimately, oneself.

"Is there a Christological aspect?"

You mean the role of Jesus? Isn't it obvious? He is the host. He is the one bringing the bountiful feast. He fully understands the joy of yielding to the Lord. He invites everyone to the feast, even the sinners, since they too can yield to the Lord and enjoy the bounty of God.

God's bounty is not a matter of winning (trophies) or bestowing blessings (wealth, safety, and the like). That is an overliteralization, though a natural one, since I am particularly by one's side when one is hard-pressed. But the blessing is the very presence of God—no, not that exactly, but the participation in the divine realm. This is the Kingdom of God. You understand, I trust, the joy and peace and sense of direction that this represents.

"But what about the claim that Jesus is the Son of God and is God incarnate?"

Don't you see that this does not matter? Jesus brings the message, in a very pure form. What more do you want?

"Well, the idea is that God came to earth, suffered like a human, and died for our sins—his sacrifice, in effect, paying our debts incurred by our sins."

Let's parse that. Why does God need to come to earth? God is already "on" earth and "is" earth and is "in" you and "is" you.

"But it could still be another important act for God to become a person in the flesh, couldn't it?"

Yes, sure, but what would that mean? That, of all creation, I was "especially" embodied in Jesus? Of all creation, I was "especially" ensouled in Jones? What would that do?

"Well, it would certainly bring You closer to mankind. The Old Testament God seemed distant."

No, He didn't. Where did you get that? Not from the Old Testament. I am all over the place—unfurling the heavens, talking to Noah, to Abraham and to Moses, to the Prophets and Job and Daniel. Do you think John the Baptist or Jesus thought I was distant? I am closer to you than you are to yourself. That is not just a figure of speech. It is literally true.

"But it is felt that God's becoming man is essential to His sharing our suffering and sacrificing Himself for our sins."

Then let's go on to parse the rest: first, that God "suffered like a human." I already suffer like a human. That is clear from the Old Testament story. That is why Genesis says I regretted ever having made the world. Do you imagine that I felt no pain at the betrayal of Adam and Eve, which stands for the betrayal of all mankind, that I did not suffer for the sins of Israel, whom I loved, (indeed) of every sinner, all of whom I love, of everyone cut off from Me, when I feel totally and fully—and without psychological mechanisms of repression—all their suffering? I suffer more than a human being can ever know; that is, My suffering is greater than a human can ever experience.

And the last part, namely, that I became human so I could "die to pay for everyone's sins." That doesn't even make sense. Sins are not debts to be "paid." They are a condition to be healed, rectified. The solution is not for Me or someone else to suffer or sacrifice or otherwise "pay" for them or "redeem" them. It is for each person to become more perfectly attuned to Me. There are many ways a person can do this—living uprightly, lovingly, even more intuitively and appreciatively, even, in a sense, more quietly. Some hear My voice clearly. Some walk with Me through all the travails of life. Others love their wives and husbands, and children and neighbors. Still others have a meditative or even aesthetic understanding of what life is all about, of the nature of the world. I am present in all these modes (of experience) and each one moves the individual, and his or her community, closer to Me.

So, no, the world does not need to be "saved" from sin—though people do a lot of sinning, of falling away in different ways, and they need a lot of "saving" in the sense of getting on the right track.

"So Jesus is not the 'Son of God' or 'God'?"

I didn't say that. You have a particular story about Jesus, God, and the people, and I have told you that (it) is not a very apt story.

You can't get to the truth by starting with some theological nos-
trums and trying to force divine reality into that box. This is true
not only of Christian theology but of others as well. The theological
phase of revelation is as often a setback as it is a breakthrough.

57

My love is itself the help

Get in tune with Me.
I quiet myself and try to tune in to God.
Don't you feel how I am reaching out to the world?
"Yes, with a kind of longing, a yearning."
Yes.
"But what kind of longing or yearning?"
Just sit still, and get in tune with Me.
"It feels very much like unrequited love—a love reaching out for the other person's good, but the person who so much needs that love is distant and unresponsive."
Yes. Now come into Me again.
"I'm having trouble, Lord, because I start thinking. The sense of yearning and of distance reminds me of the artist who creates an artwork, thereby stamping an object with the artist's own subjectivity, but since this subjectivity now has objective reality, it becomes an object independent of and standing over against the artist."
Yes, that is very apt. I *am* the world in some sense, and yet I "stand against" the world and face it and try to interact with it and redeem it.
I don't like hearing this. God sounds too distant, too alien, standing opposite the world. And you and I and all the people in it just seem like problems to be fixed—or redeemed like bad debts. I keep

wanting a Grand Swoon in which we and the Divine are entwined, something with more crescendo.

But it is not my role to tell God the answer. It is my job to be quiet and listen. So I pause and try to reconnect with God. Then an image comes to me.

"Lord, now I have a sense more like a mother bird with her little ones nestled in her bosom and surrounded by her wings. That sense is more nurturing, less distant—of God having given—and *still giving*—birth to the world . . ."

Yes!

". . . and still nurturing it within a womb or nest, and hovering over it and loving it and yet feeling that the world is now independent, self-preoccupied and rejecting of the love and help God provides."

Yes, that is getting close.

"Then Your story is the story of that birth process?"

Yes, but don't get too literal about your images. I am not just a big incubator. But the aspects of coming-to-be, of nurturing and guidance and drawing forth toward fuller realization, of My love and offering of help, and of independence and distance and rejection and being ignored, are all present.

"So Your story is the story of this coming-to-be of You and the world in tandem, and the central drama is Your love for a world that tends to reject or ignore You?"

No, that is not right at all. There is a drama inherent in the action of the world, the action within the world, the action of individuals and institutions and nations. That drama unfolds on its own. You (people) and I are participants in this flow of action, and it is up to us to meet it successfully. We are partners.

"But that seems like a very different story from the first sense I got of yearning, a kind of unfulfilled love."

No, they are part and parcel of the same story. The world is a world of action. That is the plane on which it is all decided. The world—all Being—moves forward, moves up or down, depending on action on that plane. My love is instrumental in helping creatures meet the challenges of that plane of action. It is not just that, out of

My love, I want to help them. My love is itself the help, but it has to be received in order to be effective. I can work through people, I can meet the challenges of action through people, I cannot do it alone. And people cannot do it alone. They cannot even have a decent life alone.

"That sounds as if action in this world unfolds entirely on its own, driven by our actions and only partly by Yours. I keep wanting to have God preside over destiny, not the other way around. I want a strong sense of Divine Providence."

No, you have to give that up. I do not write the script. We are all players trying to discover our lines. I have a very special role and it involves guiding the human players toward the right action.

"But we have never talked about any overall plan that must be enacted or challenge that has to be met."

No, those are not apt ideas. There is not a single trajectory of action or one big problem to be solved. The world of action consists of many actions, some of which are personal to oneself; others involve the people you love, family and friends; others larger institutions and entities such as nations. No one plan (arena of action) is more important than the others. It depends on the mission of each individual's life.

"Does each individual have a single, overall mission?"

No. Sometimes you can sum up the challenge of someone's life in a nutshell, but no, every day presents many challenges, and they must all be met. They are all important. I am a partner in meeting them.

"And so Your story—and the story of the world—is not an upward march through a necessary series of phases?"

No.

"It sounds as if we should not look for a grand design but focus on the particular ways You disclose Yourself, interact with people and nature, and give them love and guidance, and on how You have developed through these interactions."

Yes, that is My story. It is the story of how I have tried to help people move forward and meet the challenges of their lives, and how we are partners in that effort, and how I develop just as people do.

"But then there is no destiny, no Providence, no Divine Plan, no goal toward which it is all pointing?"

I didn't say that. But you have to give up your fixation on a means-end understanding, a goal-oriented outcome in time, like the finish line of a race. There is a purpose, a telos. Not every purpose is a finish line.

Worlds

I have done it many times in the eons of eternity

58

These messages had sent tremors through my worldview, but only once was I so upset I stopped praying. It was early but I have delayed mentioning it.

Reincarnation had first come up when I started reading Proust's *Remembrance of Things Past*. Later I was prompted to revisit that page. *Reincarnation* was underlined. The question came to me: "Lord, have *You* done this more than once?" Nervously, I added, "Please don't mislead me, Lord."

Yes. I have done it many times in the eons of eternity. By your categories, it is very strange—because, remember, time itself comes into being with My "creation." And it ends—not meaning merely the end of things but of time itself. And so one can barely time (or date) which of My emergences comes first.

Like an animal in a fight-or-flight moment, I froze. Then a deep breath and a search for a more acceptable answer. "Isn't there a level of divine awareness that stands above this process and endures?"

That is true.

Well, that's something. "Lord, does God at this level of awareness have a history? And, if not, does this level of God see the different divine emergences as a succession?" I was searching for a temporal framework.

Questions crowded into my mind. "Lord, are there two different beings, God and the God beyond God—or just different levels of the one God?"

Remember the word *reincarnation*. It is like the same person through different lives.

"Okay, the God to whom I pray is one of many reincarnations of the God beyond God. But, Lord, when we reincarnate, we stand above our different lives and observe them, right?"

In a sense, you do (your Self behind the self does). But My self-conscious level (God's Self behind the self) does not forget—though the emergent level (the God of any particular world), in a sense, does (forget). It is as if it is a different personality, beginning anew (in a newly created world).

"Is that why there are non-God-centered religions?" I was thinking the God beyond God might be like the impersonal Brahman.

Yes, it is complex, but it is connected.

The strangeness and disappointment of it all! Endless worlds, endless gods, the God of this world not the ultimate God. I paced around, slumped into a chair, got up, sat down, and complained. Have greater piety, I was told, this too is okay. But with potentially infinite eons, in endless cycles, we would never get anywhere. There could be no purpose to the world, to human life at all!

No, that there is more than one eon does not mean that we will not get anywhere, any more than the fact that there is more than one century on earth. There is a meaning to the whole and we will talk about that later.

How to find my bearings in this whirl of gods and worlds? My inner compass was spinning. I felt queasy like a bad carnival ride.

I took a walk to calm down, to get into the frame of a relaxed willingness to take in whatever I might be told. "Lord, You were talking about Your own multiple reincarnations." My notes record what happened next.

"At this point, I am carried to what feels like a beginning-of-the-world stage. It seems as if I am looking at an almost-void through the eyes of God or the God behind God. It seems that God has emotions—because there is a heavy, almost sad feeling to the scene."

That is right. . . . Keep looking.

I am taken back to the cosmogonic beginning. There is a feeling of great sadness, as if for a previous life and world, a burden of incalculable sadness, as if all the world's tears had gathered on one lowland plain, and a Dorian Gray–ish personality showing the gnarls of a misspent life.

By contrast, a newly created world offers a chance to do it better. While the God behind God seems distant, neutral, uninvolved, our God is saying, "Lord, please don't let me live that kind of life again. Protect me from those mistakes. Let me do it over, better. I'm sorry, so sorry." Then I see the emerging world of lights and sounds and colors and shapes. It is all a turmoil, lively, bright, and chaotic. Then the image fades.

"Lord, I hate this idea that You reincarnate."

That shouldn't worry you so much. Everything comes into being and passes away. Otherwise it wouldn't be alive. Didn't you already ask whether something—some kind of Self—survives My successive incarnations and the answer was Yes?

I know it is disturbing to you to think of your whole universe as merely one among many. In part, that is just egocentrism—the idea that humans have, even on an individual level, that "my" story must be "the" story. But also there is a perfectly good sense in which your story—(the story) of your life, of your world—is *the* story. Each one encapsulates the whole moral struggle for good versus evil, for completion of the world. In what way this is so will become clearer to you later. Think of war narratives where (for example) the tiny band at Burnside's bridge—I thought of Chamberlain's troops defending Little Round Top—enact the entire struggle by defending their spot of ground. The battle is not just the *result* of many individual struggles; it is *contained* in each. Each is a mirror, or replica, of the whole.

"Then there is a God behind God, something like an Atman?"

Yes, you could say that. I am not as much a divided self as you humans are. I enter the world fully even though I have to start over each time.

"I am comforted by the idea that there is an enduring Divine Self behind the reincarnations."

Good.

I felt better but not good enough. I had been told to "tell God's story"—bizarre assignment enough!—and God's story had burst through every dike protecting the believable from the unbelievable. I had reached my limit. I stopped praying.

If I am to have a presence in each world, I have to enter it again

59

I stopped praying but continued to read. It seems that ideas shocking to me are commonplace in other religious traditions. In *Myth and Symbols in Indian Art and Civilization*, Heinrich Zimmer tells the story of the Parade of the Ants.

To show he is the greatest of all the gods, Indra builds the most spectacular palace ever conceived. Shortly thereafter, a Brahmin boy, "radiant with the luster of wisdom," arrives at the sparkling palace. With a voice "as deep and soft as the slow thundering of auspicious rain clouds," the boy compliments Indra on this splendid edifice. "No Indra before you has ever succeeded in completing such a palace."

"No Indra before me? There have been other Indras?"

The holy boy explains, "Who will count the universes that have passed away, or the creations that have risen afresh? And who will search through the infinities of space to count the universes side by side, each containing its Brahma, its Vishnu, and its Shiva? Who will count the Indras in them all?"

As they talk, Indra and the boy notice ants, row upon row, marching in line and column across the palatial floor. The boy laughs. "Why did you laugh?" "Oh, I laughed because of the ants. Each was once an Indra."

That there have been countless worlds is not a new idea, even in the West. In the Renaissance, Giordano Bruno argued that, since God is completely actualized, He must create whatever He conceives.

Since God is infinite, and thus has an infinity of conceptions, He must create infinite worlds. Since each world needs salvation, there must be an infinite number of Christs, one for each world. When these ideas reached the Vatican, they—and their author—went up in flames.

The notion of multiple universes existing, perhaps in a parallel reality, has been given new life by the Many-Worlds Interpretation of quantum mechanics. Instead of saying, as the Copenhagen interpretation does, that subatomic particles have no location until observed, which is impossibly puzzling, some theorists prefer to say that all possible locations are real, but in different worlds—a *Back to the Future* cosmology.

In fact, God's reincarnation is consistent with other things I had been told—that at the creation, God too came into existence—with a mission much as a human being has. All along, I had mentioned the idea of a God beyond God, which I had seen in Tillich. It suggests that, behind the personal God of our experience, there is a more ultimate God, or dimension of God, that is the Ground of Being, the fundament of reality. Presumably, that would be the God who reincarnates. And if there is a Self behind the human self, there could be a God behind God—a kind of Atman of God.

After six months and a long sigh, I started praying again, and listened.

The world has existed many times, (there have been) many worlds. This idea (that I reincarnate), which seemed so bewildering to you at first, is quite obvious, once you accept that there are different worlds. If I am to have a presence in each world, I have to enter it again. But it is more than that. I am reborn—in a sense, I start all over again.

That is what I have described to you—or allowed you to co-experience—My rebirth, a "surprise" each time, and the slow dawning on Me of My situation.

The line went dead. "Lord, did You stop or did I lose the transmission?"

I quieted myself and tried to become receptive. "Lord, tell me what You want me to know."

There is a "moral" dimension to the coming into being and passing away of worlds.

"That is why I wondered about a sequence or progression."

Remember that I have told you that, with (multiple) lives, it is like an author who, having written a novel, now turns to poetry. It is not a linear development; it is more a matter of touching all the bases. The worlds are like that. Each world fills out a different destiny, a different scorecard, a different dance card.

"Are people—individuals—carried over from one world to another?"

Yes. Individuals have many lives, going back into many worlds. That enables them to fulfill their destinies.

"Destinies in relation to what? We don't even have one world with one God anymore. And the God beyond God sounds completely impersonal."

Not quite right.

"But You have always said You were a Person but also more than a Person. The latter aspect must be impersonal."

More than a Person is not the same as impersonal. The ultimate ground of My Being transcends the personal, but that can be a misleading point. It has to do more with what an ultimate ground is than with the nature of the particular being in question.

"I thought it meant that there is much more to You than the Person I experience."

That is also true. I manifest Myself to you in a limited way. Each particular manifestation is limited. You should never assume that this simple conversational Person is all there is to Me. I also light the stars and move the heavens, I generate matter and motion, I draw life forward toward its end, and many more things.

"What about the yogic path to spiritual liberation, becoming one with the Brahman by detaching from desires?"

Yes and No. Getting in touch with the you that is Me, with that highest level of yourself, is liberating. There is a kind of freedom that operates at that level, not found at lower levels. But immortality is not exactly the goal. Reincarnation goes on forever. There is not an end-point. My reincarnations will go on forever. There are an infinite number of combinations and permutations. They all have significance; none is redundant—any more than, if you were to live one life forever, individual moments and experiences would lose significance or be merely redundant.

So the goal is not to break the chain of reincarnation. It is to fulfill your spiritual destiny and, through that, the spiritual destiny of the world (and) of Me.

There are infinite
worlds to live

60

In the Hindu "trinity," Brahma is the Creator, Vishnu the Preserver, and Shiva, who represents Time and Fate, is the Destroyer. In one story, Shiva is disappointed the world he made is not perfect and goes into profound meditation to make it so. Brahma rebukes him.

When I was studying India, I asked, "Lord, what am I to understand about Shiva?"

Destruction is part of what the universe is about. Shiva's displeasure is at the imperfection of a world Shiva had wanted to make perfect. It was not a reasonable desire, as Brahma knew. The world cannot simply be *made* perfect in one fell swoop. It was a kind of pride that made Shiva think that all that was required was that he meditate in a pure state. He tried to make the world perfect by withdrawing from it. But the world can be made perfect only by engaging it. That means that, meanwhile, the world will contain imperfections and must be perishable—not only because they (things) perish due to their imperfections but also because imperfect things must be destroyed and replaced by something higher.

"Is that why You reincarnate?"

Yes, with each world, I have to reenter it. I am not perfect either and so I have to perish and be reborn.

"Lord, You once told me, 'When you achieve balance, there is no reason to be born again.' Is this true for You as well?"

No, there are infinite worlds to live.

"But then it's pointless."

No, the process itself is the point.

"Lord, I am getting the following picture: the Atman of God is One and, in some sense, exists outside particular worlds, of which there is a succession or multiplicity; and the Atman of God enters into each particular world as a personal God."

You seem to understand the Atman well—you have experienced it yourself—and the relation is similar to (that of) the transcendent (Atman) and the empirical self (in human beings). The Atman of God has qualities similar to the Atman of the self, or Soul—total awareness, but disinterested and wise and all-knowing, but concerned and loving and attuned. This is the God's-eye view you had when you felt it possible to survey all humanity and to love each individual personally.

"Why isn't the Atman of God sufficient in itself?"

That is just as it is for human Souls. It is in the nature of Soul (or Soul-stuff) that it must be incarnated to grow. It is, in a sense, nothing until it has been incarnated.

The Atman of God must be incarnated to be actualized and to develop. And, like human souls, it cannot develop fully in a single life. Part of this is just logical: God must actualize many possibilities; each world actualizes only one.

"Religious philosophies describe God as perfect and therefore needing no embodiment and no development."

You already know from your reading about the Platonic forms— (that there is a question) "why are they (the Forms) exemplified at all, since they are more perfect than the embodiments?" and (there is) the puzzle of why a perfect God would create a material (hence imperfect) world at all—that something is wrong with this assumption (that God is perfect).

In short, if Plato's forms and the Christian God are perfect and self-sufficient, why is there a world at all? What could possibly be the reason for a perfect being to create an imperfect world? The hypothesis of a perfect being fails to fit the fails to fit the fact of an imperfect world.

"God is perfect" is empty talk. It means nothing. It seems to (mean something), and it serves a purpose in piety, but it literally means nothing. The Atman of God must be actualized in an empirical God, the God of a particular world. And, just as a particular world is limited and has, of all the logical possibilities, just one set of characteristics and boundaries, so the God of a particular world has just one set of characteristics, just one personal history, just one set of triumphs and failures.

"God has failures?"

Of course, you know that already. It is obvious from the story of the God of Israel and also of Jesus. Less familiarly, it is obvious from the revelations about God in other religions, myths, and such. Only the metaphysicians claimed that God was "perfect."

"But isn't the Atman of God perfect?"

That doesn't make sense. The Atman of God is not fully actualized. It has not "yet" been embodied. It is neither perfect nor imperfect, except that it is certainly incomplete.

"Lord, is entering the world a sacrifice for You?"

Yes, I am in an eternal peace. Then I erupt into the world. As I described earlier, it is like stretching limbs sore from inaction. And then I have a series of tasks and challenges, uncertain in their definition and scope, and self-discovery and self-development.

"Lord, then is it also a sacrifice for each of us to be born?"

Yes, pursue that, because it is easier for you to understand.

"Between lives, I imagine we rest and review our previous lives, see what we still need to do, and then enter life to face a new challenge. Giving up the comfortable interlude to once again risk suffering and failure would be a sacrifice."

Not quite on target. Start with the notion of sacrifice.

"Lord, isn't the core meaning of sacrifice its etymological meaning, to make sacred, make holy, mark off for God, surrender to God?"

Yes, this last is it.

"How does entering the world involve surrendering to God? I don't know if this is You or me talking, Lord, but what I get is this: Entering the world is to begin to desire, and desire is essentially a craving for possession, or for acquiring experience for the self. It is inherently selfish in this sense. One enters the world of desire and yet must renounce it and give it up to God at the same time."

That is correct.

"But to enter the world is not automatically to surrender to God. We mainly do the selfish thing. How is entering the world itself a sacrifice?"

The motive for entering the world is itself sacrificial. We—humans and Me—do not enter the world to be selfish but to live surrendering lives, sacrificial lives.

"We enter the world of desire in order to consecrate it to God. To the extent that we fail to do that, we fail in our mission. Hence, we need to go back and try again. Is that right?"

Yes. Look back at the other (of Aurobindo's four) senses of "sacrifice."

I had read, in Sri Aurobindo's *Vedic Symbols* that there were four aspects of sacrifice: "The sacrifice was represented at once as a giving and worship, a battle and a journey." Entering the world is a (4) journey that involves (3) a battle with the forces of desire, and fighting this battle is (1) a gift to God and hence (2) an act of worship.

"I suppose, then, that evil and error are mainly ways of being taken over by desire."

It is more complicated than that, but correct as far as it goes.

"That is for human beings. For You, the purpose of entering the world of desire cannot be to surrender to God. You *are* God. Can You even have desires?"

Remember that I—the God of this world to whom you are speaking—am a mere incarnation of the Godhead, the Divine Reality. I enter what is indeed a world of desires, of feelings, of decisions, of personal growth, and I sanctify the world by entering it and surrendering all to the God beyond God.

"Is that a struggle for You?"

Yes. Don't you remember the revelations to Zoroaster? I too have a divided nature and can be pulled in different directions.

Still troubled by the idea of a divided or imperfect God, I asked, "But then, Lord, how can we trust, for example, the Ten Commandments? How could Moses trust You? How can I?"

I am moving the world forward, toward its proper end (telos). I am going (forward) and might not do everything right, but I am in fact surrendering Myself to the God beyond God.

"Aren't we guided by the telos as well? But You can't trust us."

Yes, (you are guided by the telos) but mainly via Me and participation in Me and My participation in you.

I am the God beyond God—the God that is not a Person (is more than a Person)—entered into the world. The only way to enter the world is through a concrete vehicle, and in this case, the concrete vehicle is God. I enter the world to save the world, and the way to save the world is to enter it as a finite being, subject to desire, in a world of other much more finite beings, subject much more vividly to desire. I orchestrate the whole saving mission.

To say that I have a divided nature merely means that the world is not (yet) perfect. Remember that, in a sense, I *am* the world, including all beings in it. If they are not perfect and in utter harmony with each other, then to that extent there is disorder, disharmony, evil, and so forth, in the world and therefore in Me.

But it is more pointed than that. *I* have a divided nature in that I have pushes and pulls *within* Me.

"Do You mean that You are tempted to be cruel or untruthful or selfish? About what?"

"Arbitrary" is a better word. To see My "darker side," look at the God of the Old Testament, at My anger, My resentment. The story of the Flood is not literally true but it represents exactly how I felt. I was deeply disappointed, felt betrayed, and lashed out. Much like humans, I learned from that experience to have greater patience and better to love humans in spite of their failings.

You can look also at the negative traits described by Zoroaster (and) in some of the Hindu legends, Greek gods, and elsewhere.

Back to your question about trusting Me. Do you think you can do better than to trust the incarnation of the God beyond God? What ideas and high ideals you have come from Me. Do you think you can do a better job on your own?

"This sounds like the reply to Job."

Yes. There is something immature in your reaction. Like a child who idealizes his (or her) parents, you have to project Me as perfect. Notice that that is far from the universal report about Me from spiritually attuned individuals, whether Zoroaster or the authors of the Old Testament or the Vedic seers.

"So You are suggesting that we are more like partners, both growing, than master and follower?"

Don't get carried away. Your teacher doesn't have to be perfect for you to study at his (or her) feet. Your minister or guru doesn't have to be perfect to guide your spiritual growth. Again, that is immature, childish thinking.

I am the Being who has inspired the world's great scriptures and moral codes. Isn't that enough? Does anyone think that the Ten Commandments is no good just because mankind has had additional moral insights since then? Isn't the "author" of the Ten Commandments and the Sermon on the Mount and the Bhagavad-Gita and the sayings of Buddha good enough? Yet none of those works is complete and perfect. Grow up.

"Well, it is still unsettling."

Think about it prospectively. There is a great evolution taking place in the universe that includes God, humans, all life, even physical matter—a great development toward what, for the moment, we can call perfection. I am, you might say, the spearhead of that movement, the orchestrator, the guiding spirit. Is that so bad a world to be part of? Is that not a God to be, as it were, proud of?

The Atman of God endures beyond different worlds

61

"So God also has an Atman?"

I have to reveal Myself as the Atman (of human beings) and that is the step to My discovery of My own Atman. It also enables a very intimate relationship to human beings.

"Does a person's Atman relate to Your Atman?"

Yes, part of My development is to incorporate or indwell in the four phases of the introjection of Being into reality: Atman of God → God → Atman of man → man. It draws Me into Nature in a very intimate and thorough, yet pure, way.

"Okay, I think I follow that, Lord."

(Then let's go) back to (the) Atman of God. Its function is similar. It is the God that endures beyond different worlds and different Gods.

"Lord, can I communicate directly with the Atman or Soul of God?"

You know already that this is a misplaced question. The Soul (Atman) of God is incarnated in Me. There are not two of us, only one.

"I think I see. My self is my Atman incarnated. You as God of this world are the incarnation of You as God beyond this world. Is that right, Lord?"

Basically correct.

"And the purpose of my Atman's incarnation and Your incarnation is similar?"

Analogous.

And so the big question, "Is my Atman identical to You as God of this world . . . ?"

And to God beyond God.

"Hmm. I don't know how to begin to think about that, Lord."

There is not a simple identity straight through. I indwell in your Atman and in you, but in different ways I indwell in all things. I say "in different ways" in part because different things have different capacities to receive Me. In a sense, it is like different expressive instruments—think Victrolas and CDs, or simple language and rich language. In part, things are expressive mediums for Me.

"Is my Atman somehow closer to You than my empirical self?"

Of course, it is a purer medium. But don't get any idea of indirectness, as though I were filtered (to you) through the (your) Atman. No, I relate with full intimacy to you as you experience yourself, not just (to) your Atman.

The next time I prayed, I was told not to ask questions, but to go into the Atman of God. I doubted I could do it, but I closed my eyes, withdrew into an inner peace, going deeper and deeper. Here are my notes about the experience.

Feels first like a dispassionate center, very quiet, sober, presiding over and surrounded by whirling masses like vast pinwheel shapes of rotating clouds or stars. Feel a quietly, slowly pulsing energy, not sure if it emanates from the divine Atman or if it is background noise from the worlds.

The divine Atman feels very impersonal, not like an inanimate thing or vegetable, but like a very impersonal person, not cold but without much texture or definition, no traits of personality, no emotional states other than sober seriousness, no love or striving or worry, caring only in the sense of being responsible and what we would call "professional." It doesn't feel fractured, doesn't seem to lack anything. It is a bit like a telos. I thought of Aristotle's Unmoved Mover.

"Lord"—I was speaking to the Atman of God, or God beyond God—"I have the sense that I should ask what You were and are before, behind, and beyond the God of this world."

That is correct. You know what it is like. I am the Atman of that God (of your world). That God is the phenomenal self of the Self (Atman) that lies behind. The Self (Atman) of God is calm, dispassionate, quiet, tranquil, serene, blissful . . .

"That description sounds like Buddha."

Yes, Buddha had reached the Atman to a profound degree. The two experiences are very similar, parallel.

Time unfolds out of the Atman of God. That is the sense in which God is eternal.

"Eternal rather than everlasting?"

That is not the question right now. (The Atman of God is) passionless, but (has) a kind of love, beneficence, benignity. From where I the Atman (of God) stand, I see this God (of your world), Myself, emerging, unfurling the new world. I smile like the parent of a newborn child. I know there is an adventure in store for the new God.

"Do I detect a world-weary feeling in You, Lord?"

Perhaps. I have been there, done that, seen it all before. World after world, never-ending, or so it seems.

"I gather that the God of this world has something like a karma. Do You have a karma, Lord (Atman of God)?"

Yes. My karma, if we call it that, has to do with unfurling world after world, God after God, and tracing their steps, following their progress, sharing their burdens and hopes and sufferings.

"So You go through all time spinning out one world after another, one God after another, and caring about them all."

Yes, though you have to remember that time is not what you suppose it to be. It would be just as accurate to say they are all happening simultaneously. This linear frame does not apply here.

"So You are the 'Mother of All Gods'?"

Well, I don't create them—any more than your Atman creates the empirical you. But I *am* them, and I stand behind them, and I exist apart from them, in a sense.

"Why do I need to know this?"

Because this is the ultimate story, the ultimate meaning of it all.

"It has to do with Your karma?"

Yes, in a sense. I have a project to complete.

"Is this project internal to You or external to You, that is, created by Your will or independent of Your will?"

Those terms are too anthropomorphic to work here. Remember that I am, in a sense, the ultimate reality. It is in the nature of reality that the world, the totality of worlds plus Me, is here for a purpose. There is a goal.

"What is the goal?"

The goal is completeness, connectedness, to create the many and to pull them back into the one.

"Something like the richness or plenitude of being?"

Well, that was a very particular concept elaborated by a particular philosopher (Plotinus and the Neoplatonists). Don't worry about that or other philosophical analogies. Just listen and be open to let what I am telling you mean what it means.

It has to do with complexity or texture. A real world is one with complexity, texture, denseness, particularity. There is no point just to an eternal Atman—by itself a simple, undifferentiated, unrelated point, difficult to distinguish from Nothingness (hence the Buddhist confusion). That would be an unfulfilled World—let Me use the capital for the totality of all worlds and all being and all non-being—as much as if the Creator had just created a single atom.

"I am confused. Who cares whether there is density and so forth? How can that possibly matter? I expect the point of the World to be, in some sense, moral. Is the point just metaphysical?" The contrast I had in mind was something like the difference between values and facts. I was asking whether the aim of the World is to achieve certain values or just a different set of factual characteristics.

The moral occurs within the metaphysical and is conditioned by it. The point of Reality is to produce a complex, integrated Whole, suffused with Spirit, reflecting a fully developed God.

"When You say God, do You mean the Atman of God or the God of a particular world?"

Both. Each God strives for wholeness in His (Its) world. I strive for wholeness in the totality of worlds, being, and nonbeing. Achieving that integration completes Me, completes My task.

"Will it be completed or does it just go on forever?"

Remember that time is not as you suppose it. You could reframe the question as whether there is a finite number of worlds or an infinite number. For each God, the task is finite and can be completed. For the totality of worlds, it is not finite, but simply gets richer and richer.

"Isn't that pointless then?"

How would that make it pointless?

"Well, it is like Sisyphus, rolling a stone up the slope, only to see it roll down again."

No, it is not the same stone. It is like a Beethoven who lives forever and writes one great symphony after another, never-ending.

"We like an ending to a story."

Sure, there are endings as long as you tell a bounded story. There is the story of one world. There is this and that story that could be told about multiple worlds. There are stories that could be told about all worlds in terms of direction and challenge, but not in terms of completeness. Can you not write a history of the United States, even though the story could go on forever?

"Yes, I guess there is a human need for a dramatic frame around characters, goals, action, and judgments."

Yes, and My story can be told within such a dramatic frame, but that story does not exhaust the totality of reality.

62

The simple principle
of the whole of reality

"Lord, I probably need to explore more what the Atman by itself is, what its mode of reality is."

Yes.

"I sense that the Atman yearns for reality, for embodiment."

Yes.

"So the Atman is a bit isolated and disconnected from the start?"

Yes.

"And then the reason for reincarnation should follow from that?"

Yes.

"Lord, it seems that the key question is: What is the Atman in itself such that it yearns for reality and embodiment?" Unfortunately, there was an interruption before I received a response.

The next time I prayed, I was again asked to enter into God. In the usual quiet, still way, I did my best to do so. I recorded the experience.

"I looked at God from the standpoint of the Atman of God. Saw God trying to communicate with human beings—whispering warnings, inspiring expressions (like cave paintings and poetry), prompting behavior and insights, coaching people for the sake of individual spiritual development, frustrated by 'deaf ears.' Also Himself growing and developing."

And I thought: This all implies that human history is the story of man's hearing or not hearing, heeding or not heeding God's voice. He is like a director of deaf actors in a play. The experience continued.

"From the perspective of the Atman of God, our God is thrashing about, in some sense bounded and limited by, and immersed in, the material changing world. What is the attitude of the Atman of God? Serene, quiet, motionless, dispassionate (but loving in some sense), benign, well-wishing, interested in a disinterested way. Does not feel identical with our God. More like the sense that God is His agent, His boxer in the fight, the one He has put his money on, almost a feeling of pity for God's frustrations."

Until now, God's story had been about the God we know in this world. It is a moral and spiritual drama in which we and God are the main characters, and God's interactions with us drive the action. Now there is a further dimension—the Atman of God, the God of all worlds.

Later, I asked, "Is the right question, why would the God beyond God enter/create the world?"

Yes.

"Haven't we answered that already, something about needing the true grit of material reality?"

No, that is not an answer to this question. The God beyond God enters/creates the world into order to find Himself, to define Himself, to discover Himself as a Person. This is analogous to why the Atman enters the world, "inhabits" a person or "projects" a person. There is an odd way in which, prior to that, or rather without that, God (and the Atman) is nothing. You know yourself the odd emptiness of the Atman.

"Like why a poet writes down a poem or a painter paints a picture—just being in the mind is not enough?"

Yes.

"But now I'm getting queasy. It sounds as if God needs a voyage of self-discovery and we are merely tools in that effort."

Think about what you are saying. "Tools"?

"Let me put it less plaintively. God enters the world to be real and to develop to some completeness. We are not merely a means to that completeness. Interacting with us is part of the end itself, like two lovers finding one another."

Exactly!

"Or like a mother raising children. It would be odd to say, oh, the children are merely tools for the mother to fulfill her motherhood. It is a mutual interaction and bond of affection through which both grow."

Yes.

"Is the world then just sort of made up, like the grounds set aside for paintball? I thought You said, in the context of reincarnation, that we enter the world because a task actually needs doing."

Worlds are more like necessary scripts, dramas that absolutely must be enacted.

This world is a necessary arena of action. Nothing happens unless God and you are real, that is, engaged with a real material world, and engaged with evil and limitations in that world.

This *is* the world that has come into being, and so we must be engaged with it, just as if you were born an Armenian in 1900, you would be engaged in a particular set of historical struggles connected with that people and that time.

It does not really make sense to say: "But couldn't I equally well have been born in a different time and place, and doesn't that fact make these struggles trivial or pointless?" That's like discounting the fact that you love your wife because you could have been born a woman or in a different century or as someone who did not like your wife. This world is the world of your struggle and of Mine. And we each have struggles in other worlds that are just as real and compelling—and necessary.

"Lord, I get the sense of the Atman of God, the God beyond God, being pulled into this world, into creating this world. The pull feels teleological, magnetic. Perhaps it is the force of love itself."

Yes!

"I thought of Tillich's description of love as calling one another into being."

Yes!

"Prior to Creation, God is drawn into the pregnant Nothingness . . ."

Yes.

". . . to make it into something."

Yes.

"In a way, this is so simple. God creates the world in order to love it and creates human beings as suitable objects of love or partners in love."

Yes, it is simple as well as complex. $E=MC^2$ is simple as well as complex. The "mechanics" are much more complex than you realize but the purpose is not so hard to state, and love about sums it up.

So the simple principle of the whole of reality is that God creates the world in order to love it and people as partners in that love. Like Einstein's formula, everything else must be understood in relation to that. Love is the sum and substance of it all. It is starkly simple.

"Then, Lord, the purpose of incarnation, of our entering the world, is to create the otherness that makes possible a person-to-person relation to God, not a merger relation."

Yes!

"So mysticism is precisely wrong, backward."

Don't get carried away.

63

The larger story is the totality of the individual stories

"What is the Atman of God up to?"

(It) contemplates it all (and) holds it (all) in a single sensorium.

"But what does It *do*?"

It doesn't *do*. It *is*. It is inactivity.

"But, Lord, I feel the Atman of God is up to something."

Indeed. Keep feeling for this.

"I get the feeling of benign shelter, as if the thrashing about of this world and of the God of this world needs a container to hold it together and everything is safely enveloped by the Atman of God."

Yes.

"The Atman of God also feels like the egg, the ultimate source of our God . . ."

Okay.

". . . as if the world-plus-God issues forth from the Atman of God."

Okay.

I thought I should address the Atman of God directly. "I am getting an image of Your life stretching over a long, long past—but the image is immediately dissolved, as if picturing it over time is not right, and of course that is what You have said. It seems that I am supposed to enter into this experience and yet I don't know how to do that."

Don't visualize. Get the feel of it.

"The feel is of both singularity and multiplicity, but much more of multiplicity than of singularity. It is Vishnu with his many arms."

Yes! That is the image. I am like a juggler, keeping all these lives going, and yet can't you feel the singularity behind it?

"Yes, it feels like a juggler who is so expert he can do it with his eyes closed. It also reminds me of Akhenaten's picture of the Aten, the God-sun with rays streaming out in all directions and little open hands at the end of each."

Yes, that is also an appropriate picture.

"Let me just see if I can get inside Your experience. It feels very different from God. With God, I always feel the vast expanse, power, energy, activity. With You, it is much more like a still point, a small compact being, like the circus impresario inside the three circles, with high wires, clowns, and such all around him."

Yes.

"I also get a sober, serious feel."

Okay.

"But different from the personal God, who seems almost in tears sometimes, painfully aware of His incompleteness. The Atman of God just feels serious, like an experienced professional calmly engaged in crisis management. Are these terms too personal?"

No, I am a Person, just as you are. But you have an Atman, and so does God. And the Atman does not have the full range of personal characteristics an empirical self has.

"Yes, the Atman of God seems quite dispassionate, like my own Atman, surveying the experienced sensations and desires, understanding them, even sympathetic with them, but not attached to them. Is there something You are trying to do, or are You just observing?"

This is the level of Being, where doing and being are not two separate acts. This—all that is going on with gods and in the worlds— is all Me. I "do" by "being" all this. Is the electron doing or being? Its activity is what it is. It is not one thing that then bestirs itself.

"And what You are doing is moving toward fulfillment, integration?"

Yes.

"Why is there a world at all? Why aren't You integrated from the beginning?"

There needs to be a world for there to be actuality. Imagine an Atman without an empirical self. Is that complete? Remember the need for complexity, density, texture, detail. (Otherwise, I would just be) an *empty* still point, like the pronoun *I* without the rest of the sentence, a hydrogen atom in a vacuum.

As a consequence, there needs to be a "process." There is no density without resistance, traction, friction. It is that grip that defines reality.

I asked the Atman of God, "Do You also have a story? Am I supposed to tell Your story, or just the story of the God of this world?"

They are the same story. Remember God *is* the Atman of God and vice versa. They are not two people (Persons), any more than you and your Atman are two different people. One is the self in the world and the other is the Self that stands behind the self in the world. The empirical self suffers pain and disappointment; the Atman does not, except in the sense that it is rooting for the empirical self.

"I think I see what You mean. The God of this world is, you might say, You in action, You embodied in a world, You at work mending the world."

Exactly. One reason I do not seem to have much personality is that (My) personality is embodied in the world. The personality of the earthly God is My personality in this world, like someone's personality as a judge on the bench, like people in roles and in action— that *is* them, although they can also stand back and observe and reflect on themselves and do not have to be in any of those roles at a given time.

"Well, I can see how the earthly God has a story, since the world certainly has a chronology. But standing outside all worlds, how can You have a story?"

The larger story is the totality of the individual stories. Just as for the parent of several children or the coach of several players, there is a combined story.

To Me, they (the worlds) are part of one story, the story of the universes becoming whole.

"Lord, I don't know how to think about all these worlds. I don't even know what to ask."

You don't have to ask anything. Just contemplate.

"I get the sense of the worlds themselves as being in torrential commotion."

That is right, because there is an ongoing struggle there.

"A struggle between good and evil?"

No, that oversimplifies. There are forces of integration and forces of disintegration. The latter are sometimes correctly called evil. These aspects of the world are constantly contending, and the world can unravel as easily as progress.

"How do You help?"

I am integration, I am the ratio, the measure, the order, not just in an ideal sense on paper or on the plane of Platonic Ideas, but I am present in the world, via the empirical God, as its order and integrating telos and motivation.

"And You are that for all the worlds?"

Yes.

Still, I thought, it is *our* God who has a story in *this* world, and that is the story that matters to you and me.

64 The aim of many lives is not to work off karmic debts

I needed to pause and pull together what I had been told. I told the story in the first person, as if it were God speaking. I started with Creation.

Out of a yawning silence, I wake up amidst an outward explosion, shake My head, as it were, to wake up. It's like throwing My arms and legs out millions of light-years in all directions, and I try to put order and calm into all this exploding stuff. And it seems I have the power to do so, and things get calmer.

I don't yet quite know that I am an I. Nothing is present to raise that question. I have a relation to the particles, but then life emerges, and I feel Myself growing, as if I have gone from being a machine, an ordered set of moving physical parts, to being an organism, a living, breathing, pulsating thing. I relate to the atoms, but much more to living things, nurturing them, enjoying them, "playing" with them, infusing them with a sense of purpose.

I become aware of teleology, something beyond just keeping everything running and in order. There is a drift to things, a sense of direction, in a sense inherent, but in another way outside, larger than any one thing, larger than all things combined.

I lead evolutionary life upward, so that creatures become more and more interesting, and interact with Me more substantially and intimately, and this is a delight to Me. At some point, I begin to discover in a self-conscious way that I am an I, a center of subjectivity, confronting things that, while in one way part of Me, in another way are not. They have an independence, and desires and purposes of their own.

Then human beings emerge, first protohumans, borderline humans—even they are fascinating and delightful and a huge step forward—and then humans as we know them. We look at each other eyeball-to-eyeball. I discover they are persons and I am a Person. The interaction is limited, first by a lack of language and of conceptual understanding. Yet they have a primitive sense of right and wrong, they have a spiritual side, they (some of them) listen to Me, they see Me in nature around them, and I draw them forward.

The story of Adam and Eve captures much of My early feelings about them—My envy—well, that was present even if it is not in the story—and My wanting playmates. I discovered that I cannot relate to human beings in that way. First, they are not just my playthings—as a child first thinks of a pet—they are persons on their own and must live their lives themselves. Second, I am too powerful and too different for simple friendship to be possible. Moreover, while the discovery that I am a Person and what that entails is dramatic and important, I have a much larger task as orchestrator of the universe.

My experience as a source of cosmic order began at the beginning but was not a fully self-conscious role until human beings started noticing it—the Indian Rta, the Chinese Tao, the Greek Dike, the Egyptian Maat.

How does polytheism come in here? In a sense, it is a throwback to ways in which early humans responded to My presence in nature and in natural forces. That is appropriate, but it misses the whole. If that were the only way people responded to Me, I never would have developed into the kind of God I am. The Babylonians added a sense of hierarchy.

I grew in a different way through interacting with the Chinese, for whom the sense of cosmic order was so fine-tuned that it implied a right human attitude and action proper to each situation in natural and social reality. I first taught this to the seers who cast the oracle bones. Everyone wanted to know things like "Will it rain?" but I taught them to ask a different question, "What is the situation?" and

"What is the action that befits a person like me in a situation like this?"

They were not focused on God as a Person, but on the natural order and what is fitting to it. Lao-Tzu saw that the proper inner attitude is the key. That allowed Me to rest inside a person with that attitude. We could relate to one another quite harmoniously, quietly, gently, undramatically. "Be still, and know that I am the Tao." Confucius brought the same spirit to the understanding of social relationships. And so I was able to actualize My nature as the social harmony within a group, as a kind of harmonic key or the center of gravity in a painting, a kind of action by inaction.

Buddha put a further addition on it: compassion. That is very central. Love is what holds the world together. I came to see that more and more. I am not just a source of cosmic order and of moral sensitivity. The heart, even of those, is love. They would be nothing without love and they are everything with it. Later Buddhist theologians added theoretical conundrums and dilemmas, but Buddha's message was simple and resonated with people.

At some point during the last paragraph or two, I felt it was no longer me doing the talking. It was the voice who was speaking. And I had a question. "Lord, I have been presenting this summary on Your behalf, speaking in the first person, but except for mythological figures, You have not interacted with people as God in the story so far."

That started with Abraham. It happened with others as well, but Abraham not only responded to Me as a Person, but was also obedient. I had always urged people to do one thing or not do another, but Abraham was the first to take My urging to be an order, and to be an order that must be obeyed. Before that, the divine order had been a natural balance or harmony, a hierarchy or the like, or a mythological force for good (or for punishment) in a hazardous world. Now I was the source of imperative commands, and I knew that this was right. When I tell someone to do something, if he (or she) does not do it, he (or she) is not "right with God," and that entails that he (or she) is not right with the universe, with the cosmic order, or with himself (or herself).

Moses was the same way, and understood that I am One God, and not just the God of his people, but of all peoples. Monotheism was a great step forward, not because polytheism is bad, but because it (monotheism) expresses another aspect of Me, and people relating to Me in those terms (as the One God of the whole world) brought it out in Me as well. I could be their God, and protect them to ensure the survival of this truth or insight, and so I gave them commandments, to a fault as they say, and made a covenant with them. Not a "bloodless" (emotionless) act. By then, we had a history together. They were not only My instrument, but I had an emotional investment in them. I loved them. I love everybody, but it is not a bland, generic love; it is particular and I had particular feelings and protectiveness for this people. And they often loved and obeyed Me. The history of ancient Israel is the history of the ups and downs of that relationship, and they succeeded in bringing the truth of monotheism and that God is a Person to the world.

"And Jesus?"

Well, Jesus was obviously the device for bringing that message to a larger world. The message came across in a more intimate form, and did not depend on being a member of the covenant to partake of it. People found it easier to relate to Jesus than to Me, and the idea that Jesus was Me brought to flesh helped to create that intimacy. But his message was not that he was God, but it was a message of love. He is the western Buddha, and Buddha is the eastern Jesus.

Zoroaster first understood the complexity of My nature. In fact he overdid it a bit. But he helped Me to see it as well. I am not blandly all-good. I am incomplete and developing. He was not unique in seeing this: look at the Greek gods, look at Indra, look at the harsh moments of the Old Testament God. He had a very direct revelation and articulated the insight with an absolute sharpness. The world is not all good. It has a lot of misfortune and evil in it. And I am not all-good—or, as he put it, there are two gods, one good and one evil, contending with each other. I am not exactly contending against My evil side, but I am incomplete, and I am running up against My limitations and that sometimes leads to perverse consequences. There was a value to the way Zoroaster put it. In the world, good does contend against evil, and evil against good. The world, he understood, is a battleground. And I am a party to those battles, and I need people to help Me.

From India, I learned another side of Myself. Long before Lao-Tzu had written about the inner attitude to the Tao, the seers who wrote the Upanishads had made a major discovery. They had succeeded in contacting Me through their inner selves. They had discovered the Self behind the self, and they had discovered—and I discovered, when they connected with Me in this way—that the Self behind the self, which they called the Atman, is Me, which they called the Brahman. "The Atman is the Brahman."

This was a revolutionary step in the human understanding of the divine reality, and it was a critical evolutionary step in My self-understanding. I had always whispered in man's inner ear. I had put thoughts in his (or her) mind, so that sometimes there was no difference between what he (a person) was thinking and what I was "thinking in his (or her) mind." And I knew that, in a sense, I am everything. But I am not everything in the same sense. I am Atman in a special sense. It is a very special point of identity between Me and a human being.

I think the following is still God speaking.

And I began to see the implications. Not only man has a Self behind the self, the Atman, so do I. There is an Atman of God. Man's Atman is, in a special sense, identical with Me. My Atman is, in a special sense, identical with a God beyond God. Notice that the Atman is the person—do not multiply entities here. But I am God incarnated in this world. And I realized that I am not only incarnated in this world, I am reincarnated in it. I—or the God beyond God who is incarnated in Me—has reincarnated in many worlds. I came to realize this and, in dialogue with Indian seers, I came to understand the full implications.

For some reason, the next paragraph talks about God in the third person, but it is still not me speaking.

The structure of life's purpose became clearer. It is not just following God's plan, as it had been to the ancient Israelites; it has a karmic structure. God's plan always sounded as if it might well be arbitrary, especially if God is assumed to have free will and to be omnipotent and the court of last resort.

[In fact, I was told on another occasion, By the way, this stuff about God's (absolute) freedom is for the birds. I don't have any more freedom than anyone else.]

But it (God's plan) has its own internal structure and logic. Actions have consequences. They have consequences not only in this life, but also in one's lives to come. Why should they not? We are talking essentially about moral consequences, and since the self is the incarnated version of the Self that carries on to another time and life, then that Self carries the karmic consequences into the next life.

But the aim of many lives is not to work off karmic debts from previous lives, but to meet the challenges of a variety of lives. That helps the individual grow. It helps the world develop. It helps God to grow.

One of the things you have to remember is that time is not what you think it is. The closest you have come to understanding it is the concept of the simultaneity of times. That is not really accurate—for one thing, it conceptually depends on the concept of time it is supposed to replace—but it is a good way to begin to shake up the linear thinking.

But life is lived on this empirical plane, where there is a struggle. This is where I engage in the struggle as well, as *The Thirteen Pet-alled Rose* [by Kabbalist Adin Steinsaltz] explains.

This was hard for the Indian seers to understand. They took a wrong turn at karma. They grew heady over the experience of meditation, of direct contact with Me through the Atman-Brahman identity, and they lost sight of the ground beneath their feet. They started to deny the reality of things, to view the sole purpose of life as being escape from it. In the process, they developed many valuable doctrines, including nonattachment. But they needed to be brought down to earth. I kept sending this message to them but they had trouble accepting it. Enough heard that it is reflected in the Mahabharata. Pure saintliness gets Yudi in trouble. Portrayed there are the dilemmas of action. They apply to Me just as much as they did to Yudi. One is genuinely compromised by the necessities of action, but that does not lessen its necessity. Managing that is one of the tasks of human and divine life.

That's the basic story.

Victory

The victory is now and the struggle is now

65

In one of the prayers about Creation, I had been told,

It is not quite right to say that I "always" existed. I did come into being, and before Me, there was only Nothing, and there is a sense in which I was present in the Nothing. There was no time, in the usual sense, then—there was no matter, no energy, no events.

"Lord, the simultaneity of times would make this all very different. God emerged out of Nothing, but the time of that emergence is, in some sense, simultaneous with now. If so, God is emerging *right now*."

Exactly! Now you're on the right track.

"And Nothing would also be simultaneously present at the 'same' time as now, that is, at all times. If so, Nothingness would represent a permanent possibility of annihilation."

You're on the right track.

"Lord, I feel I am supposed to pray about the really big context."

Yes, that's right. There is a much larger picture. . . .

"I get an image of that 'pregnant Nothingness' and the sense that everything springs from that and returns to it."

Now set aside the time aspect of that.

Okay, I was supposed to picture it without the passage of time. "Lord, I get two different images: first, a static image of everything in a timeless realm of essences."

No.

"Second, a simultaneity of times—that everything is *happening* but at the same time, at a simultaneous moment."

Now take that to all times and all universes and all gods.

Well, I didn't know how to do that, so I tried a different tack. "Lord, I read again the prayers about Zoroaster and Your double-sidedness. Maybe that is relevant here."

Yes! The Whole, God and All beyond God, Being itself, is double-sided. This means different things at different levels of being—for the atom it is one thing, for a human another, a god different yet, and the God beyond God still different.

"So we experience it in human beings as good and evil, incompleteness, and so forth. And we understand God's divided nature on that analogy. Is that right?"

Yes, that is fine, but there is a bigger picture.

"Are You talking about being and nonbeing?"

Just listen. It is more like a fault line, a place where tectonic plates rub together, a point or line of friction. It is fought out in every world and at every level.

"I take it one side is good and the other bad, or if these concepts are too anthropomorphic, that it is important that a certain side win?"

Winning is even more anthropomorphic. No, the tension stays and goes on and, in the simultaneity of times, is fought "all the time."

"Well, is it in some ways like good versus evil, order versus disorder?"

Good versus evil is more apt because it is not just the challenge of entropy or disorganization.

"I get the sense of a deep inner blockage, as if something needs to come out or possibly be dissolved, but it is very difficult to dislodge or bring to fruition—I'm not sure which image is more apt. Oh, yes, Lord, it is like labor pains."

Exactly!

"But labor pains are not about good versus evil."

We won't worry now whether they are or are not. You are right

that something is aborning and it is blocked by obstacles in the world.

"In all the worlds?"

Yes—to Me, all the worlds is the (total) World.

"It feels as if You are trying to bring something out of all these worlds. But I also sense that You succeed—simultaneously with the struggle."

Yes, that is exactly right. That is why your inadequate time sense (inadequate concept of time) has been such an obstacle. The struggle is happening right now, yesterday's and tomorrow's struggles are happening right now—and the final victory is happening right now.

"The Kingdom of God is here now?"

Exactly.

"Is there some way for us to get in touch with that 'final victory' level or dimension?"

Yes! That is also Me. You access it through Me.

"Is it important that we relate to the level of being (if that is the right way to put it) on which the final victory occurs? Does our relating to the victory level contribute somehow to 'winning the struggle'?"

Yes, oddly enough, the victory is now and the struggle is now, and yet the victory depends on the "outcome" of the struggle.

So our usual ideas about time are inadequate. There is some sense in which all times are present "now." How to understand such a concept? Then I received an image. It was like God looking down at an infinite stack of transparent snapshots, each taken a second apart from the previous one, the most recent on top. Somehow God, looking down, can see right through them all and thereby see all times simultaneously. "Lord, instead of a horizontal image of moments being lined up, left to right in a historical timeline, this is a vertical image."

Yes!

Then it occurred to me: teleology is vertical. The aim or meaning of the moments of our lives is evident in their *vertical* dimension, simultaneous in their relation to God. God looks down, while the moments of our lives, *in their meaning*, face upward toward God.

Yes!

"I sense that it is not that things are 'drawn' upward."

That's correct.

"It is more that they all 'point' upward, toward the top—not the top in the sense of the most recent snapshot, but top in the sense of the meaning of the whole stack as seen from above, from God's vantage point."

That's better.

"As if each moment or event is reaching, as if with arms outstretched, toward the top, toward God?"

Yes.

"But it's not actually to *merge* upward but just to be *fulfilled* by that connection to the top?"

Yes.

"But it seems more as if each moment actually *has* its fulfillment up top, in the Godward direction of the whole stack of moments, rather than its having to *connect* to the top."

Yes, the connection is by an aspiration from below.

"You mean the moments below get fulfilled by their relation to or drawing in or exemplifying the top?"

Yes.

"Reaching for or turning toward the top?"

Yes.

"Actually reaching, arriving, merging with the top?"

No.

"So, Lord, I don't have to actually 'reach' God? I, in this moment, just have to let myself be 'fulfilled' by God? Or to live completely in terms of fulfillment by God?"

Yes, that's better.

That made me think of St. Thérèse of Lisieux, the Little Flower. "I believe that if a little flower could speak," she said, "it would tell very simply and fully all that God had done for it." She described herself as only a tiny thimble of faith, but one filled to the brim.

"Lord, would St. Thérèse's little thimble of faith be an example?"

Yes, perfect.

"It's as if the challenge isn't to connect two different beings, a person and God, much less to merge. It is just somehow to realize or 'take in' the fullness. Fulfillment has a normative or qualitative pull, as a turning toward God."

Yes.

"It's like a plant flowering as it basks in the sunlight. Its fulfillment is down here, not in actually reaching the sun."

Yes. Exactly. The fulfillment is on the earthly plane. Now look at Jesus again with this in mind.

Yes,
(the Kingdom of God
is already present)

66

How does Jesus talk about fulfillment? He speaks of the Kingdom of God. The great New Testament scholar J. P. Meier, explores the relevant texts in volume 2 of *A Marginal Jew: Rethinking the Historical Jesus*. While the term sounds static and territorial, he says, it is actually dynamic. It means reign, rule, or kingship—"the dynamic notion of God powerfully ruling over his creation, over his people, and over history." The term does not so much define a concept as tell a story, one that "stretches from the first page of the Bible to its last" and teaches that "God as Creator has ruled, is ruling, and always will rule over his creation, be it obedient or rebellious."

According to Meier, an important moment in God's story is "(Deutero-)Isaiah's rethinking of God's kingly rule in terms of forgiving love" which "resonates in the message and activity of Jesus." He cites Isaiah 43:1, 3-5.

> Do not fear, for I have redeemed you;
> I have called you by name, you are mine. . . .
> For I am the Lord your God,
> The Holy One of Israel, your Savior. . . .
> Because you are precious in my sight,
> And honored, and I love you. . . .
> Do not fear, for I am with you.

The message of Jesus is quintessentially stated in the Lord's Prayer. The shorter version (Luke 11:2-4) begins:

> Father,
> Hallowed be your name,
> Your kingdom come.

When the petitioner prays, "Hallowed be your name," what is being asked for? The key, says Meier, is that "God sanctifies his name by manifesting himself." The prayer asks God to manifest Himself in His kingly power.

"Your kingdom come" relates to Zechariah 14:5-9, where "the promise that Yahweh [the Lord] will come is closely connected with the eschatological battle against all the hostile nations gathered against Jerusalem." Zechariah writes that, after winning the battle, "Yahweh will become king over all the earth. On that day Yahweh will be one and his name [will be] one." Thus, the meaning of the first half of the Lord's Prayer is: "Father, reveal Yourself in all Your power and glory [= hallowed be Your name] by coming to rule as king [= Your kingdom come]." This request implies that "in some sense" God is "not yet fully ruling as king." This fits Jewish scholar Jon Levenson's understanding of the Old Testament: God is holding back forces of chaos that continue to resist His rule.

According to Meier, Jesus goes a step beyond the tradition when he links God as king with God as father. Both are positions of authority, but one is distant and fearsome, the other is intimate and loving. Jesus' use of the term *abba*, which has the intimate feel of a word like *papa*, is without precedent in Jewish practice. "Measureless divine might, about to explode in the final act of human history," says Meier, "is accessible even now in prayer by those who enjoy intimacy with the divine king, who is also their loving father."

There are three requests in the Lord's Prayer: Give us this day our daily bread, forgive us our sins, and lead us not into temptation. The bread petition resonates with the eschatological banquet—the great feast that celebrates the Lord's final triumph. In the Jewish apocalyptic tradition, the slain Leviathan (representing Chaos) is to be served to all the faithful. For Jesus and his disciplines, it was acted out in the table fellowship, the most famous instance of which is the Last Supper. The prayer asks that this final celebration be given "this day," right now.

Meier discusses the Beatitudes and considers the most authentic version to be what is called the Q version, a presumably lost text that appears to have been known to Matthew and Luke but not to Mark. The earliest form was probably a simple triad.

> Happy are the poor, for theirs is the kingdom of heaven.
> Happy are the mourners, for they shall be comforted.
> Happy are the hungry, for they shall be satisfied.

At this point, I paused to pray. "Lord, these three verses are all in the present tense. The poor, the mourners, the hungry *are* happy. This sounds like a celebration of current fulfillment—of fulfillment right now."

Yes!

On the question of when the Kingdom of God will arrive, Meier finds "a notable absence of phrases" saying that the Kingdom of God is imminent. One of the few is Mark 9:1. "Amen I say to you that there are some of those standing here who shall not taste death until they see the Kingdom of God (having) come to power."

"Lord, this fits with what You have told me. Given the simultaneity of times, and the nature of fulfillment as an orientation to God, the final victory—the Kingdom of God—would be present to all those who turn their souls upward toward God. Is that right, Lord?"

Yes.

Meier goes on to discuss "whether Jesus viewed this final arrival of God's kingdom as purely future or whether he also claimed that in some way the Kingdom of God had already arrived—however partially and symbolically—in his own words and actions." Reviewing the present/future conflict, he reports that scholars such as C. H. Dodd and Marcus J. Borg reject the idea that the parables of the Kingdom of God refer to the future. E. P. Sanders and others place the Kingdom of God entirely in the future. But it might not be a question of either-or.

In Matthew 11, John the Baptist asks, "Are you the one who is to come [literally, the coming one] or should we wait for someone else?" Jesus does not reply directly but suggestively points to the public record of his miracles—preparing us, Meier says, "for the insight that this is how God's kingly rule of Israel in the end time operates concretely and is experienced right now, through the ministry of Jesus."

Then occurs an extraordinary statement (Matthew 11:11): "There has not arisen among those born of women one greater than John; but the least in the Kingdom of God is greater than he." It is not Jesus who is said to be greater than John, but *anyone* who is in the Kingdom of God, anyone, as Meier explains, "already in the new, eschatological state of affairs, the new type of existence made possible by the Kingdom of God." Moreover, "the least" is "not simply promised a kingdom that will arrive at some future date. He exists in the Kingdom now as he experiences the power of God transforming his life."

For Jesus, "human beings were not basically neutral territories," says Meier. Rather, "human existence was seen as a battlefield dominated by . . . God or Satan." Each person had to choose "which 'field of force' would dominate his or her life, i.e., which force he or she would choose to side with." Neutrality was not a possibility.

Asked by the Pharisees when the Kingdom of God is coming (Luke 17:20-21), Jesus answers, "The Kingdom of God is not coming with (close) observation. Nor will they say, 'Behold here or there.' For behold, the Kingdom of God is in your midst." Since Jesus is addressing his adversaries, the Pharisees, the point seems to be that the Kingdom of God is even in their midst.

"Lord, this seems consistent with what I have received. The Kingdom of God is right here, everywhere, now."

Yes.

"Since *entos* ("in your midst") can also be translated "within," many interpreters prefer an interiorization or spiritualization of the Kingdom of God. But, Lord, in light of what I have received, it is not just an interior phenomenon. It is the whole of life and action."

Yes!

Mark (1:15) reports that, after John the Baptist was put into prison by Herod Antipas, Jesus said that "the Kingdom of God has drawn near." This is a statement in the perfect tense, denoting an action that has both occurred and continues to occur, like saying of a train pulling into the station, "The train is arriving."

Jesus is criticized, in Mark 2:18-19, because his disciples are not fasting. He replies, "Can the wedding guests fast when the bridegroom is with them?" Meier explains that, in early Judaism, fasting was prohibited on certain holy days, such as days of joy and celebration. "Jesus says, in effect, this is a time of celebration, since the Kingdom of God is with you now!"

Yes, My reign is the presence of My authoritative love. And it is present already, and all of nature knows it. You just have to open your eyes and open your heart.

"Jesus' admonition to 'keep awake; for you do not know when the time is' seems to portend the near future."

No, that's a mistake or misunderstanding. "Keep awake" stresses the urgency of attunement to God. "Don't know the time" is not right. Every time is *the* time.

It is the pivot on which turns the fulfillment of the world

67

"Meier likens the Kingdom of God to a field of force."

Yes, that is good (apt).

"I thought You said it had to do with divine presence."

(It is) presence of a particular kind, the presence of divine authority.

"I expected You to say something more dynamic like 'force' or 'energy.'"

The divine look is itself force. I see how everything is, relate to it in terms of its rightness or fittingness or fulfillment or lack thereof, and I am most fully present to it if it is right, and less so if it is not. This is what "divine judgment" is. You might say (call it) My authoritative smile or frown, but like a king's smile or frown at court, My presence has authority and force, not the force of making people react in a certain way, but the ontological force of divine presence.

Ontological here seems to mean, not a causal relation of A making B happen, but the force of redefining a situation or state of being—creating, as Meier put it, a new field of force.

"I find this difficult to track, Lord. Everything that matters—suffering, the struggle of right against wrong, the teleology, the fulfillment—occur on the historical or horizontal plane of before-and-after. But they are also present in the vertical dimension where everything is now?"

I didn't say it was all now. The concept of now belongs to the horizontal sequence. But there is another respect, another angle of vision, in which they are all simultaneous, therefore accessible at any given moment or at no "moment."

"So the action is still temporal and that is real."

Surely.

"So there is some sense in which moments of our lives 'seen from above' in the vertical perspective are 'pointing upward' or 'reaching toward.' If it is not a reaching to merge, it must be a reaching for the divine presence."

Yes.

"It sounds as if the connection comes more from below, as if we first have to show our faces to God."

Okay.

"Like the Little Flower, St. Thérèse, it is as if we have to turn toward God and soak up His presence, like a flower receiving the Sun."

Yes.

"And the main challenge is to let God in."

Yes.

"We experience our lives in the horizontal dimension, but You see our lives in the simultaneity of its all happening at once, like a great chorus, and somehow our being fulfilled."

The fulfillment just *is* the drawing upward. There is not some perfect moment hidden there that makes it all okay. The symphony of everything reaching up toward My glowing presence *is* the fulfillment, the triumph over evil, over negativity, over the void. Can you relate to that? What makes a symphony great, or a great novel or drama? It is not one perfect moment. Even less is it the ending. It is the totality making a masterful whole.

"I'm afraid that all this leads to the idea that evil is an essential part of the whole, the way dissonance is in music and Lady Macbeth is in the play. For me, that is a world turned upside down."

Yes, I know, and I understand (and) sympathize with why you are uncomfortable. But it is not that God is beyond good and evil. We have already discussed that I have to cope with My own dark or incomplete side. The fight for good over evil in the world and in the heart of each individual is crucial. That is the crucial plane of action. It is the pivot on which turns the saving or healing or fulfillment of the world and of Me. And for this, as I have said, I need human partners.

But we have also discussed the need for friction. Why is there a material world, with its tendencies to decay and its resistance to purpose? Why don't I come into the world as "perfect," or make you "perfect," or create a world that is "perfect," or indeed not create a (material, hence imperfect) world at all? But to be a world is to be material and to be material is to be flawed and resistant. And to be a person is to be an actual personality, an individual with a history and (with) particular characteristics, and to have a personality is to have strengths and weaknesses, and that is precisely the drama of life, not just the drama but the basic ontological process of the world. (That is) what it is all about.

So you need to relax your preconceptions on this subject. The fact that evil, including human evil-doing, has a place in the world is not the same as saying it does not matter or is an illusion or anything like that. In fact, in a sense, nothing else does matter. Everything, even loving Me or My loving you, has this struggle, and the crucialness of its right outcome, as a reference point.

"But it sounds as if Lady Macbeth is to be praised, because she is fulfilling the divine purpose, when she talks her husband into murder?"

No, it is as if you are not listening to Me. It is necessary to defeat or overcome Lady Macbeth and one's own murderous instincts. That's what life, the whole world, is about. But it is also necessary to live in a world, and with a self, in which murderous instincts are a force and, being a force, sometimes prevail. To say that the murder is "part of God's plan" is to confuse the two levels of analysis or of reality.

"What is Your attitude to the murderer? Do You think, 'Oh, Lady Macbeth is fulfilling My plan,' or do You think, 'The rat, she is getting away with murder'?"

What do you think (I would say)? Haven't I explained this already?

"Okay, You would condemn her."

Yes.

"But still love her?"

Of course. When to condemn and when to love are two different questions. Sometimes, the evil that bothers you the most is that perpetrated by someone you love. All evil is like that for Me.

He is like
the master switch

68

Suddenly the pieces of the Impossible Puzzle snapped into place.

"Lord, I am looking at Jon Levenson's 'The Future and Presence of Cosmogonic Victory' in *Creation and the Persistence of Evil*, and the things he says fit exactly what You've been telling me!"

Yes.

"One: acts of obedience to the commandments, mitzvot, make the eschaton, the fulfillment—in New Testament language, the Kingdom of God—happen *right now*."

Yes.

"Two: the struggle of order versus chaos, good versus evil, occurs up and down the levels of the cosmos."

Yes.

"Three: there is a negative or incomplete side to God."

Yes.

"Four: human effort or partnership is essential to, or at least a key part of, the overcoming of incompleteness."

Yes.

"Five: faith in God means faith in His ultimate, not proximate, goodness. At the end-time, or in the vertical dimension, or just in the final analysis, God is good and evil is conquered. But at the present time, or in the horizontal dimension, or looking at less than the full picture, God and the world are both works in progress."

Yes.

"Six, from the vertical view, both the struggle and the victory are present now."

The last is okay if you remember that those time words can be misleading.

"In a similar way, both the battle and the final victory are present throughout the entire vertical spire of all times seen from 'above' or from God's perspective."

Yes.

"But how to understand time and the vertical dimension?"

Stop trying to picture it and think about it.

"Well, even after Einstein, we still can't *picture* time as the fourth dimension of space. But it can be laid out mathematically. However, the vertical spire doesn't seem like a dimension in that sense."

Right.

"No, it's more like a point of view. You can look at events or time-slices horizontally or vertically."

Yes, that's much better.

"And neither displaces or is superior to the other."

Yes, that's important. Just because there is a vertical or simultaneous dimension does not make the horizontal (temporal) less real or less important. In some ways, your old idea of a novel was more apt. The story is sequential, but it is all there (simultaneously) in the book (that can be opened at any place).

"Yes, but that makes it sound predetermined."

Yes, but any vertical perspective is liable to that misunderstanding.

"Because human life is a series of *real* decisions and actions, not a finished novel? And actions have unpredictable consequences, and You are as much engaged in the contingency of the horizontal as we are?"

Yes, that's exactly right!

"Is there anything else here I need to understand?"

Look at Jesus again in this light. "The Kingdom of God is here." And why Jesus has a cosmic role. He is not just present in first-

century Palestine. His presence is a cosmic event. He was/is more fully Me than any other human has ever been. So he represents—is—My full presence in and to the world, and it's a loving presence.

So, by being "fully" God, Jesus brings God's full presence into the world. And bringing God's full presence into the world is a cosmic event, connected with the arrival of the Kingdom of God. And it is a loving presence. Is it also a fighting presence?

Very much so.

"Do love and the conflict with evil, inner and outer, go together?"

Of course, in myriad ways. You do not love the world unless you fight the evil in it, and love is itself a weapon or instrument in that fight.

"And Jesus . . ."

What do you take his mission to be?

"There I am quite puzzled. To bring a message of love—to *embody* love?"

And the Kingdom.

"The 'Kingdom' of love?"

Just love?

"Well, of divine love, as well as the Divine in us loving one another?"

Yes, now you're getting somewhere. The contrast is not love versus war. Both are necessary. It is that the ultimate triumph over evil and incompleteness is to be in tune with the God inside you and to express that divine love to others. That is not incompatible with your having to fight them. These are two separate issues.

"What about Jesus' overall role? Is it for his time and place only or for the whole world and all times?"

What do you think?

"Well, maybe the contrast is not valid. Perhaps every action by every person is for both. One is moving one's own scene and also contributing to the divine turning or redemption of the whole vertical spire."

Yes!

"So every person can help actualize the divine fulfillment?"

How is (Jesus) different from you or (just) anybody?

"He has a bigger impact on the whole, I suppose because his will is one hundred percent the divine will. Lord, I sense I'm supposed to think about Christ, about the meaning of God's incarnation in person. It is still puzzling. If God is in everything, and is everything, then how can some people be more God-filled than others?"

That's the right question.

"It occurs to me, Lord, that I have a case study of the question in myself—the difference between my God-filled moments, when I am in God or He is in me, and other moments when I am less close to God."

Yes.

"The analogy that comes to mind is when a person is 'more himself' or 'more herself.'" I was thinking of the evening before our wedding. Abigail was apprehensive about losing the autonomy and identity she had as a single professional, indeed professorial, woman and becoming Mrs. Somebody-Else. "Who will I be?" It was as much accusation as question. "You will be more yourself than ever," I replied. I somehow knew that and I think today she would agree.

"Lord, perhaps the difference between being not quite oneself and more oneself might be analogous to the difference between being less God-filled and more."

Yes.

"In my experience of Jesus, his role is mainly that of a spiritual helper, trying to open my heart to love and to God. But he also seems to 'stand in' for God. For example, I can pray to him and supposedly it is as good as praying to God."

Of course, you can pray to anyone (with the right spirit) and I will hear your prayer.

One of the Hindu texts says that, if you address a sincere prayer to the wrong god, it will automatically go to the appropriate god.

"Lord, I was told earlier that Jesus is something like a Bodhisattva, a fully enlightened person dedicated to helping others on the path to enlightenment. Is that right?

Yes.

"The Buddhist concept is tied to a particular conception of enlightenment as the path to Nirvana. Lord, You don't mean that Jesus is a Bodhisattva in this particular Buddhist sense, do You?"

That's right (I don't).

"So Jesus' impact is not ontological, but more like the master teacher and guide."

It is both. He is like the master switch. He does not just point you toward contact with Me. He achieves it, embodies it.

"Lord, didn't Jesus have an ontological impact beyond being God-filled?"

No, being one hundred percent God-filled has that impact.

"In addition to being God-filled, Jesus had a particular function?"

A good way to put it.

"The function was a 'saving' function?"

Don't lapse into standard Christian language. It will just entangle or confuse you.

"Well, Lord, I am getting nowhere."

No, you're getting somewhere.

"I can understand the way in which any good person contributes to the order of the world, and reflects or interacts with Your divinity, but . . ."

If you can understand that, you can understand Jesus.

"He is in some way a connector or the connector?"

Yes!

"Is it that he transmits divine energy?"

Not so much that.

"A conduit . . ."

Yes.

"A high-conductivity conduit?"

Yes!

"He is a superconducting medium, means, or intermediary for people to relate to God?"

Yes. Not just people, but *the world*. Remember I relate to everything, including the atoms. He helps connect Me to it all.

"Yes, I see, Jesus as conduit is cosmic, ontological, and 'simultaneous,' and connects to the Whole across all times."

Yes.

"Well, then, back to the difference between the respect in which You *are* the world and the respect in which You need to *connect* to the world."

Don't you see? The side of Me that is Self needs to connect to the side of Me that is Other. These are real differences (Self and Other), not just an illusion. The difference needs to be real and to remain real, (hence) without merging. But (the two sides) also need to be related, connected. In human beings, the connection is through love. For matter, it is through something analogous to love (forces).

"So Jesus is the—or perhaps a—conduit or connector to the 'victory level,' the Kingdom of God?"

Yes!

The old walls
between religions
would collapse

69

Religious historian Wilfred Cantwell Smith spoke of "religion in the singular." It is a mistake, he believed, to think only in terms of separate religions that come in complete packages. Religions are not, and never have been, hermetically sealed. He gives a simple example of the interpenetration of religions: the sojourn of St. Josaphat. He was a Christian saint. Or was he?

In his *Confession*, Leo Tolstoy reported that his spiritual awakening was sparked by reading *The Lives of the Saints*, especially, the story of the saint known to Latin Europe as St. Josaphat. The Russian version of his life was taken from a Greek source. It is the story of a young prince who renounces worldly power and wealth and wanders in the wilderness in ascetic piety. The Greek version was actually taken from a source in Georgia, where it had been transformed into a Christian version from an Islamic source. The Moslems had gotten the story in Central Asia from the Manichees, who had absorbed the stories of several traditions, this one from the Buddhists. It was, in fact, the story of the Buddha. And the name Josaphat derived, by transpositions in several languages, from the word *Bodhisattva*. Thus, Smith concludes, "for a thousand years, the Buddha *was* a Christian saint." Smith is not debunking St. Josaphat. On the contrary, he is asserting the historical *fact* that the living truth of this story is woven into the texture of many religions.

Smith's point, which he illustrates with many examples, is that we should think of "religion in the singular" as an encompassing reality that involves all "religions in the plural." And he draws a further conclusion, evident in the title of his best-known book, *Towards a World Theology*, that theology should likewise be more encompassing, not just the articulation of a single tradition.

"Lord, what about the idea of a world theology?"

Yes, great!

Theologians often define theology as the interpretation of a canonical body of scripture of one's own tradition. The idea of a world theology seemed to take this idea one step further. "Lord, would this then be a theological interpretation of a more comprehensive body of scriptures including sacred texts from multiple traditions?"

Yes.

"This is an exciting idea. And it fits my philosophical turn of mind better than this project of 'telling Your story.'"

Well, don't go off on your own.

"You mean, a collection of texts is just a collection of texts, and me or someone else elaborating on them is just a human product?"

Something like that. You must pray at every step of the way, and you must make no bones about it to the reader that that is what you are doing. The collection itself (the selection of texts) must be inspired, guided, and so must the interpretation, the highlighting of those parts of the texts that are truest.

Suddenly, I had a different reaction. I had put a lot of time into preparing *God: An Autobiography*. "Is that project now to be replaced with one quite different?"

I would like you to do both, at least for now. Continue work on the *Autobiography*, but with an eye to the other project down the line.

"Lord, this really seems like *the* spiritual project for the twenty-first century."

Yes, that is exactly right. That would be a dynamite book, and very much needed at the current time. Your job would be to get the debate started. The old walls between religions would collapse in a minute.

The following fall, I was told to give a talk that included some of these prayers. I chose a meeting of the American Academy of Religion, but could I really quote "the voice of God" in a paper to a group of scholars? I could barely make myself do it.

I set selected prayers in the context of what philosophers call the problem of the diversity of revelations. Put simply, if there is one God, why are there so many religions? I argued that the aim of theology should be to understand as much as we can about God or the ultimate spiritual reality. If so, then the theologian should take into account all self-revelations of the divine reality, not just those in a single tradition. I dropped the term *world theology* because it sounds like an effort to impose a single religion on everyone. Instead, I spoke of Theology Without Walls as a kind of exploratory theology.

When I started quoting the prayers, and it became clear to listeners that this was supposedly God talking, they shifted uneasily in their chairs. After some restless minutes, they seemed to relax and just take it in.

Nervously I battened down the hatches and invited questions. A young Chinese woman had her hand up. "I am so glad to hear this," she said. She was now studying Catholic theology but complained that her Christian teachers had condemned the tradition in which she was raised and had tried to alienate her from her Chinese family. "I value the wisdom of my elders," she said. Someone else asked, if what I had said was right, what is the next step? How should we worship? I had only prepared for hostile questions. This one took me by surprise, but the answer came to me immediately. "You worship where God finds you."

After the meeting, I prayed about Exploratory Theology or Theology Without Walls.

I want You to share with the world what I have told you, My story. Your task is not to start (a new project called) Exploratory Theology—that is a sideline, a byproduct, an offshoot. Your job is to tell My story, as it is told to you.

I felt somewhat reproached, as if I had been going off on a tangent all my own, and I protested. "Lord, You are the One who told me to give this paper."

Remember that your job is just to do or not do whatever I ask of you each day.

"Okay, Lord, what is my assignment today?"

The world needs to hear My story anew. That has many aspects, can be done in many ways. One of those ways is theology. I want you to write My story as a *story*, as I tell it to you. I have given parts of the story to different people at different times. The whole now needs to be told. Theology is another way to tell My story in nonnarrative, or less narrative, form. It will be valuable too.

"Do You want people to piece the whole together out of the parts?"

What I most want is for people to listen to Me.

"And to listen to what You have told various people over the ages?"

Yes, that is part of listening to Me.

"Doesn't Theology Without Walls fit with that?"

Yes, but the listening is also important. This is not the place to discuss continuing revelation, but that is what it amounts to—not just your efforts, but those of others, even ordinary theologians (who do not hear God's voice in their ear) as well.

"The reason for putting some prayers at the end of my AAR presentation was to provide examples of listening?"

Yes.

As a lifelong agnostic, I had not been paying attention to what was happening in religion. When I looked around, I saw the walls already coming down. Interfaith dialogue is no longer just peacekeeping. Participants are sharing spiritual truths with one another. People who are turned off of doctrinal religion are finding a new kind of spirituality that draws on multiple traditions. Spiritually attuned individuals are looking over the walls and finding genuine insight in other faiths. In *The Seven Storey Mountain*, Catholic Thomas Merton reports finding spiritual wisdom in a Buddhist monastery. Bede Griffiths, a Catholic monk who lived in India for twenty-five years, concluded in *The Cosmic Revelation: The Hindu Way to God* that "the modern Christian view needs to be complemented with the constant awareness which the Hindu has of the eternal dimension of being." Religious philosopher Raimon Panikkar considers himself both a Christian and a Hindu, each without reservation. Irving Greenberg holds the astounding view, for an Orthodox rabbi, that Jesus was indeed resurrected, but God veiled the eyes of the Jews so they would reject Jesus. In his view, God needs both religions—one emphasizing the horizontal (partnering with God in history); the other, the vertical (the relation to the Word that is with God and is God).

"Lord, the walls are collapsing already, but without anything clear to put in their place."

Yes, that is right.

But then I wondered if perhaps the task is simpler. We don't need to have a comprehensive theology taking in the truths of all religions, but just to recognize the contribution of each religion. That would not require that we surrender or even revise our current religions.

They (the two alternatives) are identical. Once you say that one religion captures the horizontal and the other the vertical, and that both are essential, then you have a comprehensive conception that goes beyond a single religion.

That is a different question from the question of devotion, ritual, and the like. The same theological truth can be celebrated and lived in different ways. The division of labor (among the different religions) can even continue, with people selecting the vocation that fits their talents or history or calling, but understanding it in a new way, not as the exclusive path, but as an essential path contributing to the whole.

Following instructions, I had read and prayed about Jesus but not subsequent Christianity, Buddha but not Buddhism, and so on. "Lord, am I still supposed to stop at that cut-off point?"

Yes.

"But Your story continues beyond that point, doesn't it?"

Yes.

"Will there be a sequel?"

Maybe yes, maybe no, maybe by someone other than yourself.

"Am I being fired?"

No, of course not. But I have already given you a very big task, and we have talked about more than one book, so don't bite off more than you can chew.

"What about the idea of an expanded canon encompassing a selection of the world's scriptures?"

That is still a great idea. You need to just pick out the parts that you find most meaningful—truest from our conversations—and that will be a guide to seekers.

"Now I have another worry, Lord. It is one thing for me to tell Your story, quite another thing to initiate an effort at Theology Without Walls."

Why are they incompatible?

"The methods are opposite. Theologians give arguments. They don't claim that they heard it directly from God."

What if listening to Me is part of the method?

"Well, I suppose any theology or formation of a scriptural canon must be inspired in some sense. Otherwise, it would be like developing a science without ever looking at data. Or writing a history of art without looking at any paintings. You need an eye as well as a mind."

Another current development is the emergence of comparative theology. Theologians from one tradition study others to gain spiritual insights that will help them become better theologians within their own faith.

"Lord, where are You leading me with regard to comparative theology?"

You know the answer to that. This is the next stage in My relation to mankind.

"Since people will be looking at the same texts with the same mental frames, why think they'll come up with anything different?"

You know both of those presuppositions are not true. They will look at a broader range of religious experience, and they will look at it with much more relaxed theological frames and fewer vested institutional interests.

"Doesn't the *Autobiography* relate somewhat oddly to the Theology Without Walls project? On the one hand, I will be posing a question for theological inquiry: how best to understand the wider range of revelations. On the other hand, I will already be answering the question by reporting what God Himself has told me. Lord, what is the relation of the *Autobiography* to Theology Without Walls?"

God: An Autobiography gives a kind of model for how it might be done.

"Because theology cannot just be an intellectual enterprise, but requires spiritual attunement?"

Yes.

"Ah, what we need is not the right *theory* about God, but to figure out how we are supposed to *respond* to God."

Yes, that is exactly right.

70

You stand
on the threshold
of a new spiritual era,
a new axial age

You are now at a different time in history, not only because literate and thoughtful human beings have had an additional two thousand years of experience with Me, but also because you stand on the threshold of a new spiritual era, a new axial age, in which, for the first time, spiritually attuned individuals will draw their understanding of spiritual reality, not just from the scriptures of their own religious tradition, but from the plentitude of My communications to men and women.

The upshot will not be a bland acceptance of all so-called scriptures and theological traditions, as if they all said the same thing. As you can see, they do not. But the more accurate of them can be fitted together in a meaningful way. This is not just a conceptual puzzle-solving, as if the challenge were purely intellectual: how to fit the largest number of pieces into a single coherent story. It is, most fundamentally, spiritual: how to sense which writings and experiences are truly sensitive to the divine reality and how to put them together in a way that is spiritually meaningful, whether or not it seems "logical."

"Lord, are the world's religions converging on the cutting edge of spiritual development?"

Yes, that's right. It's time for them to come together. Not merely putting the pieces together, but in a dynamic way, a way that lends itself to forward development.

"What do You mean?"

As people from different traditions appropriate or take in elements from other traditions, they will make something of that. It won't just be a passive reception; it will be a creative, very dynamic process. For example, as a Christian takes in the "truth" of the Atman—truth in scare quotes because the Hindu truth of the Atman is not the final truth—it leaves the Christian perspective out, for example—understanding of the Atman will be shaped and expanded and connected to other elements not present, or not so fully present, in the Hindu tradition. As the Hindus or Chinese fully take in the personal God of the Old Testament, as they take in the reality of Jesus, they will be transformed.

"Resulting in a single world religion?"

There is no way human beings will all subscribe to a single religion, any more than all philosophers agree. But they will no longer be hermetically sealed, looking at one another over tall, thick walls, sending bullets or, when you're lucky, flowers back and forth. But it will be a creative ferment in which religions feel free to borrow freely from each other, and individuals will feel free to borrow from all religions, and create their own creeds and rituals.

"Will this mean the end of the old religions?"

Of course not. The early Christians absorbed Greek philosophy and still remained Christians. There are many other examples of religious syncretism, some of which resulted in new traditions, others of which were fully absorbed by an existing tradition.

"Once religions and individuals take in truths and revelations from each other, will that be the end of the process?"

Of course it won't be the end. There will be new developments and new communications from My side, and new developments and events and consciousness from the world's side. The cutting edge (of spiritual development) will continue.

We had left Washington and, of course, no longer spent late afternoons on the banks of the Potomac, but on a visit to the city, I returned to the spot where I had first met God. While it is a beautiful setting, it does not have the aura of a sacred place. Instead, one hears the clicking of wheels on the bicycle path and the shouts of kids throwing Frisbees. But it is still a good place to think, and I asked myself, "What do you know when you know God?" After all my prayerful experiences, the central assumption of my training as a philosopher no longer seemed adequate. I was taught that knowledge consists of propositions. For example, Maria knows that the proposition "Paris is the capital of France" is true. So here is Maria and there is Paris (or a fact about Paris), one thing (Maria) standing in a cognitive relation to another thing (Paris). The relation is based on a third thing, a body of evidence. It is a distant and purely intellectual relation. Most arguments for or against the existence of God assume this model of knowledge.

But is that the correct model for knowing or understanding God? The knower and the known—God and the person experiencing God, attuned to God—are not quite so separate, so distant from one another. And the knowing or understanding relation is neither abstract nor purely intellectual. It is existential, participatory, and transformative. It is a saving or liberating relation.

One of the existential facts about relating to God is that, in spite of His reassurances to the contrary, He seems hidden. Even when He is most available, most fully present, it is not the way, across the river, the Lincoln Memorial is present. Some call it a matter of faith, but that sells the experience short. It is not groundless belief. It is just that, to use St. Paul's phrase, "the evidence of things unseen" is elusive, hard to nail down. The life of faith is living in light of that divine presence that one never captures, never holds in one's hand. Perhaps it is precisely this elusiveness that makes the knowledge of God transformative. To be aware of God at all, you have to reorient your life.

"Is this right, Lord, that what one knows when one knows God is not an inert fact, it is a living Reality that places demands on us and transforms us . . ."

Yes.

". . . as if this were Your sole reason for being?"

Yes!

Acknowledgments

I would like to thank my agent, John Loudon of LoudonBooks, my executive editor, Ann Delgehausen of Trio Bookworks, my publicists, Sarah Miniaci and Mallory Campoli of Smith Publicity, and my "home team"—Lauri Kempson, Jessica Cortes, and Laura Buck—for their talent and commitment.

About the Author

Jerry L. Martin has served as chair of the National Endowment for the Humanities and of the philosophy department at the University of Colorado at Boulder. He has testified before Congress and appeared on radio and television. He is a contributor to the Good Men Project and coordinator of the Theology Without Walls project at the American Academy of Religion.

In addition to a number of scholarly articles on epistemology, the philosophy of mind, and public policy, he is author or coauthor of major reports that have been cited in hundreds of newspapers, including the *New York Times* and the *Washington Post*.

He was founding director of the University of Colorado's Center for the Study of Philosophy and Social Policy, state president of the American Association of University Professors, advisor to the Colorado Commission on Higher Education, founding president of the American Council of Trustees and Alumni, member of the Governor's Blue Ribbon Commission on Higher Education in Virginia, Andrew W. Mellon Congressional Fellow, Distinguished Georgia Humanities Lecturer, and adjunct professor at Georgetown University and the Catholic University of America.

Martin received his Ph.D. from Northwestern University and an honorary doctorate from the Thomas More College of Liberal Arts.

He is married to Abigail L. Rosenthal, professor emerita at Brooklyn College of the City University of New York, author of *A Good Look at Evil* and the forthcoming *Confessions of a Young Philosopher*.

www.godanautobiography.com

Connect with the author and other readers
at the *God: An Autobiography* website. It's a place
to make comments, ask questions, and share experiences.
You can also keep up with book news and author events,
see YouTube videos of Dr. Martin discussing life issues,
and read his ongoing reflections on the book.